Paul Janowiak, S.J.

Foreword by Edward Foley, Capuchin

The Holy Preaching

*The Sacramentality of the Word
in the Liturgical Assembly*

A PUEBLO BOOK

The Liturgical Press, Collegeville, Minnesota

A Pueblo Book published by The Liturgical Press

Design by Frank Kacmarcik, Obl.S.B.

Library of Congress Cataloging-in-Publication Data

Janowiak, Paul, 1951–
    The holy preaching : the sacramentality of the Word in the liturgical
  assembly / Paul Janowiak.
      p. cm.
    "A Pueblo book."
    Includes bibliographical references and indexes.
    ISBN 0-8146-6180-7 (alk. paper)
    1. Catholic preaching. 2. Jesus Christ—Presence. 3. Catholic
  Church—Liturgy. 4. Catholic Church—Doctrines. I. Title.
BX1795.P72 J36 2000
264'.02—dc21   99-042558

The Holy Preaching

Kay,
may the Word we shared
may the Word we shared
both feed the Church.
Paul Janowiak, SJ.

To my parents and my family
and to my Jesuit brothers,
who so faithfully live the life they profess.

Contents

Foreword

In one of the more startling lines of the Constitution on the Sacred Liturgy, the Council Fathers assert Christ's presence not only in the eucharistic species, but in the ministers, the community, and "in his word since it is he himself who speaks when the holy scriptures are read in the Church" [n. 7]. Though this declaration is well grounded in the teachings of the early church, the teaching about Christ's presence in the proclaimed and preached word is an underdeveloped part of our religious imagination and our sacramental theology.

Many Roman Catholics instinctively believe that Christ's presence in the eucharist, especially under the species of bread and wine, is the full and true presence of Christ. The other modes of Christ's presence asserted by the council are often viewed as pale reflections of the fullness of the eucharistic presence. Part of this confusion may stem from the conciliar instruction itself which notes that Christ is "present in the Sacrifice of the Mass not only in the person of his minister . . . but especially (maxime) in the eucharistic species" [n. 7]. To many it sounds as though there is a greater density or authenticity to Christ's presence in the eucharist, thus suggesting almost a quantitative distinction between eucharistic and other modes of divine presence. The assertion of the special import of Christ's presence under the eucharistic species, however, is not an assertion of more or less presence. Rather, it is an announcement of the more or less importance of that mode of presence for the tradition and faith of the Church. If Christ is present then Christ is present, with no divine holding back whatever the mode of Holy self-communication.

In contrast to a quite developed theology of divine presence in the Eucharist, contemporary Roman Catholicism is marked by a relatively underdeveloped theology of the word. Those segments of Christianity which did concern themselves in a particular way with theologizing on the word—notably those influenced by the word theologies of Luther and Calvin—have been separated from us since the sixteenth century. As Roman Catholics struggle in this post-conciliar era to realize the full sacramentality of the word, we are challenged to expand our theology of presence so that it might be fully catholic. This broadening of sacramental theology—anticipated in a council which asserted the very sacramentality of the Church—is not and cannot be to the detriment of our authentic eucharistic theology, but must redound only to its benefit.

It is this task that Paul Janowiak has admirably accepted in this important volume on the sacramentality of the word. Happily this work has not been undertaken in any narrow or insular manner, for the author does not consider the sacramentality of the word as some self-contained or isolated aspect of divine self-communication. Rather, this consideration of the sacramentality of the word is a self-conscious attempt to retrieve and assert a theology of the word in the context of the sacramental community. Thus while the author carefully outlines a sacramental theology for liturgical preaching and proclamation, he does so with such breadth and insight so as to contribute commendably to the broadening sacramental discourse that marks this moment in our Church's life.

Three aspects of this work are particularly noteworthy for this reader. First of all, *The Holy Preaching* is thoroughly Catholic. This reimagining of the sacramentality of liturgical proclamation is rooted in the work of three giants of twentieth-century Roman Catholic thought: Otto Semmelroth, Karl Rahner, and Edward Schillebeeckx. Ironically, while each of these giants attends to the sacramentality of the word in their own works, this aspect of their theologizing has been widely overlooked. The author's reading of these giants is at once thorough and critical. It is this careful combination of precision and critique which provides a sound foundation for the author's own theologizing as he weaves together the tradition and contemporary theory with unusual competence.

While thoroughly Catholic, this work is also utterly ecumenical. Such ecumenicity is achieved in two distinctive ways. First of all, by plumbing the depths of the particularly Roman Catholic tradition, the author provides a solid basis for a fruitful dialogue with the Christian traditions which have more emphasized the salvific nature of word. Without a careful exploration of one's own tradition, it is virtually impossible to have a credible dialogue with another. Paul Janowiak prepares for a true ecumenical encounter by first acquainting Roman Catholics with the riches of their own tradition on the sacramentality of the word. This undoubtedly renders us more suitable and viable dialogue partners in the ecumenical venture.

After exploring our own tradition, however, the author then takes the welcome turn of broaching the works of Luther and Calvin, which he views as critical resources for enriching a Roman Catholic understanding of the sacramentality of proclamation. The juxtaposition of the writings of Semmelroth, Rahner, and Schillebeeckx with those of Luther, for example, suggests that the Reformer's treatment of God's word contributes much to Schillebeeckx's understanding of the kerygmatic nature of revelation. Furthermore, Luther and Calvin's word theologies can greatly enrich the teaching of Rahner and Semmelroth on the dynamic nature of the revelatory word.

While thoroughly Catholic and utterly ecumenical, this work is also strikingly contemporary. In true correlational mode, the author makes a well-considered turn to contemporary literary theory in order to discover what it can contribute to our understanding of scriptural proclamation and preaching. In particular, his use of the New Historicism and reader-response criticism highlights the fact that such proclamation is a dynamic social event and a creative transaction. Maybe, most striking of all, this exploration of contemporary literary theory provides new language for understanding how the assembly has active agency in the proclamation process. Such theories also provide new lenses for seeing that the reading and hearing of sacred texts is not an individual enterprise, but ultimately and essentially a communal act.

Thoroughly Catholic, utterly ecumenical, and strikingly contemporary: *The Holy Preaching* beckons us into a rich and challenging journey. It is a well-guided pilgrimage into sacred proclamation that respects the mystery yet proffers understanding; engages the individual reader, while never abandoning its social-ecclesial context; explores the conceptual but always at the service of the pastoral. This is not the last word on the sacramentality of proclamation, but it is unquestionably a good word, and I for one am profoundly grateful for it.

Edward Foley, Capuchin

Prologue

"Jesus then rolled up the scroll, gave it back to the assistant and sat down. And all eyes in the synagogue were fixed on him. Then he began to speak to them, 'This text is being fulfilled today even as you listen.' And he won the approval of all, and they were astonished by the gracious words that came from his lips" (Luke 4:20-22).

The reform of the liturgy that followed upon the promulgation of the Vatican II's Constitution on the Sacred Liturgy emerged from decades of scholarly research and pastoral reflection in the fields of sacramental and liturgical theology. The implementation of the document in the intervening years immersed the sacred rites in the concrete experiences of believers, whose hungers and hopes, resistance and faithful trust now bring the Church to a new millennium. We worship very differently from the generation of worshipers before us. The contemporary context in which we express the primary symbols of our ecclesial identity demands and expects such change. Yet, such shaking of the foundations unsettles us. We need a symbolic and ritual home to which we return, when the rigors of living in a world gnaw away at our shared traditions and communal identity. Christ's presence to us in the Eucharist provides that foundation and encounter without which we cannot live. The reform of the liturgy expressed the profound hope that our worship might continue to be "the outstanding means whereby the faithful may express in their lives and manifest to others the mystery of Christ and the real nature of the Church" (CSL 32).

Too often in our shared history, believing Christians have divided the ecclesial body over the meaning of Christ's abiding presence to us and for us. We have narrowed our vision, separated ourselves from one another with differing doctrines and emphases, and often tried to control the Mystery that is always, first and foremost, a gift of God. That is why the Vatican Council II called the Church to recapture a way of worshiping that reflects the multivalence of that divine presence, a saving deed of God which is alive to us in the power of the Holy Spirit. Christ is present, the Constitution on the Sacred Liturgy insists, in a complex, integrated whole: in the sacramental elements, in the ritual proclamation of the word, in the one who presides in the name of the community, and in the assembled Church that prays and sings (CSL 7). This presence reveals itself in dynamic activity—persons celebrating and participating and responding in faith—rather than in static categories or aloof interpretations. Such a vision captures the heart of the earliest tradition and it calls us all, in succeeding generations, to make our common identity whole again. This sacramental re-imagination has proved difficult to realize. This book provides one way to weave our disparate threads back together.

Christ's presence in the word, in particular, has become a common expression for us, even in traditions where sacramental life has eclipsed that understanding. Yet, how that presence in word expresses itself and how our actions at the table or font fulfill its proclamation remain ambiguous for most of us. Understanding proclamation and preaching as an *event* rather than a *closed text* uncovers the heart of the arguments posed in this book. It revisits the traditional categories of sacramental theology through the lens of theologians who themselves had been formed in a Neo-Scholastic framework, but who were re-imagining how such categories could expand to embrace an ecclesial grounding for these expressive acts. Part I of this book traces the work of Otto Semmelroth, S.J., Karl Rahner, S.J., and Edward Schillebeeckx, O.P., as central figures in this regard, especially as its relates to the proclamation of the word within the liturgical assembly.

Building upon this foundation, Part II offers a critical assessment of two contemporary literary theories (New Historicism and Reader-Response Criticism) in which the interrelationship between a common text, its readers, and the prevailing social context provides the focal concern. We then use these insights as a way of understanding Christ's presence in the word, a complex circulation of grace-filled energy whose elements are the Scriptures, the assembly, the preacher and lectors, and the ritual enactment in which it takes place. The communal hearing of the word, the role of the ministers in that proclamation, and God's grace at the heart of it all move the assembly toward the table in grateful praise and thanks. This is true communion in the body and blood of Christ.

The title of the book comes from the life of the founder of the Order of Preachers, St. Dominic Guzman. Early in the evolution of its founding, Dominic called the community "The Holy Preaching" or "The Preaching of Jesus Christ." Every talent and gift, along with every action on behalf of its common mission, contributed to their communal identity as preachers of the word. That shared identity reflects the early Church's understanding of itself as the body of Christ. The four-fold presence of Christ in the Eucharist mirrors that web of interrelationships that culminate in a unified proclamation to the world of God's saving acts in Jesus, through the power of the Holy Spirit. "The Holy Preaching" communicates both who we are and what we do. This communal dynamic reveals the underlying thesis of everything that follows in this book.

I would like to thank my mentor and friend, Kenan Osborne, O.F.M., for guiding me through my thinking about the ritual presence of Christ in the word. The example of his life and faith embody everything he shared with me in our study together. I also express my appreciation to John Baldovin, S.J., Dr. Michael Aune, and Mary McGann, R.S.C.J., who accompanied me and supported my work, as well as Fr. Patrick Howell, S.J., my colleague and companion in the Society, whose art of reading and critique always proved a grace to me. I would also like to name the liturgical communities in which I have served and the students I teach as partners in this study. Their faithful enactment of Word and Sacrament provides the context from which I speak. Finally, I owe an immense amount of gratitude to Edward Foley, Capuchin, who believed in this book and encouraged me in numerous ways to take a risk and join the public discussion about things we both treasure. My hope is that communities of faith, through their lives of worship and service, may continue to respond to God's Word of grace, the Lord Jesus, so that we might be "The Holy Preaching"—the body of Christ, broken and poured out for the life of the world.

PART I

1

Worship and the Mystery of God's Action in the World

A long, complex, and circuitous road led to the official reform of the Roman Catholic liturgy at the Second Vatican Council. Even four decades after the promulgation of the Constitution on the Sacred Liturgy, that evolution continues to beckon and challenge. Worshiping communities, pastoral liturgists, and liturgical scholars are still encountering the ambiguity of a reform whose dynamism, like the spirit of the liturgy itself, feeds upon a mystery, which first and foremost is God's gracious activity in our midst. This divine initiative permeates all life and reaches into the depths of human experience through the gift of the incarnate Word made flesh, whose saving presence is sustained in us through the working of the Holy Spirit. Liturgical worship highlights this saving dialogue between the mystery who beckons and a people who respond. The mystery is embedded in this complex interchange of ritual word and action. Liturgy proclaims one Word and work of God.

To try to understand sacramentality, the presence of Christ, and the relationship between that presence and the proclamation and preaching of the Scriptures in the midst of a liturgical assembly, one must begin with a simple acknowledgment of this mystery. If anything, it makes the momentous reform of the last century a part of something larger than scholarly reason or powerful prelates or dazzling popular movements. The hungers of believing people and their identity as the body of Christ—their festive celebrations of joy, their rituals of grief, and even their liturgical passivity—share a prestigious place within the mystery as well. We have come to acknowledge that *how* and *why* people worship really does mean something theologically.

Historical and social realities shape the inquiry as well. The tragedy of world wars in the first half of this century shifted the arena of liturgical experimentation and nuanced its development. A broadening cultural awareness of the diverse ways people engage this world and understand the mystery forged this mix. And, of course, there are the human foibles and heroics, sometimes fueled by petty jealousies and misinterpretations, which sharpened the arguments and invigorated a liturgical movement whose momentum would radically affect the way the Church understood herself and the world she serves. Everything is interwoven.

That is why we begin with this mystery—God's presence and action in the world—as the ultimate background of this investigation into liturgical proclamation as a sacramental act. Furthermore, as Vatican II insisted, God's saving acts in Jesus are expressed in the liturgy through a fourfold presence of Christ: in the minister, in the elements, in the ritual proclamation of the word, and in the assembled Church that prays and sings.[1] This interrelated mode of presence was a bold departure from common understanding and actual practice. True, Roman Catholic theology, through its history, had investigated and appropriated the presence of Christ in the elements and in the priest acting *in persona Christi*. What had been and continues to remain ambiguous is how Christ is present in the gathered assembly and in the word proclaimed. These were the questions that Protestant theology had raised centuries earlier.[2] The Roman Church, without denying that presence, had obscured the issue by continuing to worship in a manner in which the praying assembly and the proclaimed word seemed extraneous to the central and real presence of Christ located in the consecrated species through the action of the ordained priest.

How did such a declaration about the presence of Christ in sacramental worship come to this richer synthesis, after centuries of such a narrow focus? The synthesis is rooted in history and time, and so some key events and figures from the liturgical movement of the last century help to situate this discussion of sacramentality, liturgical

---

[1] Constitution on the Sacred Liturgy [CSL] 7.

[2] See Frank Senn, *Christian Liturgy: Catholic and Evangelical* (Minneapolis: Augsburg Fortress Press, 1997) esp. ch. 4, "Word and Sacrament in Luther's Reformation," 299–322. For a Roman Catholic appropriation of Luther and Calvin in the renewal of preaching and proclamation, see the final chapter in this book.

proclamation, and the mysterious ways of God. Within the first half of the twentieth century, a dramatic new framework for understanding both sacramental theology and pastoral, liturgical practice seemed to coalesce. Such a convergence, along with the persons who inspired it, allows us now to focus on what it means to say that Christ is present "in his word, since it is he himself who speaks when the holy Scriptures are read in the Church," as the Constitution on the Sacred Liturgy, no. 7 asserts. As Annibale Bugnini remarked in his monumental study *The Reform of the Liturgy: 1948–1975*, the events of the past decades are not cosmetic changes or theological victories of one position over another, but a statement of a great theological and ecclesial reality unfolding in the Church during these years, through the guidance of the Spirit. The pastoral emphasis, Bugnini noted, is distinctive to the theology that emerged:

"The participation and active involvement of the people of God in the liturgical celebration is the ultimate goal of the reform, just as it was the goal of the liturgical movement. This involvement and participation is not limited to externals but reaches to the very root of things: to the mystery being celebrated, to Christ himself who is present."[3]

What are the key moments and persons in this liturgical movement which laid the groundwork for the conciliar reform and what were the issues that stirred the inquiry? The brief, historical overview which follows will show the unique underpinnings of the Vatican II liturgical reform: systematic theology informed by pastoral praxis and vice versa. The discussion concludes with some theological issues that effect liturgical renewal in the mid-twentieth century. This lays the groundwork for Chapter 2, where the work of sacramental theologians in the years before the council provides an ecclesial foundation for worship and a communal hearing of the word which is inseparable from any liturgical action that follows. In short, God's presence and action in the world was clarified in the interplay between *lex orandi et lex credendi:* the practice of worship and the reflection upon that experience, in dialogue with the tradition, continued to unfold the mystery at work in our midst. The liturgical reform, this history shows us, is on solid sacramental ground.

---

[3] Annibale Bugnini, *The Reform of the Liturgy (1945–1975)*, trans. Matthew J. O'Connell (Collegeville: The Liturgical Press, 1990) 5.

FROM LITURGICAL MOVEMENT
TO LITURGICAL REFORM: 1909–1969

The year 1909 is generally considered to be the birth of the modern liturgical movement as an organized body, although Abbot Prosper Guéranger's "return to the sources" at Solesmes from 1833 onward began a process of liturgical change and study whose spirit can later be detected in the "Parochial Liturgical Movement" and the 1909 Catholic Lay Congress in Malines, Belgium.[4] At that congress, the Benedictine Lambert Beauduin addressed the need for participation of the faithful in Christian worship. His prior pastoral experience as a parish priest before entering the abbey, his passionate interest in ecumenism, and his love for the liturgy he experienced at the Abbey of Mont Cesar, where the congress was held, galvanized an attitude stirring for almost a century. The movement that Beaudin and his colleagues were initiating built its foundation upon initial attempts in France and Germany and, on a wider scale, with Pius X's attempt to renew the faithful through "the foremost and indispensable fount" of the liturgy and through more frequent reception of communion.[5]

In the years preceding World War I, Beauduin's "liturgical study weeks" occurred yearly after this first Malines Congress. These "study weeks," in addition to the publication of pastorally oriented journals like *La vie liturgique,* which published the Sunday Masses for the dioceses in Belgium, and the bi-monthly *Questions liturgiques et paroissales,* all helped the popular pastoral movement begun by the monks of Mont César to reach more and more people. The emphasis, as Dom Bernard Botte notes in his personal reflections, was pastoral but not "practical" in a rubrical, manual style.[6] The movement was

---

[4] For the consensus concerning 1909 as the beginning of the movement, see Josef Jungmann's "Commentary," *Commentary on the Documents of Vatican II,* vol. 1, ed. Herbert Vorgrimler (New York: Herder and Herder, 1967) 2; Bugnini, *The Reform of the Liturgy,* 6; I. H. Dalmais, *Introduction to the Liturgy,* trans. Roger Capel (Baltimore: Helicon Press, 1961) 71; Bernard Botte, *From Silence to Participation: An Insider's View of the Liturgical Renewal,* trans. John Sullivan (Washington, D.C.: Pastoral Press, 1988) 10; Virgil C. Funk, "The Liturgical Movement," *The New Dictionary of Sacramental Worship* (Collegeville: The Liturgical Press, 1990) 697.

[5] Pius X, *Tra Le Sollecitudini* (Restoration of Church Music) 28, and *Sacra Tridentina* (Decree on Frequent and Daily Reception) 76 in *Official Catholic Teachings: Worship and Liturgy,* comp. James J. Megivern (Wilmington, N.C.: Consortium Books, 1978) 18, 27.

[6] Botte, *From Silence to Participation,* 22.

attempting "to reestablish contact between the altar and the nave" and was taking aim at the poor training and spiritual preparation of a generation of honest, hard-working priests for whom liturgy had always been taught and perceived as a prescriptive duty to perform instead of a "source of life for them and for their people." The pastoral emphasis of these first few years of the "Parochial Liturgical Movement," as the Dominican liturgical scholar I. H. Dalmais called it,[7] characterized this movement from that of earlier attempts in France and Germany. Once again, issues and events "interweave" and the stunted success of the nineteenth century finds new and lasting expression in a wedding of scholarly research with the concrete worship experience of Catholics in everyday parish life. This pastoral emphasis explains why the movement blossomed into concrete reform during the next fifty years, instead of becoming the professional monopoly of artists, antiquarians, or social activists. It was a correct response to the signs of the times and the life of the whole Church.

During the war most organized work halted, but what had begun in Belgium and especially at Mont César began to spread to other countries. For instance, the Benedictine Abbey of Finalpia in Italy published the journal *Revista Liturgica,* and *Jahrbuch für Liturgiewissenschaft* sprang up from the Abbey of Maria Laach in Germany.[8] Dom Odo Casel, a monk at Maria Laach, greatly influenced liturgical thinking with his reflections on the mystery of the liturgy and the mystery of Christ, both in his journal articles and his famous *The Mystery of Christian Worship.*[9] Casel's views were widely discussed and often criticized and corrected in many circles, especially regarding the relationship between Christian worship and Greek mystery cults and Casel's questionable exegesis of St. Paul.[10] However, an important stage in the movement was being born here, namely a theological underpinning for ecclesial sacramentality in which, as Dalmais notes, "the worshipping community enters into participation

---

[7] Dalmais, *Introduction to the Liturgy,* 171.

[8] Botte, *From Silence to Participation,* 30–1.

[9] Odo Casel, *The Mystery of Christian Worship,* trans. Burkhard Neunheuser (Westminster, Md.: Newman Press, 1962). For a brief and clear expression of the importance of this work, see Dalmais' *Introduction to the Liturgy* and the works he cites, such as Th. Filthaut, *La théologie des mystères* (Paris: Desclées, 1954).

[10] See note 7 and also Funk, "The Liturgical Movement," 698, for just a few of these critiques. Hints of that critique are evident in Pius XII's encyclical *Mediator Dei* 8 (November 1947).

in the redeeming event which is evoked."[11] Botte's recognition of the importance of Casel's work emphasizes the shift in the theological imagination taking place which will have an important contribution to make to proclamation's sacramentality: Casel's notion of mystery "allows for the liturgy a coherent overall vision which does not distinguish rites according to the modalities of their effects, but, quite the opposite, brings them together in unity."[12] One of the effects of the disagreement and dialogue over these thoughts, according to Josef Jungmann, actually ended with the German bishops' establishment of a liturgical study group at the Bishops' Conference in 1940. Such gatherings of theological scholars and pastoral practitioners gave a vehicle for reputable liturgical scholars to respond to attacks against the movement and provided a stamp of official legitimacy in wider Church circles.[13]

Other notable figures during this time immediately after the war were Anton Baumstark at Maria Laach, Pius Parsch at Klosterneuberg in Austria, and Dom Antonio Coelho at the Portuguese monastery of Singeverga.[14] Of particular note for the American liturgical movement was the return, in 1926, of the Benedictine Virgil Michel to St. John's Abbey in Collegeville, Minnesota.[15] After visiting the sites of the renewal at monasteries in Europe and studying with Beauduin at the Benedictine College in Rome, Michel initiated the immensely popular and influential *Orate Fratres* (the forerunner to *Worship*) and The Liturgical Press, with its printing of Beauduin's book *La piété de l'Eglise* and short pamphlets on liturgical topics entitled "The Popular Liturgical Library."[16] The relationship fostered at Collegeville between the liturgical and catechetical movements in the United States would have a lasting effect on Catholic parish life and liturgical renewal, a relationship which distinguished the American liturgical experience from their European counterparts. The Catholic Action social movements in Europe and, to a lesser extent, in the United

[11] Dalmais, *Introduction to the Liturgy*, 64.

[12] Botte, *From Silence to Participation*, 32.

[13] Jungmann, "Commentary," 2.

[14] Botte, *From Silence to Participation*, 32–3.

[15] For a social history of the liturgical movement in the United States and how it has shaped contemporary liturgical scholarship, see Keith Pecklers, *The Unread Vision: The Liturgical Movement in the United States of America, 1926–1955* (Collegeville: The Liturgical Press, 1998).

[16] See Funk, "The Liturgical Movement," 702, and Botte, *From Silence to Participation*, 33.

States also strongly wedded social movements and the young with this renewal. Because of the youthfulness and newness of these outlooks, burgeoning attempts at the Dialogue Mass, vernacular singing, and active participation began to create an environment of creative possibility that was to bear fruit officially only years later.

Related fields of theology invigorated and accelerated the movement. Abbot Marmion's biblically inspired eucharistic piety represented a shift to the growing importance of Scripture in the overall celebration of the liturgy,[17] fed as well by a similar revival of the Church Fathers and their mystagogical preaching texts. Finally, during these interim years between the wars the Jesuit Josef Jungmann and Anglican Dom Gregory Dix begin their long and fruitful scholarly careers. The momentum of scholarship and pastoral experimentation was building.[18] All of these offshoots begin to be funneled in a common direction, which the interruption of World War II and its savage and tragic preoccupations only temporarily stilled and redirected, especially among the French.

The "Centre de Pastorale Liturgique" was born near the end of this war and signaled a new phase of predominantly Dominican direction for the movement, followed after the war by similar efforts in Germany at Trier.[19] Colleagues like Roguet, Martimort, Duployé, Chavasse, Gy, Dalmais, Botte, Daniélou, and Bouyer began gathering liturgists, theologians, and parish priests for study sessions at the Centre, and the publication of *La Maison-Dieu* began shortly after the liberation of Paris in 1944. Pius XII's *Mystici corporis* (1943) on the union of the faithful with the mystical body of Christ fed this ferment and prepared the way for official favorable recognition of the movement itself in his encyclical *Mediator Dei* in November 1947.

The international study meetings beginning at Maria Laach in 1951, and including the seminal Assisi Congress in 1956 (three years

[17] Classic examples of this integration of liturgy, personal devotion, and the central role of Scripture are *Christ in His Mysteries* (London: Sands and Co., 1939) and a devotional book entitled *Words of Life: On the Margin of the Missal* (St. Louis: Herder, 1939), with quotations from his main works to accompany liturgical feasts.

[18] In their 1960 book *Liturgy and Contemplation* (New York: P. J. Kenedy and Sons), Jacques and Raissa Maritain pay tribute at the outset to Virgil Michel and the North American Liturgical Study Week at which they recently had played a major role. Their contribution to the movement, they insist, is to give a "systematic form" to the pastoral issues raised.

[19] Jungmann, "Commentary," 2–3.

before the Vatican Council II was called) on the theme of "the pastoral nature of liturgy" began to set forth themes and principles that were formalized in the promulgation of the Constitution on the Sacred Liturgy seven years later.[20] The reform of the Easter Liturgy (1951–56) and the revision in the rubrical codes in the Missal and the Breviary in the early sixties[21] were mere preludes to the great events to come. The Easter Triduum and the renewal of the Liturgy of the Hours, both of which seem so foundational to our contemporary liturgical worship and sacramental identity, trace their renewed life and momentum to these creative years before the council.

At the time the windows were thrown open by John XXIII in January 1959, the Second Vatican Council itself now became the key event and place of focus for the liturgical movement and reform. This included the establishment of the preparatory commissions for the council in 1960, the actual debates on the schemas in 1962 and the important inter-session work that followed, and the final approval of the document in November and its promulgation of the first decree of the council, the Constitution on the Sacred Liturgy, on December 4, 1963.

The Consilium, which was the committee for the implementation of the decrees formed by Paul VI in February 1964, and the subsequent subsuming of the commission into the new Congregation for Divine Worship in 1969, occupy the years after the council and usher us into the present time of continual implementation and further renewal. The seminal and untiring work of people like Annibale Bugnini, who himself weathered the storms of official caprice and growing resentment at the depth of the task of reform, is a testimony not only to the deep love for the liturgy by those who labored for this reform, but points to the equally long, complex, and circuitous road that still lies ahead.

Throughout the entire movement during these years the mystery was deepening. The task of implementing the reform would prove to be equally as challenging. In particular, the sacramentality of liturgical proclamation and preaching still remains largely untapped and

---

[20] Bugnini, *The Reform of the Liturgy*, 11–12. Note especially the importance Bugnini places on two lectures at the Assisi conference, Josef Jungmann's "The Pastoral Idea in the History of the Liturgy" and Augustin Bea's "The Pastoral Value of the Word of God in the Sacred Liturgy," published in *The Assisi Papers, Proceedings of the First International Congress of Pastoral Liturgy, Assisi-Rome, September 18–22, 1956* (Collegeville: The Liturgical Press, 1957) 18–31.

[21] Jungmann, "Commentary," 2–4.

suggests a fruitful vein to pursue if we are to be true to the Gospel and to God's activity in our midst, in the power of the Spirit.

With such a cursive overview to highlight the issues, a more intentional look at the theological climate out of which the liturgical movement emerged and its effect on the eventual re-articulation of sacramentality and the proclamation of the word can now be outlined. It is the environment out of which the Constitution on the Sacred Liturgy was promulgated as the first fruits of the Second Vatican Council's rich deliberations.

THEOLOGICAL ISSUES AND LITURGICAL RENEWAL IN THE MID-TWENTIETH CENTURY

The Inheritance of Scholastic Categories and the Liturgical Critique

Recovering the dynamic nature of the four-fold presence of Christ that was the hallmark of the conciliar reform required a re-imagination of the ways the Church understood the nature of sacramentality and its ritual expression. Static metaphysical explanations from the manual tradition could not adequately articulate the eventful character of this broader vision. The limitations of a sacramental theology in the scholastic tradition, however, must not obscure the positive and lasting contributions such a methodology made to Catholic theology between the thirteenth and twentieth centuries. Peter Fink, s.j., has noted in particular "the distinction between sacrament and sacramental" and the insistence on rooting the effectiveness of the former in "the [then-] seven distinct liturgical actions that displayed and continued the saving mission of Christ."[22] The priest and the worshipers had important sacramental roles as well, at least from a categorical perspective. The requirement that the priest intend to do what the Church does *(ex opere operato)* and that the recipients be receptive and open to the grace being offered in the sacrament *(ex opere operantis)* were provisions for God to act freely and personally through Christ in the lives of believers. However, many of these categories had been forged in the furnace of metaphysical debate, in response to

[22] Peter E. Fink, "Sacramental Theology after Vatican II," *The New Dictionary of Sacramental Worship,* 1107–14. See also a detailed and contemporary analysis in David Power, *The Eucharistic Mystery: Revitalizing the Tradition* (New York: Crossroad, 1992), or, for a somewhat more critical view, Bernard Cooke, *The Distancing of God: The Ambiguity of Symbol in History and Theology* (Minneapolis: Fortress Press, 1990).

popular devotional movements and medieval sensibilities that had raised questions about the presence of Jesus in the sacrament, apart from the eucharistic context. Over the centuries the "sacrament" had become increasingly an object of devotion, a treasure to be grasped, rather than a participative reality that feeds and strengthens and unites. Lay evangelical movements questioned the authority and morality of ordained priests who controlled access to such a sacramental presence.[23] Aquinas' complex metaphysical categories were a clarification and a rethinking of questionable sacramental notions as well as of the necessary authority structures underlying the ecclesial expression of these vessels of grace. The Thomistic system was grounded in a faith and a committed life and a liturgical fidelity that could never be contained in the strict confines of such categories; yet the system itself provided a splendid "reason" to the mysteries so close to his heart. This context of faithful practice and embodied faith made the system cohere. However, the more these categories were estranged from that dynamic faith life and were used, instead, for polemical debate and as litmus tests for orthodoxy and rubrical purity, the more they strayed from their original intent. Set apart, they ossified what was (and is) at heart a dynamic encounter between God and humankind into an objective reality "which could be observed and analyzed from without,"[24] its mystery quantified and explained reasonably and definitively. This reification of sacraments has obscured liturgical celebration ever since.

It is important to emphasize that Aquinas had used Aristotelian categories both to preserve the past and to create something new. In the same way, Roman Catholic theologians in the mid-twentieth century began to rethink and reexamine their inherited sacramental tradition in the context of new insights and methods for studying the tradition, especially in light of the issues and concerns of the modern world. The liturgical movement outlined above highlights the complex web of pastoral, scholarly, and human issues that were converging. It indicates that worship had drifted from its fundamental grounding and meaning. The Church's liturgy, in many ways, was not doing what it intended to do, no matter how precise the rubrics

[23] An insightful and clear description of the issues in the medieval Church and how they emerged as a context for Aquinas' thought can be found in David Power's *The Eucharistic Mystery*, Part IV, "Eucharist in the Later Middle Ages."

[24] Fink, "Sacramental Theology after Vatican II," 1108.

or how detailed the manuals that explained them. In addition, receptivity and openness to the "grace" of the sacraments by well-intentioned, faithful people still seemed primarily a passive response to a commodity handed out or withheld, devoid of the personal, redemptive mystery it proclaimed.[25] The four-fold presence of Christ needed a broader arena of encounter.

The Liturgy's Role in the Shift toward an Ecclesial Sacramentality

If Scholastic theology from the thirteenth to the twentieth centuries was moving toward a more individualistic understanding of the sacramental encounter with Christ *(Christus solus)*, one could also characterize Roman Catholic theologians in the mid-twentieth century as part of a process of retrieval of the sacramental community, a rediscovery of the earlier Augustinian image of *totus Christus*— "Christ in the midst of the church, together with the church which is gathered to himself."[26] This symbolic shift highlights the primacy of the *communal* encounter as the locus of revelation between God and humankind; it suggests that the Church's rites themselves are the *expression* of such a sacred, dynamic, and multidimensional meeting. A communitarian understanding of the Church and her worship was aided, quite understandably, by the renewed interest in biblical sources and the early Fathers taking place at this time.[27] What were recorded in these texts were notions of covenantal relationship and communal identity, enlivened in the patristic community by a vital experience of the presence of Christ amid rites vigorously enacted.

All of these images provided a vision of the Church very different from the experience of most Roman Catholics at this time. This is not to romanticize the Fathers and the faith of the Church in these early centuries: superstition, unquestioned authority based on systems no longer viable, a focus at times on the literalness of the scriptural

---

[25] For a personal reflection on the experience of "assisting" at the Mass of his youth, which highlights concretely the estranged experience of worshipers that fostered the beginnings of the liturgical movement in the twentieth century, see the first chapter of Botte's *From Silence to Participation.*

[26] Fink, "Sacramental Theology after Vatican II," 1108.

[27] Among the works that note this rediscovery of early sources in detail is Volume 1 of A. G. Martimort's *The Church at Prayer: An Introduction to the Liturgy*, trans. Matthew J. O'Connell, with contributions by I. H. Dalmais, P. M. Gy, P. Jounel, and Martimort (Collegeville: The Liturgical Press, 1987). Each contributor was a key figure in the Centre Pastorale Liturgique in Paris. An extensive bibliography is provided.

witness, and an unnuanced notion of sin and evil certainly were operating as well. But underneath all this, the scriptural witness and the later sermons and accounts of Church life and worship—such as Justin's *First Apology*, Hippolytus' *Apostolic Tradition*, or Egeria's journeys[28]—suggested a worship not only different in social expression and cultural sensibility, but grounded in an entirely different symbolic foundation than currently existed. The locus of revelation is clearly rooted in a gathered assembly, rather than in the private individual. Even more, the sense of the presence of Christ in that gathering, manifested in the actual enactment of the events of redemption within the rites themselves, was not so much the result of proper matter and form, but of a vibrant, holy encounter. And yet, some veil or separation was indisputable in the Tridentine liturgy before the Vatican II reform. Its liturgical enactment masked the intimate presence of Christ within the assembly, an anomaly that the third-century Origen, for example, would not have understood. Preaching on the Lukan Emmaus passage to the Alexandrian Church, Origen said:

"We shall understand the meaning of the Law if it is Jesus who reads it to us and makes its spiritual significance clear. Do you not believe that in this way the meaning was grasped by those who said: 'did not our hearts burn within us while he talked with us along the way and while he opened to us the Scriptures.'"[29]

God's presence, moreover, was not just christological in its expression in early texts such as this. Read from a liturgical hermeneutic, and not just a doctrinal one, many patristic accounts portray an ecclesial body whose very identity is grounded in the divine indwelling, through the power of the Spirit.[30] This ritual perspective yielded new

[28] For example, see Justin's well-known account, "On the day which is called Sunday . . ." in his *First Apology* C. 67.6 in Migne, *PG* 6.429; for Hippolytus, *Traditio apostolica,* English trans. Burton Scott Easton (Hamden, Conn.: Archon Books, 1962) or G. Dix's *The Treatise on the Apostolic Tradition of St. Hippolytus of Rome* (London: SPCK, 1937); and *Egeria's Travels,* trans. John Wilkinson (London: SPCK, 1971).

[29] Origen, S.C. 71.26; quotation in Thomas K. Carroll, *Preaching the Word: Message of the Fathers of the Church,* vol. 11 (Wilmington, Del.: Michael Glazier, Inc., 1984) 44.

[30] For an excellent compendium of such passages, particularly as they apply to mystagogical catechesis, see Edward Yarnold, *The Awe-Inspiring Rites of Initiation: The Origins of the RCIA* (Collegeville: The Liturgical Press, 1994).

insights into figures like Clement of Alexandria, for example, who proclaimed that the liturgy itself expressed the interrelationship between the life of the Church and the movement of the Holy Spirit, a theme to which the twentieth century returned anew with relish: "Breathing together is properly said of the church. For the sacrifice of the church is the word breathing as incense from holy souls, the sacrifice and the whole mind being at the same time unveiled in God."[31]

As a result, sacramental theologians, in particular during the time of the contemporary liturgical movement, began to reflect more earnestly on the dissonant contrast between the Church as a dispenser of grace as opposed to the locus of gracious encounter. They understood with increasing clarity the limitations of scholastic categories in the Tridentine doctrines concerning sacraments and worship. The emergence of Odo Casel's mystery theology,[32] noted earlier, is but an example of the direction sacramental thought was taking: the sacramentality of Christian life as a whole and the unity of worshipers in the redemptive action of Christ.

Such theological ferment expressed a profound shift from the prevailing image of *Christus solus* ("Christ alone, present in the ministry

---

[31] Clement of Alexandria, *Stromata* VII.6, *Ante-Nicene Fathers* 2:526f.; quotation in David Power, *The Eucharistic Mystery: Revitalizing the Tradition* (New York: Cross, 1992) 117. In this chapter, Power makes an important statement about the nature of patristic preaching that would serve well in the current reappropriation of the earliest traditions as a part of liturgical reform: "The [paschal] mystery is manifested through the way in which word and sacrament belong together" (106). Patristic preaching as a whole, and mystagogical catechesis in particular, are used by both Power and Edward J. Kilmartin (*Christian Liturgy I* [Kansas City: Sheed & Ward, 1988] 288–90) as examples of this symbiotic relationship between assembly, preacher, liturgical ritual, and the sacred mysteries of the paschal event. Key to this integration is the ecclesial and communal mode of address and rhetorical intention of the patristic preachers.

[32] Odo Casel, *The Mystery of Christian Worship and Other Writings* (Westminster, Md.: Newman Press, 1962). The German editions of Parts I and II were originally published in 1939 and 1959. Casel notes this dynamic relationship between God and humankind in this mystery:

"The shared work of God and man belongs to the mystery; its author can only be a God-man, and this work gives entrance into the eternal, divine, life, here already 'in promise,' while its fullness is reserved for the time to come. The mystery gives a most intimate, real union with God; the Father begets, the Logos joins himself to us as bridegroom; Agape, God's own love, is the mark of this mystical union. Only the new alliance could bring the mystery and through it reveal the inmost heart of God, his love" (31).

of the priest, and acting on behalf of the people"[33]) to *totus Christus,* in which the Trinitarian dynamic of God's mighty acts in Jesus (Acts 5:30-32) ground God's action in the world and Christ's presence in the Church through her worship and service to the world. The sacramental theology of the manuals that explained the liturgical activity appeared increasingly inadequate, both from the perspectives of the earliest tradition and of contemporary thought. *Christus solus,* outside of a Trinitarian relational context, proved to be an impoverished symbolic foundation for the Church's life and mission. Moreover, a sacramental power divorced from the locus and enactment of that divine encounter rendered the liturgy itself a mere tool for "effecting" grace through the hands of the priest, while believers merely watched from outside the arena of sacred action. Finally, the listless and unimaginative state of preaching in Roman Catholic worship at this time seemed inexorably linked to a profound lack of understanding by both priests and the faithful, not only of the multivalence of scriptural texts, but also of the relationship that the proclamation of the word had to the rest of the sacramental action that followed. Doctrinal polemics with Protestants simply were no longer enough to keep Roman Catholic theologians from investigating the dialogic relationship between Word and Sacrament; the multidimensional presence of Christ needed a rich assimilation of both. In short, the sacramental "system" was in need of profound reform.

Two Specific Areas of Inquiry that Affect an Understanding of Sacramentality and Proclamation

The promulgation of the Constitution on the Sacred Liturgy, along with the continued reform it has engendered, was born out of this continuing and often ambiguous interplay between people's faith and worship. Its vision was clarified by pastoral and theological reflection on the part of scholars, who themselves were in dialogue with related fields of theology, as well as cultural and ritual theory. Increased ecumenical cooperation broadened the conversation. Even concerted attempts by Church authorities to monitor and safeguard the ecclesial tradition kept the issues alive and contributed to this critical reflection.

Two theological issues in particular emerge as germane to this present study of the word as a sacramental act, and they will be dis-

[33] Fink, "Sacramental Theology after Vatican II," 1108.

16

cussed in Chapter 2 by examining the works of three representative sacramental theologians of this period. First to be explored will be the evolving notion of *sacramentality*, particularly as expressive of the ecclesial character of the Church's liturgical enactment. Following upon that, the complexity of *proclamation* as a grace-filled action of the Church will be clarified in light of the specific sacramental understanding articulated. These ecclesial and sacramental notions of proclamation will lay groundwork for a contemporary reappraisal of liturgical proclamation and preaching from a specifically Roman Catholic perspective. The prevailing assumption in this book affirms the integral, ritual relationship between what is proclaimed and heard in the Liturgy of the Word and the Liturgy of the Eucharist which follows.[34] That relationship itself expresses the four-fold presence of Christ in worship.

In Chapters 3 and 4 of this work, the sacramentality of proclamation will then move outside its comfortable theological boundaries. Liturgical praxis will dialogue with current *literary theory* to investigate further how the actual *event* of proclaiming biblical texts in the midst of a worshiping assembly is part of this sacramental encounter with God in Christ. What is happening, for example, in the assembly and in the preacher that reveals Christ's presence in the word? How do sacred texts proclaim the power of the word throughout the rest of the liturgical celebration? The final chapter will then summarize the study and offer some conclusions and implications regarding liturgical proclamation that have emerged from this conversation between sacramentality and literary theory.

The circle of conversation did not end with the advent of the Second Vatican Council. St. Paul's labors to uncover the mystery hidden for generations that has "now been revealed to his holy apostles and prophets by the Spirit" continue to be shared by ministers of the Gospel and by the whole People of God. We are "fellow heirs, members of the same body, and sharers in the promise in Christ Jesus through the gospel" (Eph 3:6). Re-imagining ways to proclaim that mystery unveils God's gracious activity in our midst.

---

[34] The focus of the discussion of sacramentality in this study will be on the Eucharist, although implications are immediately recognizable in the celebration of all the other sacraments. For the primacy of the Eucharist in "making the work of our redemption a present actuality," see the Constitution on the Sacred Liturgy 2.

2

The Church as *Totus Christus:* A Renewal of Sacramentality and Proclamation

Sacraments are not things. They are, first and foremost, events that express and celebrate God's saving acts in Jesus. The focal moments of this eventful proclamation—what we traditionally understand as the seven sacraments—reveal the true nature of the Church as a dynamic body of believers who encounter God in this holy meeting. The liturgy employs elemental things like words and gestures, water, food and drink, and uses them in faithful memory to announce a new reality and to lead us into a future filled with hope. This is the heritage of the Church handed down by our Jewish and Christian ancestors.

Through the passage of time and the blurring of ritual memory, these foundations were lost. As we saw at the end of the last chapter, pastoral theologians and their colleagues in systematic theology, from the 1940s onward, stirred the conversation again regarding the nature of the Church and the meaning of her liturgical practice. From different starting points they were asking similar questions: "Who are we and why do we do what we do?" This imaginative shift in ecclesial identity and expression is at the heart of twentieth-century sacramental theology and the liturgical reform.

Three representative theologians elucidate Roman Catholic thinking on sacramentality in these years prior to the council: Otto Semmelroth, S.J., Karl Rahner, S.J., and Edward Schillebeeckx, O.P. They were not only focal figures for much Roman Catholic understanding about sacraments and the nature of the Church, but they did so from an important perspective. They labored from within the tradition, committed to the painstaking process of theological inquiry and historical development. Despite the radical new questions they were asking, they saw themselves as faithful to the Church, and indeed worshiped and lived out their faith in a community of believers whose very identity they were investigating. Consequently, the pastoral underpinning that fueled Beauduin's "study weeks" in the years before World War II is a similar foundation for their sacramental investigations in these decades prior to the council. From its beginnings, liturgical reform has not been an exercise in scholarly passivity.

The distinctive lens employed in the investigation of these three theologians is their emphasis on the sacramentality of the word and the liturgical implications that accompany their ecclesial understanding of sacraments. To imagine Christ present in the word, "when the holy Scriptures are read in the Church" (CSL 7), transforms the paradigm: proclamation is no longer an objective text, but an event. All three sacramental theologians raised the question of the proclamatory nature of the Church and her sacramental life. Study of their work, however, has largely ignored the specifically liturgical questions regarding proclamation that follow from their initial study. To be sure, proclaiming the Scriptures and breaking open the word to reveal the presence of Christ in the midst of the gathered assembly was understood by Semmelroth, Rahner, and Schillebeeckx as a sacramental act. Each had different emphases and strategies to look at what could only be considered uncomfortable territory for Roman Catholics in the first half of this century. Their own pastoral praxis in the Tridentine rite did not provide a fertile place where the rule of prayer could inform their theological insights. Decades later, questions concerning the sacramental character of the word and the eventful nature of liturgical preaching have resurfaced with vigor among worshiping congregations and scholars alike. To affirm that Christ is truly present in the word and to appreciate how that presence is expressed in the liturgy are the theological issues that draw us back to their work to look for untapped veins of rich treasure.

SEMMELROTH: WORD AND SACRAMENT AS INDISPENSABLE EXPRESSIONS OF THE NATURE OF THE CHURCH

The Jesuit Otto Semmelroth's two works, *Church and Sacrament* (1960) and *The Preaching Word: On the Theology of Proclamation* (1962),[1]

---

[1] Otto Semmelroth, *Church and Sacrament*, trans. Emily Schossberger (Notre Dame, Ind.: Fides Publishers, 1965), and *The Preaching Word: On the Theology of Proclamation*, trans. John Jay Hughes (New York: Herder and Herder, 1965).

provide a clear and easy entrance into the issue of sacramentality and the theological ideas which will shape the eventual reform of the liturgy a few years later. In both works, the proclamation of the word as sacramental activity is central to his understanding of the Church as *Ursakrament* (original sacrament).[2] Semmelroth's theological context reflects the concerns of post-war Europe, where modern believers were questioning the identity, rights, and value of the individual person. The creative challenge to Semmelroth was to relate that personhood and its inherent freedom to the corporate structure and life of the Church. Semmelroth explored the necessary correlation between the individual and communal character of shared faith, by which he clarified that the sacraments and the Church are "a 'collective unity' which exists prior to the individual decisions" of faith. The personal and the communal dimension are not in opposition to each other.[3] For contemporary persons of faith, the importance of this methodological guideline continues to challenge us, because unresolved issues of personal identity and ecclesial expression remain in tension and skew the corporate nature of liturgical enactment.

Three arguments will come to the fore in both books as a response to this *Sitz im Leben*. They are presented here using Semmelroth's own terms, which use traditional sacramental language in a fresh, new way. First, the Church is a "sign" which "stands for something beyond itself"[4] and which is, therefore, "both subject and object of our faith."[5] Second, the Church is a "basic sacrament" and her "sacramental life functions," as Semmelroth calls the individual sacraments, are understood in their fullness only in the context of "the sacramental mystery of the Church whose actualization they are."[6] Third, the proclamation of the word and sacramental worship are "complementary functions" of a "single work," a "many-in-one-form

[2] Kenan Osborne, in his book *Sacramental Theology* (Mahwah, N.J.: Paulist Press, 1988), notes that Karl Rahner first referred to the Church as a "radical sacrament" in an unpublished manuscript circulated prior to Semmelroth's 1953 book *Die Kirche als Ursakrament,* but that Semmelroth himself "deserves the credit for making this term theologically acceptable" (10).

[3] Semmelroth, *Church and Sacrament,* 18–19. The decades since the council have demonstrated that this tension between personal freedom and corporate identity continues to be a major faith issue for contemporary Christian catechesis.

[4] Ibid., 31.

[5] Ibid., 11.

[6] Ibid., 9–10.

of the Church's life."[7] As such, the grace bestowed in sacramental enactment flows from this "unified whole."[8]

In liturgical proclamation, that unity is present in *both* the content
and in the actual act of proclamation. Sacred text and ritual action are
conjoined in a multilayered act of preaching. As a liturgical act, the
biblical word proclaimed in the gathered assembly plays a pivotal
role in the two-fold dialogue of Word and Sacrament that images the
totality of Christ's redemptive activity, his incarnation and saving
death. Taken together, the dynamic union of Word and Sacrament
makes the fullness of the paschal mystery present in the life of the
Church.[9] Exploring in greater detail these three key issues in
Semmelroth's ecclesiology of worship will clarify the apparently ambiguous relationship between the Liturgy of the Word and the
Liturgy of the Eucharist. What is more, Semmelroth's tightly drawn
arguments demonstrate how the multivalent presence of Christ in the
liturgy—in the elements, the proclaimed word, the praying assembly,
and the presider—cooperates in this unified proclamation.

The Church as "Sign" of the Divine Encounter

The all-embracing mystery chooses to encounter persons in relationship. Such communion is the eventful nature of divine activity.
According to Semmelroth, the Church is always pointing to this richer
reality whose fullness is in God. At the same time, it expresses God's
relationship—in and through Christ's incarnation and self-sacrifice—
with all of humankind. As both subject and object of faith, the Church
"is a community of those who, as true believers, accept God's revelation, but it is also part of the content of that revelation."[10] The visible
structure of the Church, clerical and lay, the mystical and institutional,
the Church of love and the juridical office, mirrors this two-fold nature. Although this suggests merely an apology for a hierarchical
structure of power, which Semmelroth obviously accepts as an inheritance of his time, the sign quality of an ordered communion of persons
who point to the presence of mystery obviates against either a "too-
worldly" or "other-worldly" interpretation of God's saving activity.[11]

---

[7] Semmelroth, *Church and Sacrament*, 41; *The Preaching Word*, 232; *Church and Sacrament*, 9.

[8] Semmelroth, *The Preaching Word*, 232.

[9] Ibid., 226ff.

[10] Semmelroth, *Church and Sacrament*, 11.

[11] Ibid., 30–1.

It assures that the Church is rooted in the world while she proclaims all things redeemed in Christ. Consequently, what happens in the liturgy and what is preached to the assembly actually participates in the grace-filled action of God's saving events in Jesus. "Signs can only exist," Semmelroth notes, "where there are persons to be addressed who can interpret them and in whom the effect represented by the signs can operate."[12] Speaking specifically of preaching, he insists that this activity "is never the bare communication of facts, but always direct address."[13] However, as part of such a dynamic signification, the Church participates in a "noteworthy ambivalence" because it is "placed at the center of our religious consideration" and at the same time "stands for something beyond itself."[14] The Church both "manifests" and "camouflages" the mystery proclaimed.[15]

As the sign, then, the ecclesial body is caught up in the mystery and the reality of God's action. "The Church is the historical setting of [humankind's] redemption by Jesus Christ."[16] *Because* there is an encounter, a presence and a grace are at work. Hence, the Church as sign of the divine encounter, according to Semmelroth, is inseparable from its nature as "a great common sacrament."[17] This ecclesial grounding for sacramental and liturgical theology affirms a lost patristic heritage and situates worship and sacramental life in its communal context. That is why we move now to the second issue in Semmelroth's project to re-integrate Word and Sacrament into a single proclamation.

The Church as Basic Sacrament of God's Redemptive Action

The Church, in its "symbolic purpose" and in its visible structure as a society, "contains this distinctive divine quality"[18] that it signifies. This is the classical definition of a sacrament since the time of Augustine, expanded in a way that places the eccelsial body as the

---

[12] Ibid., 101.

[13] Semmelroth, *The Preaching Word,* 189.

[14] Semmelroth, *Church and Sacrament,* 31.

[15] For this terminology I am indebted to Kenan Osborne. "Camouflages" (rather than "hides" or "conceals") is more descriptive of God's activity in the Church, especially in the liturgy, because these ecclesial realities are not withholding or keeping out the fullness of God's life from the world. Rather, as a "sign," the Church cannot contain it.

[16] Semmelroth, *Church and Sacrament,* 19.

[17] Ibid., 81.

[18] Ibid., 35.

primary metaphor for every other sacramental act. As such, the Church is not a place where an individual goes to receive sacraments, a "warehouse" which is of interest to a person "because of the objects stored there."[19] It is an arena of encounter. And in this encounter, every dimension—the vertical, the depth, and the horizontal—are played out in both the structure she embodies and the content of her message.[20] Not one of these three dimensions is exclusive of the other: the relationship between God and God's people, the reality of Christ's presence within the community as the body of Christ, and its witness to the salvation experienced in it and offered to the world is one proclamation of redemption. All the individual sacraments make present in some form the "encounter with the glorified God and realizes his mediation."[21] They are expressions of "the sacramental mystery of the Church whose actualization they are."[22]

As the arena of encounter and the three-dimensional expression of the Triune life of God, the Church as a sacramental communion in the body of Christ does not "stand by" or "administer" while God and an individual person "find each other in the Church." Semmelroth uses the image of a person "holding something in physical closeness within the clasp of his arms" to describe "the living union" between God and the Church in which an individual person is invited to share in a sacramental encounter.[23] As a basic or "source" sacrament, "the Holy Spirit, in the power of grace, animates the body of the Church as a soul" and the individual's encounter with its liturgical and sacramental life "is at the same time an immersion into the living union with God, that is, into grace."[24] As "God's will to save," the Church is the "life sphere" into which the individual sacraments gather all women and men. Such engagement, body and soul, images Christ's own life and witness.

Furthermore, if this three-dimensional nature permeates the life of the Church, then its liturgical life, and particularly the Eucharist as "the life center of the Church,"[25] is the sign of that same unity of divine activity and grace. Those who participate in the mysteries par-

[19] Ibid., 82.
[20] See ibid., 19–28.
[21] Ibid., 34.
[22] Ibid., 9–10.
[23] Ibid., 85.
[24] Ibid., 86.
[25] Ibid., 84.

ticipate in the redemptive act announced by Christ's presence in the world. Hence, this saving presence is not one-dimensional but permeates the people, events, and words that make up the action of corporate worship. Semmelroth's attempt to integrate the totality of Christ's self-offering (the paschal mystery) with the liturgical action is also what yokes together the Liturgy of the Word and the Liturgy of the Eucharist. A simple, unified vision of the activity of Christ and the worship of the Church falls together, as we will see in the third and final point.

Word and Sacrament as a "Single Work" Bestowing Grace

The two-fold dynamic of Word and Sacrament together reflect the fullness of the redemptive event. Therefore, these two expressions of the divine encounter with humankind cannot be separated. Semmelroth argues that the complementary nature of Word and Sacrament is a natural expression and "sign" of the dynamism of God's word. He explains that the initiating gift is sent forth into the world in the incarnation and returns to its source by means of Christ's self-sacrificing response back to the Father, an offering in which we are invited to share. This two-fold structure of the liturgy is a "representation of the salvation event"[26] in its entirety; its unity as a "single work" is rooted in the fact that the incarnation and the sacrifice of Christ are both part of a single redemptive event. The dialogue commences in the heart of God and is completed in God by Christ, who continually, through the power of the Spirit present in these mysteries, calls all believers to the same fullness.

The liturgical proclamation of the word, both content and enactment, appears from this argument to be a sacrament in its own right. However, Semmelroth notes a theological problem here. The Church definitively decreed at Trent (Denz. 843a)[27] that the seven (and exclusively seven) sacraments are the only means at the Church's disposal by which grace is "effected." Therefore, according to Church doctrine, proclamation cannot have "its own saving effect along with the sacraments."[28] Semmelroth, however, avoids the dichotomy of endless Protestant-Catholic polemics over the nature of grace bestowed

[26] Ibid., 38.

[27] Semmelroth uses this reference to Denzinger in *Church and Sacrament*, 55, n. 6. The more definitive statement that the number of sacraments is "seven, no more and no fewer" is found in Denzinger (DS) 1601.

[28] Semmelroth, *Church and Sacrament*, 55.

in Word and Sacrament precisely because he has had to find a way to incorporate Catholic doctrine into his schema. He correlates the liturgical proclamation to the sacramental dynamic as a whole. His logic is simple and convincing and deserves closer scrutiny.

Semmelroth is convinced that in the proclamation of the word "the same elements which are inherent in the sacraments seem to be present."[29] For example, the word of God carries with it a "divine guarantee"[30] of God's faithfulness (the *ex opere operato* of the sacrament). In addition, both the preacher and the hearer need to be open and receptive (the *ex opere operantis*) to the "self-revelation of God" contained not merely in the content but in "the actual event of the church's preaching of God's word."[31] This attention to enactment is perhaps Semmelroth's most important contribution to the sacramentality of proclamation: the preaching *act* itself "expresses symbolically that element in the incarnation and life of Christ which complements and supplements that other act expressed in the administration of the sacrament."[32] The act of proclamation makes present or invites the community into the reality of that incarnational event which is literally "God's own sermon" to us. The content must always reflect this sacred trust as God's word; but, equally, the event itself "is a symbolic act even without considering content."[33] Furthermore, it is not limited to the preacher's words alone, but embraces the whole range of biblical text and all who proclaim and hear it, who then respond at its completion with a profession of faith and a confidence in God's desire to hear their communal intercession.

Because of Trent's clear delineation of the sacraments alone as "the instrumental cause and source of the grace of justification,"[34] simply equating the obvious graces of Word and Sacrament or positing an "eighth sacrament" were not options for Semmelroth. Rather than separating Word and Sacrament as independent sources of grace existing "side by side" that would thereby offer the believer "a choice between them," there is, rather, one "effect" that is accomplished by a "complex total action," whose reality "possesses a certain imperfect similarity to the Triune God him-

[29] Ibid., 55.
[30] Ibid., 51.
[31] Semmelroth, *The Preaching Word*, 201.
[32] Ibid., 222.
[33] Semmelroth, *Church and Sacrament*, 57.
[34] Semmelroth, *The Preaching Word*, 208.

self."[35] The sacraments "effect grace," he says in agreement with Trent, but the reality they announce and proclaim comes to its grace-filled completion in the fullness of Word and Sacrament, a "redemptive dialogue in which God and [humankind] are a living unity joined in a personal confrontation."[36] In these saving acts, Christ is both "word" and "answer."[37] The German original is even more dramatic here: Christ is both *Wort und Antwort*." The conjunction of the two events, located in the person of Christ, expresses a profound theological affirmation about God's salvific plan, which the liturgy embodies and conveys. The single work of Word and Sacrament and the corresponding question of the bestowal of grace in relation to the proclamatory event, therefore, are both accounted for in his struggle to take the concerns of Trent seriously:

"For this grace proceeds from what has happened in Christ, that is, from his incarnation considered as a word, and from his sacrifice considered as an answer, the two partners in the dialogue being God and [humankind]. But both are portrayed in the single and yet dual process of preaching the word and the cult celebration of the sacrament."[38]

The sacramentality of liturgical action, therefore, is an image of the *totus Christus,* and this action of Christ is Trinitarian in nature and ecclesial in its manifestation. Even more, the whole liturgical celebration—Word and Sacrament together—becomes the sign of the redemptive event made present in the worshiping assembly and the empowering grace at work in the life of the Church. The assembly and the one who presides, the Scriptures read and the bread and wine shared in grateful memory cooperate in this sacramental proclamation, a dialogue whose word and answer shape the identity of the People of God into the body of Christ, broken and poured out for the world.

RAHNER: THE CHURCH AS THE ABIDING PRESENCE OF CHRIST, THE PRIMAL SACRAMENTAL WORD OF GOD

Just as Semmelroth focused attention upon the sacramental mystery of the Church, in which Word and Sacrament are indispensable expressions of God's redemptive dialogue with humankind, his

---

[35] Ibid., 211–2.
[36] Ibid., 232.
[37] Ibid., 230–2.
[38] Ibid., 237.

Jesuit colleague Karl Rahner expanded and deepened this dialogue at a more primordial level. He explored how underlying this mystery of the Church was the presence of "a word of grace, reconciliation and eternal life: Jesus Christ."[39] Rahner's contributions to contemporary systematic theology embraced christology, anthropology, soteriology, and ecclesiology. These were not, however, independent areas of concern for him. God's decisive action in creating, sustaining, and redeeming the world takes flesh in Jesus Christ. Part of this one divine initiative is the presence of Christ constituting the reality of the Church's life and worship. From this unique relationship, Rahner explored the Church as "the continuance of Christ's presence in the world." The Church, Rahner explains, is the "fundamental sacrament"[40] and "this one word of grace and this one grace of the word," Jesus Christ. The Church rooted in the word is not "God's class-room where Christians are taught how to behave," Rahner insisted. Rather, the word expresses an event, a person, and a relationship with the whole world. Liturgical proclamation is not a preparation *for* anything; it is embedded in the body of Christ and proclaims in space and time the salvation God offers the world.

Two of Rahner's prolific writings focus this discussion of the nature of the Church and the sacramentality of the word. *The Church and the Sacraments* (*Kirche und Sakramente,* 1962) and the essay "The Word and the Eucharist" ("Wort und Eucharistie," 1960)[41] are both concerned with this notion of sacramentality rooted in the utterance of God's definitive word in Jesus. The Church's identity with this living word is fundamental, abiding, and symbolic. It is the "visible and tangible form in which something that appears, notifies its presence, and by so doing, makes itself present, bodying forth this manifestation really distinct from itself."[42] This presence of the word in the Church, situated within humankind and the world as a whole, and prophetically spoken in history through the Church, creates an argument for sacramentality that cannot be divorced from the event and

[39] Karl Rahner, *The Church and the Sacraments,* trans. W. J. O'Hara (New York: Herder and Herder, 1964) 15.

[40] Ibid., 21.

[41] Rahner, *The Church and the Sacraments;* Karl Rahner, "The Word and the Eucharist," trans. Kevin Smyth in *Theological Investigations,* vol. IV (New York: Crossroad, 1982) 253–86. The essay was first found in *Aktuelle Fragen zur Eucharistie,* ed. Michael Schmaus (Munich: Max Hueber Verlag, 1960) 7–52.

[42] Rahner, *The Church and the Sacraments,* 37.

moment of proclamation that announces its presence. "Word and sacrament constitute the Church," Rahner said emphatically.[43] In light of that relationship, we will explore four issues in Rahner's notion of sacramentality to investigate precisely how the proclamatory word is part of the nature of the Church itself, and, hence, "renders the grace of God present."[44]

The relationship between sacramentality and proclamation in Rahner's thought must begin with a proviso that Rahner himself states in his introduction to "The Word and the Eucharist" in *Theological Investigations,* IV. He attempted to treat the question "in the perspective of the sacrament of the altar." Like Semmelroth, he was breaking new ground here for Roman Catholic theology at the time. At the same time, he admitted, "a unanimous answer is still lacking."[45] Consequently, the following issues are presented in order to focus some light on that relationship, while acknowledging that the conclusions remain speculative and were not definitive in his theology by any means. The points follow upon one another: First, Christ is the "primal sacramental word of God,"[46] by which Rahner means "the actual historical presence in the world of the eschatologically triumphant mercy of God."[47] Second, the Church is the continuation of that perpetual presence of God's mercy in Christ and, hence, is a "fundamental sacrament," in which "the sign and what is signified are united inseparably."[48] Third,

---

[43] Rahner, "The Word and the Eucharist," 254. He goes on to lament as "really astonishing that we Catholics provide no space, no systematic place for a theology of the word in the average theology of our schools, in the Latin manuals, etc." We are only beginning to appreciate that lament decades later as the hunger for the word increases in our liturgical communities.

[44] Ibid., 260. The "grace of God" was expressed earlier in terms of Christ: "now in the Word of God, God's last word is uttered into the visible public history of [humankind], a word of grace, reconciliation and eternal life: Jesus Christ" (*The Church and the Sacraments,* 15; see n. 62). Elsewhere (see "Sacramental Theology" in *The Concise Sacramentum Mundi,* 1487), Rahner refers to the "mysterious presence, occurring in *anamnesis,* of the saving event of Christ that took place once in history (Christ's incarnation, death, and resurrection), as real *signa rememorativa* and as a personal (intersubjective) encounter with the man Christ." He goes on to refer to Schillebeeckx on this point. This issue will be covered below.

[45] Rahner, "The Word and the Eucharist," 253.

[46] Rahner, *The Church and the Sacraments,* 18.

[47] Ibid., 15.

[48] Ibid., 23. Osborne notes in *Sacramental Theology* that the terms "fundamental" and "basic" sacrament are not consistent terms in Semmelroth, Rahner,

the Church is the starting point for his notion of *opus operatum*, which
he defines as "the supreme degree of the Church's actuality, as the act
of its self-*realization*," rather than as a "static and substance-like" grace
apart from that act.[49] Fourth, the Church, "through preaching by divine
command, is always likewise the hearer."[50] This word of God that the
Church hears, affirms, and preaches "must always and everywhere be
considered as ordained to [the] sacramental word,"[51] for it is part of the
character of the "one whole word of God." The whole "reality" is
present and effective in each phase of that process.[52] The logic that follows in these points is tight and progressive, but they unfold a dynamic
relationship between the incarnate *logos* of God and the preaching
Church which raises the stakes on the nature of the liturgical act of
proclamation and the sacramental word.

Christ as the Primal Sacramental Word of God

The notion that Jesus Christ is the sacrament of God is of importance to Rahner's sacramentality because it effectively unites the saving mystery of God to the concrete historical reality of this world.
Rahner is emphatic that the grace poured out in Christ makes a claim
both on God and the world by its particularity, because, in the incarnation, "redemption cannot be arrested or canceled," although individuals are free to refuse it. Jesus' historical, enfleshed existence is
"both reality and sign, *sacramentum* and *res sacramenti*, of the redemptive grace of God" now manifest in the world. As such,

"The grace of God no longer comes (when it does come) steeply down
from on high, from a God absolutely transcending the world, and in a
manner that is without history, purely episodic; it is permanently in

---

and others. The point here is that Jesus' sacramentality is the foundation for
the nature of the Church. Michael Skelley, in *The Liturgy of the Word: Karl
Rahner's Theology of Worship* (Collegeville: The Liturgical Press, 1991, p. 141),
mentions that Rahner employs *Ursakrament* in *The Church and the Sacraments* to
speak of the Church, but in later works reserves that terminology for Christ
and calls the Church *Grundasakrament* (basic sacrament). In my view, this later
shift strengthens the argument for a sacramentality of the word that posits
Christ's presence as a theological fact.
   [49] Rahner, "The Word and the Eucharist," 274.
   [50] Ibid., 253.
   [51] Ibid., 278.
   [52] Ibid., 279.

the world in tangible historical form, established in the flesh of Christ as a part of the world, of humanity and of its very history."[53]

Consequently, Jesus is both this *sign* "in which God made known his irrevocable mercy that cannot be annulled by God or [humankind]"[54] and is himself the *reality* of that grace revealed by "coming where *we* are for the very first time."[55] Furthermore, he abides here still in the Church, "in the flesh of the one human family."[56]

This spatio-temporal presence of Christ as sacrament has important implications for preaching as an event in this "self-communication of God," because the word arrives and its reality is made present when "proclaimed and accepted" in the event of its sacramental utterance.[57] The text and the proclamation are never static and generic, but specific, personal and participatory, because it is part of the "one whole word" and the "historically real and actual presence of the eschatologically victorious mercy of God" that abides in the Church.[58] The locus and context of that word uttered by God to the world defines the Church, and it leads to the second consideration of Rahner's sacramentality of the word.

The Church as Fundamental Sacrament of the Eschatological Redemptive Grace of Christ

The "institutional, hierarchical build of the Church" is only the "juridical constitution of something that must already be there for it to

---

[53] Rahner, *The Church and the Sacraments,* 15.

[54] Ibid., 18. The divine initiative cannot be "annulled" because God is faithful to God's promises and true to God's own self. Rahner does not mean here that the promise has escaped the realm of both God and humankind and has a destiny of its own. Rather, the promise is particularized and personalized in this relationship between God and the world, whose concrete expression is Jesus. God, he says, "did this by effecting it in Christ, and effected it by making it known."

[55] Rahner, "The Word and the Eucharist," 261.

[56] Rahner, *The Church and the Sacraments,* 18. The emphasis here is on the humanity of Christ, because it is related, as well, to the Church's historical, visible presence as a particular community of persons, not some abstract notion with no historical referent. As K. Osborne has noted in *Sacramental Theology,* "the more that the very humanity of Jesus is seen as sacrament of the divine, the more clearly one joins humanity and divinity" (78).

[57] Rahner, "The Word and the Eucharist," 261.

[58] Rahner, *The Church and the Sacraments,* 14.

be given such a constitution."[59] We can see a clear shift in ecclesial foundations in this assertion that changes the acting agent of proclamation and changes the nature of the event itself. The Church is first of all the "people of God," a particular community of persons called and saved by the mercy of God in Christ. Because the eternal Word took flesh, "those who are sanctified all have one Father" (Heb 2:11), and in Christ "an actually real unity by the will of God." Even though there is a visible, structured body, which is acknowledged by the individual response of persons to that "call of all [humankind] in that one Adam to a supernatural destiny,"[60] they "are in fact preceded, even chronologically, by a consecration of the whole of [humankind] which took place in the incarnation and death on the cross of the eternal Word of the Father."[61] Through the gift of the Word made flesh, humanness assumes priority over juridical structure when articulating who the Church is and how the Church acts.

The emphasis upon the redemptive events of Christ as prior to the gathering of the community and any future structures it embodies is key to Rahner's understanding of the Church as fundamental sacrament. This priority ties the Church intrinsically to these saving events in such a way that the Church is both a sign that points to God's acts in Jesus on our behalf and, at the same time, is herself the reality or expression of that grace offered to the world. It underlies the close connection between Jesus as "the primal sacrament of the mercy of God" and the Church as the historical locus of that abiding grace. As Rahner noted:

"The Church, in its concrete reality, is the permanent sign of the fact that God does not merely *offer* the grace of his self-communication but that in the triumphant efficacity of his grace . . . [God] also powerfully brings about the acceptance of this offer. Grace is not merely in the world; it is not merely there as an offer: since Christ and through Christ it is also in fact triumphantly there."[62]

The liturgy and the proclamation of the word within it take on, then, an efficacy that is drawn precisely from their ecclesiological foundation and not because of their "matter and form" per se. There is a

[59] Ibid., 11.
[60] Ibid., 12.
[61] Ibid., 13.
[62] Rahner, "The Word and the Eucharist," 272–3.

"priority" in Rahner's logic which was intentional: it begins with God, who utters this word of grace and mercy, which is spoken to the world in the historical specificity of Christ, whose paschal mystery, in turn, consecrates the whole of humankind.[63] Such overflowing grace continues in the Church, who is itself "the well-spring of the sacraments."[64] God's saving acts in Jesus are embedded in the nature of the Church, and sacramental life is expressive of this Paschal identity. As Kenan Osborne has explained, "an 'analogous' relationship between the Church as a sacrament and the other sacraments is not adequate. It is this 'well-spring' in a strict sense approach to the Church which describes the Church as a 'basic sacrament.'"[65]

The Church, Rahner maintained, is a "fundamental sacrament" not by some "vague borrowing of the concept of sacrament known to us already from the current teaching about sacraments." Rahner's warning confirms that he understood the radical shift from manual theology that he was making. Rather, Christ as primal sacrament abides in the Church in "a presence in which sign and what are signified are united inseparably but without confusion, the grace of God in the 'flesh' . . . which cannot be emptied of what it signifies and renders present."[66] The role of proclamation and preaching, by virtue of its being an identifying act of the Church, will share in this intrinsic relationship between God's word uttered in Jesus and the Church's intrinsic nature as "reality and sign."[67] In addition, the permanence and irreplaceability of the "grace of Christ" reflects a new articulation of the classic notion of *opus operatum*, in which the proclamation of the word becomes a part of "the structure of the Church's own nature," rather than a word "about" the mystery which is proclaimed. "Fulfilled in our hearing" is a consecration of the Church in her basic identity as the body of Christ. We now address this third point.

The Church as the Starting Point for the Notion of "Opus operatum," *an Act of Its Self-Realization*

The liturgical proclamation of the word as a moment of grace within the Church as fundamental sacrament suggests a fresh look at the notion of *opus operatum*. Preaching and proclamation is not a

[63] Rahner, *The Church and the Sacraments*, 13.
[64] Ibid., 18.
[65] Osborne, *Sacramental Theology*, 91.
[66] Rahner, *The Church and the Sacraments*, 23.
[67] Ibid., 15.

prelude *for,* nor does it talk *about,* something that is real. It is an act of the Church through which the redemptive presence and grace of Christ is heard and affirmed. But how does one *know* this and why is it important? How are human utterances understood to be sacramental? The possibilities for misinterpretation are enormous. Arguing for a notion of sacramentality that "takes the Church as the starting point,"[68] Rahner raised a perplexing point about the distinctive efficacy of sacraments in the classic understanding:

"For the meaning of *opus operatum* is not at all very clear. If one simply says that *opus operatum* is the operation which produces grace in virtue of Christ, without merit on the part of the agent of this operation or on the part of the subject on whom it is performed: then we must recall that all grace comes by the power of Christ, and that there are non-sacramental occasions on which grace is given without any merit. . . . Thus the notion of *opus operatum* alone is not of itself adequate to demarcate a sacrament in contrast to anything else."[69]

This point is of particular importance in a consideration of the sacramentality of the word, because Rahner was looking at the relationship "between the efficacious word of God in the Church in general, and the efficacious word of God which we have in the sacraments."[70] Starting from Trent's attempt to demystify the grace conferred in the sacraments as automatic or "magical" (Denz. 849, 850f.), Rahner affirmed the council's insistence "that God has linked his grace once and for all to the making of this sign" so that there is a connection "between sign of grace and grace signified."[71] He noted as well that Trent expressly taught that there is, in addition, "the need for inner receptiveness and for appropriation in faith of the grace conferred" (Denz. 797f., 819, 849). Yet, given the clarity of that dual quality of sacraments, "the Council teaches the necessity, if the sacrament is to be received by an adult, of a right disposition."[72] This surfaced a dilemma that will ground his own insistence on the Church as the starting point for any discussion of grace and sacraments.

---

[68] Ibid., 34.
[69] Rahner, "The Word and the Eucharist," 270.
[70] Ibid., 271.
[71] Rahner, *The Church and the Sacraments,* 25.
[72] Ibid.

"Consequently the sacrament in its concrete reality involves, like the *opus operantis* (the dispositions of the recipient), an element of uncertainty about grace, of doubt about its factual efficacy. With the sacrament a person knows just as little as he does with his merely 'subjective' actions performed in faith, whether it has really given him God's grace. Just as little and just as much."[73]

There seems to be a gulf between the sacrament as a sign and the sacrament as a cause of grace. To bridge this gap, one must reunite the reality *(sacramentum)* and the sign *(res sacramenti)*. This links the argument with our first point above, Jesus as "primal sacrament," as "both reality and sign . . . of the redemptive grace of God,"[74] and the second point which followed, the Church as "fundamental sacrament . . . [which is] the one abiding symbolic presence, similar in structure to the incarnation, of the eschatological grace of Christ."[75] The grace of Christ and the historical, tangible reality of the Church constitute the sacramental presence. The acknowledgment was simple, but profound.

This abiding presence of Christ in the Church, according to Rahner, "cannot be emptied of what it signifies and renders present, because otherwise the grace of Christ (which always remains [human]) would also be something merely transitory and replaceable," rather than God's decisive utterance on our behalf in Jesus. In "The Word and the Eucharist" Rahner used the notion of the "sacramental word" to include both proclamation of the word and the ritual action. This liturgical word is "the supreme form of the efficacious word of God," such that it "effects what it signifies, is uttered by the authority of Christ, is the word which undoubtedly represents the supreme exercise of the authority of the Church and hence also the supreme moment of self-realization."[76] Such proclamation is an ecclesial act, not a text, nor is it a single preacher's words. Furthermore, the four-fold presence of Christ in the liturgy is intrinsic to its utterance.

The communal action of the Church, gathered in holy assembly to hear the Scriptures proclaimed in its midst, distinguishes this "sacramental word" from other efficacious words. Without a clear understanding of this ecclesial and communal context, the grace of the

---

[73] Ibid.
[74] Ibid., 15.
[75] Ibid., 23–4.
[76] Rahner, "The Word and the Eucharist," 271.

sacrament imparted to an individual remains abstract and discon-
nected from the assembly's action of hearing the "sacramental
word"—and the doubt and uncertainty about God's actions on our
behalf remain. In terms of proclamation itself, the grace one experiences in hearing the word of God would seem to be unrelated to the
actual *event* of hearing that word by the assembly gathered in worship. The ecclesial link for Rahner, therefore, is essential, for it is in
and through the Church that the definitive Word of God, Jesus
Christ, is "plainly and simply" uttered *to us* and *for us* as the "gracious summons" to faith and salvation it claims to be. What is more,
this ecclesial link grounds all other individual encounters with that
word, since the Church itself is fundamentally the vessel of that abiding presence in the world.

In the end, what constitutes the sacramental word's distinctiveness
from other efficacious words and the "special form of its efficacity"
coincides, for Rahner, with the description of *opus operatum* itself. The
sacramental word has "two features which when taken together constitute, to our mind, the objective content of the concept *opus operatum*
in its unity: the word as the fullest actualization of the Church in its
absolute commitment, and the word spoken in the decisive situations
of human salvation."[77] This unity of identity and action is the "well-
spring" of all the sacraments, as was noted earlier. The Church proclaims, through her very nature expressed in the sacramental word,
not only the "offer" but the actual presence of that grace of salvation
through Christ. As such, both features of *opus operatum* are constituted
in the Church herself: "the historically audible word which proclaims
this victory and in which this victory constitutes itself present in the
world." The Church embraces both the fullest actualization of that incarnate Word in the world and through her fragile, broken voice proclaims a "word spoken in the decisive situations of human
salvation."[78] Christ's presence in the Church, therefore, employs
human words, vulnerable and prophetic voices, willing ears, and the
holy remembrance of sacred texts to announce this ultimate victory.
Assuredly, God has taken a great risk with such a human instrument.
That is the mystery that generates praise and thanks and great awe.

The liturgical proclamation of the word, therefore, coincides with
this wellspring of grace uttered in the Church when she gathers. To

[77] Ibid., 272.
[78] Ibid., 273–4.

consider grace apart from this is to forget its source, to divorce the offer from the triumphant presence, and the sign from the reality. Proclamation is an event, not a commentary or an ellipsis apart from it. Such an act "participates in the nature of the Church"[79] and cannot be understood apart from that grace. As Rahner insisted,

"For we have already seen that the Church is the visible outward expression of grace, not in the sense that she subsequently announces as it were the presence of something already there without the announcement, but in the sense that in the Church God's grace is given expression and embodiment and symbolized, and by being so embodied, is present."[80]

This ecclesial starting point for the *opus operatum*, "the unambiguous, abiding promise irrevocably made by God,"[81] leads to the final issue of Rahner to be treated here. We can affirm Christ as present in the liturgical proclamation of the word because it is part of the "one whole word of God" uttered in the Church.

Proclamation of the Word as Part of a Process of the "One Whole Word of God"

The specific issue of proclamation of the word and preaching in Rahner's sacramental theology during these years before Vatican II is admittedly ambiguous and incomplete. The novelty of the question for Roman Catholics meant that, for Rahner, "a unanimous answer is still lacking," as was noted at the outset of this discussion. His impulse to begin a discussion of the sacramentality of the word is all the more telling precisely because of the proclamatory framework of Rahner's sacramental theology. He placed great emphasis on the word "uttered" by God, who is Jesus Christ, who in turn is proclaimed in the Church by her very nature as a basic sacrament. "Thus the whole sign of grace, no matter what form it takes, must partake in the character of the *word*."[82] However, the unique action of Christ when the Church gathers to read and hear the word of God can quickly be lost in the broadness of this perspective.

As a result, we must recognize at the outset that "Word and Sacrament" are not neat categories in Rahner's "event-full" sacramentality.

[79] Ibid., 274.
[80] Rahner, *The Church and the Sacraments*, 34.
[81] Ibid., 32.
[82] Rahner, "The Word and the Eucharist," 267.

He himself admitted such a long-standing confusion in Catholic theology, and his own integral approach that founds all sacramental activity in the "one whole word of God" certainly adds to that complexity. For example, there is the perennial problem of the distinction between "the word and the element" in sacramental theology, that is, "between matter and form." This classic distinction becomes all the more complex in his thought when both "the word and the sacramental action," taken together, "participate in the symbolic character of the sacrament and hence in its quality of being *word*." His understanding of "word" is multidimensional and liturgical in character, but remains difficult to grasp, particularly when addressing the ritual activity of preaching as such. To complicate matters further, he regarded the ritual gestures and actions themselves as proclamatory. As Rahner said, "The sacramental action too has the character of the word. It designates something, it expresses something that is of itself hidden. To put it briefly, it too is a word."[83] Proper matter and form, in the classic definition, are impoverished sacramental requirements and a weak form of proclamation when the whole action proclaims grace as an integral event.

A premature conclusion at this stage would be simply to equate proclamation and sacramentality with God's word of grace, uttered in Jesus and spoken in the "decisive situations" of the Church's self-expression. Yet Rahner did not acquiesce so easily; there is a *priority and order* to this word. He insisted on a foundational context of preaching as the context out of which other sacramental words follow. In *The Church and the Sacraments,* for example, the "words of these sacraments" (which appear to refer to the words which accompany the action), demand a prior "faith and receptiveness"[84] in both preacher and assembly. Rubrical words "can therefore only ever really be spoken in the context of the preaching of the faith." The environment for the sacramental "affirmation of faith" on the part of the assembly is not only the "right and obligation" of all preachers "to produce," but the condition for the possibility of sacramental efficacy for the Church as a whole. "Thus the word God always comes as the word that is *heard* and *believed,* the word that is preached and attested because believed."[85] Preachers and ministers of the word are "testifying to the faith" when their lives radiate the Gospel they preach and

[83] Ibid., 266.
[84] Rahner, *The Church and the Sacraments,* 103.
[85] Rahner, "The Word and the Eucharist," 253.

proclaim. It follows, then, that the Church as the "Holy Preaching" (to borrow St. Dominic's term) shoulders the same responsibility before the world. Arguing for this prior attitude of "faith and receptiveness," Rahner noted that "these sacramental words *ex opere operato* encounter that disposition which is *a situation within which the sacramental words can be uttered at all and heard with faith,* and within which they have the power to produce their effect."[86]

Preaching, therefore, is both preparatory to and a *necessary* part of sacramental activity. Because of the "duality of sign and what it signifies, *sacramentum* and *res sacramenti*"[87] outlined above, an argument for the sacramentality of the word as an event of the presence of Christ is not mere speculation.[88] The Liturgy of the Word as a concrete, tangible, visible event of grace that leads to the fullest expression of the Church's actuality in the "sacramental word" appears straightforward and clear in Rahner's work at this time.

However, Rahner admitted that in practice and reflection upon that practice this sacramental quality of preaching has not been the case in Catholic tradition, "at least since the early middle ages." The primacy of the rubrical "sacramental word" (i.e., "matter and form") has led that tradition, "from the point of view of history of dogma and sacramental theology," to forget that the sacramental nature of the Church is first and foremost an "essentially-envisaged whole" and "each phase shares the being of the whole, the *whole* reality is truly present and effective in each phase." He did not disagree that the sacramental word is "unquestionably the supreme form of the efficacious word of God," but this forgetfulness of the whole process tends "to make it the *only* efficacious word."[89]

Indeed, Rahner himself seemed to fall victim to this forgetfulness in the latter half of *The Church and the Sacraments.* The eventful nature of the proclaimed word dwindled at times to a preliminary step toward a real presence in the "*anamnesis,* the words of commemoration" at Eucharist. The institutional narrative, Rahner maintained, has focal priority over all other proclamations because they are the words "in which the incarnate Word of God comes into our space

---

[86] Rahner, *The Church and the Sacraments,* 103; my emphasis.

[87] Ibid., 34.

[88] An additional reference for the importance of openness and receptivity to the word from the perspective of revelation in particular can be found in "Hearers of the Word," *Theological Investigations,* 3.

[89] Rahner, "The Word and the Eucharist," 279; my emphasis.

and time as our salvation."[90] This view resurrects a limited cause and effect approach to sacraments that his ecclesial project had taken great pains to dismantle.

Rahner came to the conclusion, finally, that "the sacramental word and the word uttered in the preaching of the Church are similar and dissimilar in all elements which characterize the word of God."[91] By being *dissimilar,* Rahner meant that preaching of its own is "the setting and accompaniment of the sacramental word" and, considered alone, has "a lesser degree of efficacity," either because "its concern is too specialized, or it is existentially addressed to a [person] only under a particular aspect." It is *similar* because preaching is part of the whole event of God's saving word, in which the "unambiguous, historical and ecclesiological presence, its embodiment and eschatological absoluteness, is called sacrament." Hence, preaching is "always aiming at this degree" and "participates in this kerygma"[92] that proclaims "the eschatologically triumphant mercy of God"[93] revealed in the redemptive event. That mercy and redemption "are inchoate everywhere in this quality of efficacious word."[94] Implicit in his distinction is the obverse warning that sacramental action itself, without the fullness of the context of a preached word that is proclaimed,

[90] Rahner, *The Church and the Sacraments,* 86. In a number of personal discussions with Kenan Osborne, he has noted the significantly poorer quality of this second section of *The Church and the Sacraments,* where Rahner focused on the individual sacraments. That lack of clarity about "word" is even more pervasive, I believe. It is my own contention that the scriptural word itself can often seem primarily as a source for what he calls "explanatory words of the Lord" (see "The Word and the Eucharist," 285) or for the context of sacramental activity described in the biblical texts.

[91] Rahner, "The Word and the Eucharist," 280. It is precisely this rich, complex nature of the word that is proclaimed, heard, and preached in faith that makes the liturgical proclamation a sacred presence. Perhaps Rahner's lack of clarity persisted because he was limiting the discussion to preaching rather than the whole ritual dynamic of the Liturgy of the Word. As will be shown below, Rahner knew there were many aspects regarding the sacramental nature of proclamation that still needed to be considered. Such considerations had to include the lived praxis of the *lex orandi,* something that the Tridentine liturgy and its lack of the vernacular did not afford him. I would add that preaching apart from the rest of the dynamic truncates the proclamation and the event-fullness of the word.

[92] Ibid., 286.

[93] Rahner, *The Church and the Sacraments,* 15.

[94] Rahner, "The Word and the Eucharist," 280.

heard, and believed,[95] is divorced from its context and the well-spring from which it takes its meaning. "We must not start by taking the two things as independent and juxtaposed realities: they are phases and moments of the same process."[96] This efficacious unity of Word and Sacrament coincides with Rahner's ecclesial sacramentality. He never considered the Liturgy of the Word, from this communal and multidimensional perspective, apart from the eucharistic table or the font. Rahner's inconsistency around the liturgical word and the sacramental word reflected his own acknowledged claim that there remains more theological work to do regarding the sacramentality of the word. Even more, his practical liturgical experience in the Tridentine rite did not express in a ritual and intentional way this unity of the process he described.

That is why contemporary reflection must return to the original vision that grounded his struggle to articulate the relationship between Word and Sacrament in the first place. We have seen how Rahner's understanding of sacramentality begins with an "event" of God's utterance. The dynamic quality of God's word animates every proclamation and every action of the Church. This uttered Word of grace "became flesh and lived among us" (John 1:14), and because of this divine initiative, "Christ is the primal sacramental word of God"[97] and the Church is "the abiding presence of this very Christ."[98] Furthermore, the historical, tangible reality of the Church is the medium through which this "supernatural reality" becomes a "human *word*"[99] to be heard and believed. This interconnectedness between God's word and the human word is essential.[100]

---

[95] See Karl Barth, *The Doctrine of the Word of God*, vol. 1 of *Church Dogmatics*, ed. G. W. Bromiley and T. F. Torrance (Edinburgh: T. & T. Clark, 1975). Barth speaks of the necessary relationship between these three aspects of the proclaimed word.

[96] Rahner, "The Word and the Eucharist," 279.

[97] Rahner, *The Church and the Sacraments*, 18.

[98] Rahner, "The Word and the Eucharist," 273.

[99] Ibid., 267.

[100] See "Hearers of the Word," *Theological Investigations*, 3, and Rahner's own note on Vatican I in "The Word and the Eucharist," 267. Michael Skelley treats of this necessary relationship between the word of God and the human word in chapter 6, "The Church and the Liturgy of the World," *The Liturgy of the World: Karl Rahner's Theology of Worship* (Collegeville: The Liturgical Press, 1991) 133–58.

At the same time, the "sacramental word"—by which Rahner meant the word and ritual actions and gestures through which the true nature of the Church is fully actualized in decisive situations regarding human salvation—is the point toward which this dynamic event moves and finds its completion in and for us, and most especially in the Eucharist. Where Semmelroth saw proclamation and sacramental activity as "word and answer," *"Wort und Antwort,"* Rahner saw both as part of one process moving toward completion as a single event of grace. This graced proclamation unfolds within history and in phases, yet each moment participates in the expression of "that essentially-envisaged whole, the decisive moment, [which] reaches its full 'manifestation'—a manifestation which is of the essence of the thing in an incarnational structure of salvation."[101] Sacramental life embodies and thereby announces this great moment and the fullness toward which it points in faith. While not opposed to Semmelroth's position, Rahner found his "word and answer" approach too limiting, too "doctrinal." Semmelroth's understanding of the advent of the word and its relationship to liturgical proclamation, while "undoubtedly correct" in its relationship to the sacramental word, lacks the eschatological expansiveness of Rahner's own approach. He preferred to see the interconnectedness of the "element of event" as the binding force that unites sacramental and non-sacramental words into one proclamation of God's victory for us in Christ. Furthermore, this integral event is rooted in his understanding of grace in the world, which can never be separated from Eucharist. Of particular importance to an understanding of Christ's multidimensional presence, Rahner noted that each element in this process radiated that presence, because "the *whole* reality is truly present and effective in each phase."[102]

Whether that distinction makes his understanding of sacramentality as it applies to preaching any clearer than Semmelroth's is not immediately apparent.[103] As was noted at the outset, Rahner admitted

---

[101] Rahner, "The Word and the Eucharist," 279.

[102] Ibid., 279–81.

[103] Near the end of his long treatise on "The Word and the Eucharist," Rahner even noted the broader distinctions concerning the sacramentality of the word that remained to be explored:

"Hence in what we have said up to this, we do not claim to have analyzed, noted, and distinguished all the elements of the word of God which can possibly be thought of and which are theologically important for our question:

that much more work needed to be done here. In the end, he maintained a "reciprocal relationship of efficacious word of God and the effective hearing of the word effected by God himself," and that relationship is necessary and absolute, so that "if one did not exist, the other could not exist, that is, be what it is."[104]

In addition, the relational context is always ecclesial, as opposed to a Reformation notion "that the act of faith alone constituted the presence of the Lord" when applied to an individual; but, "when said of the Church as a whole," such an affirmation is consistent with Roman Catholic sacramental tradition. Rahner's own reappropriation of that tradition outlined a way in which the presence of Christ in the word constitutes an ecclesial event, which is inextricably linked to Eucharist and confirmed by the ritual act:

"In other words, the word of the sacrament of the altar, which means the presence of the Lord, is supported by the faith of the Church, which hears this word and so really confers on it its true reality, that of the powerfully triumphant word—just as on the other hand the faith of the Church in the Lord present in the Eucharist is supported entirely by his word, *under which he is present.*"[105]

The first articulations of what we will later hear in the Constitution on the Sacred Liturgy on the presence of Christ in the word, "since it is he who speaks when the holy Scriptures are read in the Church" (CSL 7), were beginning to be explored here concretely, as Semmelroth also explored them. There is a presence that abides in the Church of "a word of grace, reconciliation and eternal life: Jesus Christ."[106] Ritual words and gestures, "matter and form," do not capture the fullness of this event. By his word-centered and ecclesiological

---

the word as statement and as event, the word as part of a dialogue, the word as eschatological word, the word as participation in the incarnation and redemption on the Cross, the word as anamnesis, as prediction, as affirmation and as promise, as call and answer at once, as interior and exterior word, etc. In these and other aspects the non-sacramental and the sacramental word both agree and differ" (280).

Preaching and the proclamation of the word in the liturgy participate in this rich texture of meaning, but how precisely that occurs was beyond the scope of his work.

[104] Ibid., 285.

[105] Ibid.; my emphasis.

[106] Rahner, *The Church and the Sacraments*, 15.

understanding of sacramentality, Rahner paved the way for the more attentive concern given to preaching and the ritual proclamation of the word in the reform of the liturgy about to take place at Vatican II.

Some four decades later, after much pastoral practice and theological investigation, "God's self-disclosure in word" as a moment of grace[107] is taking place anew. The well-spring of the Church and her communal worship continue to be a source of richer insight whenever the believing community proclaims again "the triumphant eschatological presence of the Lord."[108] These are the major sacramental concerns of Rahner as they effect a sacramental perspective on liturgical proclamation. Edward Schillebeeckx pursued with even greater vigor the phenomenological perspectives of the revelatory word that is located in the depths of human experience. We will now explore these contributions of Schillebeeckx as the third important figure in sacramentality at the time of Vatican II.

SCHILLEBEECKX: SACRAMENTALITY AS A HUMAN, PERSONAL ENCOUNTER WITH THE RISEN CHRIST

In his works on sacramentality in the fifteen years prior to Vatican II, the Dutch Dominican Edward Schillebeeckx attempted to address two hardened extremes of theological thought which Roman Catholic theology had inherited in the centuries after Aquinas. First of all, the Neo-Scholastic absorption with "rational analysis of the *modes* of causality" obscured the "personal action of Christ in the sacraments"[109] and the accompanying response in faith by those who passively received them. On the other end of the spectrum, Protestant

---

[107] See Rahner's "Anthropology," *Lexikon für Theologie und Kirche*, vol. 1 (Freiburg: Herder, 1957) coll. 624–5. Mary Catherine Hilkert's work, particularly *Naming Grace: Preaching and the Sacramental Imagination* (New York: Continuum, 1997), is an example of a renewed theological interest in preaching and proclamation from the perspective of twentieth-century sacramental theologians, especially Edward Schillebeeckx. Current scholarship, Hilkert notes, is a response to the hunger in liturgical communities for a "fresh word" and to the recognition of the preacher's responsibility for "naming this grace" in human experience. Such a theological project embraces the heart of Rahner's sacramental ecclesiology.

[108] Rahner, "The Word and the Eucharist," 285.

[109] "Introduction: The Roman Catholic View of the Sacraments," *Christianity Divided: Protestant and Roman Catholic Theological Issues*, ed. Daniel J. Callahan, Heiko A. Oberman, and Daniel O'Hanlon (New York: Sheed and Ward, 1961) 241–2.

critiques tended, in Schillebeeckx's view, to abandon the "objective character" of sacramentality and interpret it "existentially." Schillebeeckx found this position equally "unacceptable."[110] In the 1957 essay "The Sacraments: An Encounter with God" written as part of an interreligious dialogue in *Christianity Divided,* and in his most important work of this period, *Christ the Sacrament of the Encounter with God* [*Christus, Sacrament van de Godsontmoeting,* 1960],[111] Schillebeeckx outlined an "anthropological" approach[112] to "throw some light on the essential sacramental character of the Church from the standpoint of *intersubjectivity* or *existential personal encounter.*"[113] Schillebeeckx's fresh perspective paralleled Rahner's concern for the incarnational advent of grace in our world and drew particular attention to the historical, personal, and bodily expressions of this relationship. Later, in his systematic work in two volumes entitled *Revelation and Theology* [Openbaring en Theolgie, 1964], Schillebeeckx interrelated this sacramental structure with the Church's proclamation of the word, both of which share a "vital relationship"[114] in the saving revelation entrusted to her.

Schillebeeckx's historical, personal approach clarified some key issues regarding the four-fold presence of Christ in the liturgy and the sacramentality of the word. His vision added to the rich ferment in sacramental theology that underlies the Constitution on the Sacred Liturgy and enriched the human dimension of sacramentality and the proclamatory word. We will, therefore, consider four points of Schillebeeckx: First, God's redemptive act in Jesus takes place in *history* and "can be recognized by [humankind] as divine";[115] as such, sacramentality must deal with the recognizable, concrete world and refuse a focus that is solely interior or mystical. Second, Christ is the

---

[110] Edward Schillebeeckx, "The Sacraments: An Encounter with God," *Christianity Divided,* 245. This lengthy essay is important because it is a précis to his seminal work on the topic, *Christ the Sacrament of the Encounter with God.*

[111] The references in this work are taken from Edward Schillebeeckx, *Christ the Sacrament of the Encounter with God,* 3rd rev. ed., trans. Cornelius Ernst (Kansas City: Sheed, Andrews and McMeel, 1963).

[112] See Cornelius Ernst, foreword of *Christ the Sacrament of the Encounter with God,* xiv.

[113] Schillebeeckx, "The Sacraments," 245.

[114] Edward Schillebeeckx, *Revelation and Theology,* 2 vols., trans. N. D. Smith (New York: Sheed and Ward, 1967) I:26; hereafter, references to this work will be to Volume I, Part 1, "Revelation and Its 'Tradition.'"

[115] Schillebeeckx, "The Sacraments," 246.

bodily manifestation of the divine life,[116] which is the way God desires and chooses "to be God for us in a *human* way."[117] The mode of presence of this "living, glorified Kyrios" is always an *encounter* between living persons. In fact, the sacraments of the Church are "this very encounter itself"[118] and include our personal and ecclesial participation in its fruitfulness. Third, both the redemptive act of Christ and its sacramental expression in the Church are "a mystery of worship which is *liturgical . . .* and at the same time is the gift of redemption or *sanctification.*"[119] It bestows the grace and is the gift itself. Fourth, the Church's ministry of the word proclaims "the word of Christ himself, in the form of the apostolic word."[120] The preaching of this word and the sacraments of the Church are both "burning focal points" of the whole "visible presence of grace in the world which is the Church."[121] In the distinct manner of each, there is "a real and active presence of Christ."[122] These four points expand the dialogical, ecclesial, and unitive understanding of sacramentality and the word which Semmelroth and Rahner previously have provided.

The Historical Locus of God's Saving Acts in Jesus:
Sacramentality as Revelation

Schillebeeckx's sacramental theology begins with the historicity of God's redeeming acts in Jesus. Who Jesus is, what he came to proclaim, and how that liberating presence animates the Church today cannot be appreciated and experienced unless, "by reason of the gratuitous, saving initiative of the living God, the religious man finds himself in direct converse with his God."[123] This "mutual encounter" must touch us where we are, "created and situated in history."[124] As a result, this world is not a place from which to escape, but the locus of the divine revelation that takes place there. This encounter, which Schillebeeckx calls "revelation and religion"—God's invitation and our response in faith—is itself *sacramental.*[125] As Schillebeeckx said,

[116] Ibid., 249.
[117] Ibid., 250.
[118] Ibid., 263.
[119] Ibid., 265.
[120] Schillebeeckx, *Revelation and Theology*, 42.
[121] Schillebeeckx, *Christ the Sacrament of the Encounter with God*, 216.
[122] Schillebeeckx, *Revelation and Theology*, 45.
[123] Schillebeeckx, "The Sacraments," 245.
[124] Ibid., 246.
[125] Ibid.

"We call sacramental every supernatural saving reality which presents itself in our lives historically."[126] God acts on human life and events "through history" and God's bestowal of grace "makes history by revealing itself and it reveals itself by becoming history."[127] This simple fact of historicity is fundamental. Jesus' revelation as a human person is recognizable as a divine manifestation to those who believe. The fact of the Church, therefore, represents a "visible presence of grace,"[128] the earthly form (sacramentum)[129] by which that redemptive act is present to humankind today. Furthermore, the nature of liturgical worship itself as a participation in Christ's own worship and self-offering to the Father are real and meaningful for us, because they are rooted and take place in a historical event which has the world as the locus of its enactment. Responding to an "inward word of God calling [humankind] to a communion in grace," the human encounter with the world and its challenges focuses the liturgy as the place of meeting and of revelatory dialogue with God. Such a historical moment is sacramental and proclaims a significant word. Schillebeeckx said:

"If the God who wants to enter into a bond of personal relationship with us is the creator of heaven and earth, it implies that our being confronted with the world, existence in this world, is going to teach us more about the living God than the world alone can teach us, more than merely that God is the creator of all things. Life itself in the world then belongs to the very content of God's inner word to us . . . life itself becomes a truly supernatural and external revelation, in which creation begins to speak to us the language of salvation, in which creation becomes the sign of higher realities."[130]

Christian *kerygma*, therefore, has no voice if it is not uttered in history. Without history, no faith is proclaimed, no people hear and are grasped by its saving efficacy, no flesh is shared and saved by Christ, and no prayer of praise gives voice in thanks to its reality. Rich consequences for the sacramentality of the word and the role of liturgical proclamation emerge from this perspective: liturgical preaching and proclamation now possess a two-fold source of revelation, in both the

[126] Ibid.
[127] Ibid.
[128] Schillebeeckx, *Christ the Sacrament of the Encounter with God*, 10.
[129] Schillebeeckx, "The Sacraments," 246.
[130] Schillebeeckx, *Christ the Sacrament of the Encounter with God*, 8.

sacred word proclaimed and in the life situations out of which they are heard and lived. Proclamation is not therefore *"about* God" but reveals God. It is the locus of grace and the grace itself (i.e., the encounter). The sacramentality of the word embraces the human medium of proclamation and ritual action out of which it is heard. Even understanding and appropriating the historical tradition, especially in the sacred texts that are passed down, carry with them the character of proclamation and are kerygmatic, for it is in and through ecclesial life that faith-filled people encounter the presence of this saving reality in the sacramentality of the Church. Schillebeeckx's insistence on the revelatory reality of history raises the question of humanness and bodiliness as God's mode of encounter in the person of Jesus and leads us to the christological foundation of the human encounter with God.

The Humanity of Jesus as the Basis for an Encounter with the Lord in the Church's Sacraments

Schillebeeckx explained that the human manifestation of the divine offer of grace, which is Jesus, irrevocably changed the dialogue "between God and [humankind]."[131] It promised an advent which had its roots in the Old Testament revelation. The incarnation breaks through into that history and reveals "the perfect human respondent" in the man Jesus. *"Caro salutis est cardo,"* Schillebeeckx quotes Tertullian. It is on the flesh that salvation hinges.[132] The flesh of Jesus "is a messianic reality"[133] and "the encounter between Jesus and his contemporaries was always on his part an offering of grace in human form."[134] These human deeds of Jesus "are divine deeds, personal acts of the Son of God, divine acts in human visible form" that "bring salvation" and are, therefore, "a cause of grace."[135] The particular moments and events of this grace are the paschal mystery, "his passion, death, resurrection and exaltation to the side of the Father."[136] Schillebeeckx emphasized this bodily manifestation of Jesus because it is the foundation of all that is sacramental in the world. "For a

---

[131] Ibid., 12.
[132] Tertullian, *De carnis resurrectione,* 8; Migne, *Patrologia Latina* (MPL) 2, 806; quotation found in Schillebeeckx, "The Sacraments," 252.
[133] Schillebeeckx, *Christ the Sacrament of the Encounter with God,* 14.
[134] Ibid.
[135] Ibid.
[136] Ibid.

sacrament is a divine bestowal of salvation in an outwardly percepti-
ble form which makes the bestowal manifest; a bestowal of salvation
in historical visibility."[137] This manifestation of salvation characterizes
all that is sacramental and, in language that echoed both Semmelroth
and Rahner, Schillebeeckx reiterated that the "human shape of this
divine power," the man Jesus, "is *the* sacrament, the primordial sacrament, because this man, the Son of God himself, is intended by the
Father to be in his humanity the only way to the actuality of redemption."[138] Jesus approached his contemporaries "personally" and,
therefore, "human encounter" is "the sacrament of the encounter
with God," God's way of proceeding.[139] "Jesus' human redeeming
acts are therefore a 'sign and cause of grace,'" Schillebeeckx concluded, echoing Aquinas. Human bodiliness reveals the "inward
power of Jesus' will to redeem and of his human love."[140] As such,
these acts "cause what they signify; they are sacraments."[141]

The reason for his emphatic insistence on the sacramentality of
Jesus' humanity and bodiliness is, in part, a critical response to the
impersonal approach of Neo-Scholastic theology to sacramentality. A
revitalized and expressive sacramentality must hinge on this notion of
personal encounter. Hence the sacramental life and the rites themselves are the "bearer"[142] of that saving revelation which is Christ, not
objectified things which exist apart from that personal, ecclesial event.
In addition, Schillebeeckx spoke to the opposite perspective in some
Protestant traditions (e.g., Rudolph Bultmann), which he saw as an attempt to "demythologize" or even spiritualize the historic events of
human persons gathered in faith in this time and place in history.[143]

Following the thought of phenomenologists that influenced him so
greatly at the time,[144] Schillebeeckx noted that "in the body the soul
presents itself to another."[145] Hence, the encounter with the man Jesus
by the apostles and the contemporary encounter of believers with

[137] Ibid., 15.
[138] Ibid.
[139] Ibid., 15–16.
[140] Ibid., 16–17.
[141] Ibid., 17.
[142] Ibid., 127.
[143] Schillebeeckx, "The Sacraments," 245.
[144] Merleau-Ponty, Heidegger, etc. For an account of this influence and its
relationship to Schillebeeckx's theological project, see Ernst's comments in the
foreword of *Christ the Sacrament of the Encounter with God*, xiii–xvii.
[145] Schillebeeckx, "The Sacraments," 250.

Christ, mediated through the Church, involves "both body and soul."[146] Through tangible, visible expressions of human interaction, a "spiritual bond"[147] develops, deepens, and vivifies that encounter. Such an event bestows grace and is the grace itself. As a result, reified objects or spiritualized reminders of an interior grace—the two extremes which he critiqued—are both outside the purview of this sacramentality. However, one problem remains for believers who live in the time of "waiting" between Pentecost and the parousia: "Must we manage to get along meanwhile without bodily encounter? Must our Christ encounter occur in a purely mystical fashion, in the purely spiritual contact of faith, as our Protestant brothers in the faith suppose?"[148]

On one side, Schillebeeckx surprisingly answered "Yes." Like all persons of good will in this world, Christians wait for the fullness to come: "Our eschatological eagerness is a vigil, an advance toward a meeting, an encounter not yet complete."[149] But there is more, and it is the core of the sacramentality of Schillebeeckx from an anthropological perspective. This "active expectation of the perfect encounter" is nourished and given strength to go on *because of* the sacramental life itself. It is why the sacraments are necessary. They are life-giving and the entrance into the very life of God, rather than a luxury of faith. In this eschatological time the Church

"is sustained just as much through an encounter with the living *Kyrios* (Lord) which, though unique, is nevertheless real and quasi-bodily—this encounter takes place in the sacraments of the Church and through them. And this quasi-bodily or strictly sacramental encounter with Christ is for that very reason a pledge and anticipation of the eschatological and perfect encounter with Christ."[150]

What is more, God's "veiled" fullness in love uses precisely what is of this world—"a little bread and wine, oil and water, a warm, fa-

---

[146] Ibid., 252.

[147] Ibid., 251.

[148] Ibid., 252.

[149] Ibid., 252–3. However, the sacramental celebration itself captures the historical, personal experience of this "not-yet-ness" whenever the Church gathers to wait together, to vigil in faith for a fullness not yet experienced here on earth. The season of Lent and the dismissal of catechumens who await the Easter mysteries is one example, and the Easter Vigil itself is another. Evening prayer and funeral wakes, as gatherings of the ecclesial community, symbolically express a reality which is itself an absence that is waiting to be filled.

[150] Ibid., 253.

therly hand upon the forehead"—so that this redemptive mystery might be "effectively present to us here and now."[151] These rites and these elemental materials "are a visible expression of the celestial, saving action of Christ, the *Eschaton*."[152] In addition, the Church and the sacramental manifestation of the saving reality she proclaims is the "'medium' in a real encounter *between living men [and women]*: between the man Jesus and us [human persons] and, therefore, *as this very encounter itself*." Although "indirect," it is "also *immediate* since in the body subjectivity immediately and directly expresses itself."[153] In such a visible, tangible, and immediate milieu, proclamation as a "revelation in word" and sacramental action ("revelation in reality") are both an "*action* of the Church" where believers "meet Christ,"[154] and their ritual expression is the moment of this sacred encounter. Preaching and the proclamation of the word, as Schillebeeckx will argue below, shares in this immediate, intersubjective encounter and enables believers to recognize this divine, visible reality in their midst.[155] A holy meeting occurs when the Scriptures are read and the Church gathered in faith listens, which is the third point to be explored now in Schillebeeckx's sacramental theology.

Worship and Sanctification: The Trinitarian Structure of the Redemptive Act of Christ Present in the Church

The Trinity as a communion of persons is embedded in the personal actions of Christ's saving mysteries. Schillebeeckx finds in the fullness of redemption "the key to the sense of the sacramentality of the Church in its relation to the Kyrios, the risen and glorified Lord, and so also to the Holy Spirit." The Trinity "is our redeemer,"[156] which is revealed to us in "the *human existence* of Jesus."[157] This "divine

---

[151] Ibid.

[152] Ibid., 254.

[153] Ibid., 262.

[154] Ibid., 258.

[155] Schillebeeckx, *Christ the Sacrament of the Encounter with God*, 215.

[156] Ibid., 20. Catherine Lacugna explores the Trinity from the perspective of a communion of persons in *God for Us: The Trinity and the Christian Life* (San Francisco: Harper San Francisco, 1991). As Lacugna notes in a later essay, "The Christian community is supposed to be an icon of the triune life. In baptism we are incorporated into the name of God." See "God in Communion with Us: The Trinity," *Freeing Theology: The Essentials of Theology in Feminist Perspective* (San Francisco: Harper San Francisco, 1993) 106.

[157] Schillebeeckx, "The Sacraments," 263.

inner-trinitarian life relationship" reveals itself in what he calls the "four phases" of Christ's redemption.[158] (1) "The initiative of the Father through the Son in the Holy Spirit" is expressed for us in Jesus' self-offering love to the Father. (2) Christ responds in *"obedient* love and adoration of the Father as the human translation of his divine relationship of origin."[159] (3) God's response to this act of self-offering is the exaltation of Jesus as "the Lord, the *Kyrios.*"[160] (4) The completion of this mystery and "the cycle of loving intimacy" consists in Christ's "sending of the Holy Spirit upon the world" in this present time of the *Eschaton,* in which the Church fulfills her mission as the "visible realization of this saving reality in history."[161] The Church, therefore, shares in the worship mystery of Jesus' life and in the sending of the Spirit that invites the world into relationship with God. Sacramentality expresses in a visible yet veiled way this two-fold movement of Christ's worship of the Father and sanctification of humankind through the abundant outpouring of the Holy Spirit. In short, the "sacramental Church is itself filled with the reality to which it is giving form." This Trinitarian structure of the Church is a "historical manifestation" of the loving encounter between God and the world in Christ (worship) and of the corresponding "offer of grace" bestowed on all who share in her sacramental life (sanctification).[162] The cycle of proclamation and response, as it was for Semmelroth, shapes the entire liturgy as the work of the People of God, gathered in Christ in the power of the Holy Spirit.

This two-fold aspect of Christ's redemptive mystery is important in Schillebeeckx's schema because "this primordial sacrament [*Ursakrament*] which is Christ himself" acts in and through the Church. Consequently, liturgical action and sanctification are identifying actions inherent both in Christ's redemption and in the life of the Church. These "celebrations in mystery of the Redemption" are events, encounters, and moments of grace in which the Triune mystery of God is shared with humankind and in which redemption is made present "here and now in the world."[163] Christ is acting as both head and chief member of this Spirit-filled body of the Lord. Sacramentality defined

---

[158] Schillebeeckx, *Christ the Sacrament of the Encounter with God,* 20.
[159] Schillebeeckx, "The Sacraments," 264.
[160] Schillebeeckx, *Christ the Sacrament of the Encounter with God,* 20–1.
[161] Ibid., 47.
[162] Ibid., 51.
[163] Schillebeeckx, "The Sacraments," 265.

in this manner is "something more than that which we usually under-stand under the term 'seven sacraments'" and encompasses the nature of the Church herself as "an outward manifestation" of an "inward communion in grace."[164] Going beyond a notion of individual encoun-ters with a source of grace, Schillebeeckx's vision of sacramental wor-ship engages an ecclesial body and soul that participates in a holy communion with God and one another.

The growing consensus among theologians toward this under-standing of worship as first and foremost an activity of the Church was clearly the most formidable argument for the reform of the liturgy from its Tridentine expression. Even more, this view of the Church as sacramental in her communal identity affected the whole posture of the conciliar documents concerning her presence and ac-tion in the world. Word and Sacrament is both the source and expres-sion of that redemptive mystery made present and of the ecclesial life which expresses it (CSL 10).

And for Schillebeeckx, this worship and mission is a share in the Trinity's own dynamic life and creates the community of grace which makes that life visible:

"The Church is community of worship and community of sanctifica-tion in such a way that in the very act of giving expression to her holiness in sacramental worship she is seen to be *carrying on the work itself of sanctification*. . . . In and through the performance of a sacra-ment, Christ and his whole Church surround with prayer the [per-son] who receives the sacrament."[165]

Individual faith and devotion, even the gracious effects of an individ-ual sacrament, spring forth from this ecclesial embrace. The sacra-mentality of the earthly Church, Schillebeeckx argued, is the privileged way the human person encounters the redemptive mys-tery that God offers to us in Christ. Through her sacramental life, in-dividuals "irrevocably bear a relationship to Christ as Son and to Christ as co-principle of the Spirit, since the Church is the earthly vis-ibility of his whole mystery."[166]

One final point remains regarding the role of the individual's faith within this Trinitarian structure of ecclesial life and worship. What

[164] Schillebeeckx, *Christ the Sacrament of the Encounter with God*, 53.
[165] Schillebeeckx, "The Sacraments," 266.
[166] Schillebeeckx, *Christ the Sacrament of the Encounter with God*, 168.

the classical manuals have called the "fruitfulness" of the sacrament comes to its completion when the individual person is open to this offer of communion with God and the community of believers, which is the very body of Christ in the world. The offer is made *ex opere operato*,[167] but the "worshipping petition of Christ and his Church" becomes, in the receptive heart, also the person's own. A "real mutual encounter"[168] actually takes place that deepens with the grace it offers. The individual believer's own "longing urge of love is caught up and made part of both [the Church's] own public worship and Christ's life of redeeming love."[169] This willing attitude of heart is the foundation for what Schillebeeckx calls "the active part" worshipers take "*in the celebration* of the sacrament." Following upon that, the presence of Christ in this encounter necessarily involves the persons who share in the worship act, all the time deepening their communion with Christ, with one another, and with the Triune God whose intimacy they embody.[170]

The ramifications of Schillebeeckx's anthropological approach to sacramentality emphasize in the assembly's role a transition from a reception theology of the sacraments to a participative one. Even more, the shift from an impersonal understanding of sacraments to a personal, communal one is based on the dynamism of the Trinitarian life itself, made present and available through the worship and mission of the earthly Church. This theological underpinning affects the word that is preached and the meaning of the proclamatory act which gives voice to this revelation. This efficacious relationship of Word and Sacrament is the final point to be considered in Schillebeeckx's thought.

Proclamation as a Focal Point of Revelation in which the Real and Active Presence of Christ Is Manifest

The ecclesial life of worship and sanctification that expresses the encounter between God and humankind is grounded for Schillebeeckx in "the revelation in reality and the revelation in word, sacrament and word."[171] When speaking of the character of "priestly office" which

---

[167] For a similar and fuller treatment of *ex opere operato*, see Rahner's treatment in *The Church and the Sacraments*, 24–33, especially in relationship to preaching, 103–4.

[168] Schillebeeckx, "The Sacraments," 268–9.

[169] Schillebeeckx, *Christ the Sacrament of the Encounter with God*, 139.

[170] Schillebeeckx, "The Sacraments," 272.

[171] Schillebeeckx, *Christ the Sacrament of the Encounter with God*, 169.

"empowers us to perform ecclesial acts," Schillebeeckx notes the close relationship to these two expressions or modes of revelation: "In giving to others a participation in the divine realities of salvation the priest (bishop) must act through the visible sacrament; only in sacramental signs may he bestow grace on others and only in his audible preaching of the word can others hear the word of God within them."[172]

"Audible preaching," therefore, is a liturgical action of the Church, not a text of Scripture or the objective content of a sermon based upon that text. Furthermore, the individual preacher acts in the name of the priesthood of all believers, and it is the Church that grounds the one who speaks in the name of Christ.[173] A hearing takes place in the midst of the assembly which is related to and prepares for the encounter which takes place in the individual sacraments, particularly the Eucharist.[174] Everything about this encounter is interrelated and begins first with "Christ's visible and efficacious presence in the Church," which spreads out from this "one central point." Schillebeeckx used the image of "ripples" of a stone in a pond with the Church as its center:

"This point is the Church, the visible presence of Christ's grace on earth, and from it all movement can be seen to flow. The sacrament of the Eucharist is situated at the heart of the central point—the Eucharist is the focal point of Christ's real presence among us. Around this focal point can be seen the first radiant lights—the six other sacraments. This central mystery is, however, revealed to us only through the medium of the Church's preaching. Instructed and enlightened by *this sacrament of the word,* our vision is extended, and we can see the whole wide, continuous sphere of the Church's sacramental life."[175]

[172] Ibid., 171.

[173] The ecclesial basis for acting *in persona Christi* that Schillebeeckx asserts here was a radical departure from the prevailing understanding of the sacrament of orders. For contemporary articulations of this position see David N. Power, "Representing Christ in Community and Sacrament," *Being a Priest Today,* ed. Donald J. Goergen (Collegeville: The Liturgical Press, 1992) 97–123, and Susan K. Wood, "Priestly Identity: Sacrament of the Ecclesial Community," *Worship* 68:2 (1994) 109–27.

[174] On the community's participation in sacramental activity and the particularity of the Eucharist as an expression of that ecclesial identity, Schillebeeckx makes frequent reference, e.g., *Christ the Sacrament of the Encounter with God,* 163, 215–6.

[175] Schillebeeckx, *Christ the Sacrament of the Encounter with God,* 215; my emphasis.

The "sacrament of the word" in Schillebeeckx's anthropological approach is part of the whole action of grace through which God encounters the world in history through the redemptive activity of Christ. Its importance lies in its "outward" expression of grace that situates the ecclesial assembly for the visible expression of the "inward" mystery of the incarnate Son of God manifest in the world, and, particularly and personally, in the Church's sacramental life.[176] The proclamation of the word, however, is not merely a helpful preparation or warm-up for something else. Because of this incarnational presence of Christ,

"the preaching and the sacraments of the Church can be regarded simply as the burning focal points within the entire concentration of this visible presence of grace which is the Church, for thanks to the Eucharist Christ is really *somatikos—physically* present in her, and because of this physical presence also personally present."[177]

It is clear in Schillebeeckx's thought, therefore, that the preaching of the word[178] and the sacraments together form a focus of mutual revelation. Yet, the specific quality of the relationship between the *presence* of Christ in the Eucharist and the *medium* of preaching which necessarily reveals it was left unexplored in *Christ the Sacrament of the Encounter with God*. Four years later, in *Revelation and Theology* (vol. 1), Schillebeeckx returned to the question of preaching as revelation of the saving presence of Christ. His new analysis began with a look at apostolic preaching and its foundation for the contemporary Church's preaching. He then considered the role that proclamation plays in the interrelationship between sacraments as "revelation-in-reality" and proclamation and preaching as "revelation-in-word." Christ's active presence engages the Church within the organic unity of these two modes of liturgical enactment.

"Revelation is both a saving event and a preaching which bears upon this event," Schillebeeckx maintained in *Revelation and Theology*.[179] The relationship between the two is based upon the re-

[176] Ibid., 216.

[177] Ibid.

[178] For Schillebeeckx, "preaching the word" involves the whole range of ritual activity which includes the proclamation of Scripture, the "sermon," the intercessory prayers and hymns. See *Revelation and Theology*, 51.

[179] Schillebeeckx, *Revelation and Theology*, 25.

demptive mystery of Christ and the progressive phases of that revelation that were discussed above regarding the Trinitarian structure
of Christ's presence in the Church. Exalted as Lord *(Kyrios)* by the
Father and bearer of the Spirit upon the Church, Christ continues to
reveal the saving mystery of God's love through "the *kerygma*
(proclamation) of the apostles." Through their preaching, "the reality
of salvation appears as something that is given to us." As a result,
there is a "mutual implication of saving event and preaching,"[180]
whereby Jesus' exaltation as *Kyrios* "inaugurated the closing of the
divine revelation, and was at the same time the foundation of the
preaching which bears upon the mystery of Christ."[181] The apostolic
preaching, because of the personal and immediate reality upon
which it was based, "belongs to the constitutive phase of revelation"
and, "together with the saving reality which it passes on to the
Church," becomes for later generations "the lasting norm for the
whole of the Church's further life."[182]

The sacramental nature of the Church embraces this norm for her
proclamation, but "is itself filled with the reality to which it is giving
form."[183] The apostles' experience of the historical Jesus and their "experience of the risen Christ who appeared to them"[184] form the basis
of their apostolic witness, which has three characteristics: their actual
preaching of humankind's redemption in Christ *(kerygma),* their reflection upon the meaning of this event and the consequent witness
of their own lives *(martyrion),* and the teaching or disclosure of "the
meaning and the consequences of this revelation of salvation" *(di-
dache).*[185] The importance of these three categories for Schillebeeckx is
that they form the basis for the "revelation-in-word" in which the
present-day Church is engaged. The apostolic preaching was, "on the
one hand, a fully human activity and, on the other, an activity carried
out by the living *Kyrios* himself."[186] The Christ they had encountered
in history and the Lord they presently experienced as speaking in
their hearts was one and the same. "The apostolic *kerygma* is therefore
the historical form in which the Lord's actual inner speech appeared,

[180] Ibid.
[181] Ibid., 26.
[182] Ibid.
[183] Schillebeeckx, *Christ the Sacrament of the Encounter with God,* 51.
[184] Schillebeeckx, *Revelation and Theology,* 27.
[185] Ibid., 28–9.
[186] Ibid., 29.

as the glorified continuation of Christ's preaching."[187] The dynamic of real presence in this *kerygma* is readily apparent.

In the post-apostolic church this same presence occurs when the historical moment of preaching, rooted in Christ and in the apostolic tradition, is caught up in the contemporary testimony of the risen Christ laboring in the Church. That testimony necessarily involves participation in Christ's worship of the Father and his bestowal of the Spirit, which is the redemptive mystery that animates the Church in her sacramental life. As Schillebeeckx said:

"Christ's present speaking in the church's preaching of the word on the one hand and inwardly in our hearts on the other is not a double address, but one and the same address, in which what was said at an earlier time is really included in what is said here and now. Christ's power as Lord is revealed in the church and her preaching."[188]

The difference between the apostles' and the present-day Church's proclamations lies in the apostles' "direct and personal testimony of Christ's earthly ministry and of the *Kyrios* who appeared to them,"[189] whereas the contemporary proclamation must be faithful to what the community of believers has received from the apostolic tradition. The Church that is faithful to this charge lives in communion with that "unique and non-recurrent" experience of the apostles through which the Church now "gives visible form to a continuous speaking here and now of the living Lord." As to this immediate and Spirit-filled presence of the Lord, "the post-apostolic church is in no way different from the apostolic church."[190] The word proclaimed "when the holy scriptures are read in the Church," as the Vatican II document on the liturgy asserts (CSL 7), shapes the liturgical enactment into a revelatory moment.

The manner in which Schillebeeckx related this preaching event to the sacramentality of the Church returned once again to the notion of encounter so important in his earlier works in sacramental theology. He began with the Hebrew notion of *dabhar* (word) as a dialogue between God and humankind, in which the historical saving acts of Jesus and the "prophetic utterances" that reveal their meaning to-

[187] Ibid., 30.
[188] Ibid., 31.
[189] Ibid.
[190] Ibid., 32.

gether make up that revelation. Schillebeeckx noted the necessity in this dialogue of hearing a word addressed to the concrete reality of human living. Furthermore, the prophetic nature of the dialogue requires a human word to locate and uncover the mystery hidden within it of God's saving activity, that is, "the inward speaking of God in the historical event" which comes to "full self-awareness in the chosen people." This speaking of God "in and through a human word" comes to its revelatory fulfillment "in Christ."[191] It is that revelation in its fullness that the apostles experienced as the word of God.

The Christian *kerygma,* therefore, has characteristics that are both human and divine. Jesus' human Word is "the incarnation of a divine invitation" to faith which carries within it the multivalent dimensions of human communication. Part of the revelatory power of the incarnate Word made flesh rests in the human dynamics that are the vehicle of the sacred interchange. Following the currents of phenomenological thought, Schillebeeckx distinguished the quality of that dialogue: (1) the specific "content" which is spoken, (2) the "invitation" addressed to another person in which the "minimum requirement is attentive listening," and (3) the "self-unveiling" that thereby occurs, "a revelation of oneself and a giving of oneself."[192] In other words, how the word is communicated really matters; human communication bears the sacred revelation. At the same time, this word of Christ transcends the limits of human intercourse. It "penetrates to the most intimate core of our personal freedom" and "is *de facto* able to bring about in us the obedient response in faith"[193] which is Jesus' own response to the Father. The presence of Christ in the Liturgy of the Word communicates this revelation in reality and word:

"The invitation to faith as the inward element in Christ's speaking is the inviting power of a divine grace in human form. In this sense, Christ's word has sacramental value just as much as his saving acts. . . . It is only on this christological basis that the saving mystery of the Church's proclamation of the word, especially in the eucharistic service of the word, can be understood."[194]

---

[191] Ibid., 36–7.
[192] Ibid., 38–9.
[193] Ibid., 40.
[194] Ibid., 41.

Christ's words proclaimed through the words and gestures of liturgical proclamation carry a sacramental presence and communicate the saving mystery the Church celebrates. Consequently, just as for the apostles, the Church's proclamation is not "*about* God,"[195] but contains "the incarnation of Christ's personal word, a divine saving power." God's saving love in Jesus "is made visible and audible by Christ in the sacraments and the word of the church."[196] In answer to those who object to such a notion as the positing of an "eighth sacrament," Schillebeeckx responded that the Church is "the great sacrament from which all kinds of dynamic sacramental movements proceed." With the Eucharist as the focal point of a concentric outpouring of grace, all sacramental life is seen for the grace that it is *because of* the proclamation that announced its saving presence:

"It is only the preaching of the Church that can disclose this mystery to us and enable us to truly believe it. Illuminated by this word, we see a broad wave of sacramental activity continue to flow outwards—grace is visible for us in all the church's activities, and in the Christian life of the faithful as a power attracting others."[197]

Schillebeeckx's revelatory sacramentality takes seriously the world as the locus of divine activity, and within that arena of grace the "word of the church and the church's ritual sacraments are simply the burning focal points of this world-embracing manifestation of the Lord." This outpouring of grace is concentrated in the Church, where "Christ is truly *somatikos*, somatically—that is, physically, and therefore personally—present.[198] The presence of Christ in Word and Sacrament, he concluded, is "not a question of 'more or less,' but a difference in manner." Just as "Christ's presence in his own *humanity*" differs in manner from the *sacrament,* so also is that manner different in the *word,* which is a presence that invites the hearer to faith. Yet "there is, in all three cases . . . a real and active presence of Christ himself."

The study of the Hebrew notion of the *eventful word* and the phenomenological aspects of human communication both suggested to him "that the word cannot be separated from the person speaking," but is "a manner of being and of being present of the person him-

[195] Ibid.
[196] Ibid., 43.
[197] Ibid., 44.
[198] Ibid., 44–5.

self."[199] Christ's manner of presence in the word is one that "invites us to believe" and which comes from God and therefore bestows the grace needed for free acceptance. The interrelationship of these two modes of presence consists first in the manner of a testimonial "word of faith" addressed by God and heard and believed by the Church. This ecclesial word "becomes incarnate in the rite, with the result that this word becomes the essential core of the sacrament and of its sacramental saving effect."[200] Schillebeeckx even goes so far as to call the proclaimed word in the rite "the *forma sacramenti*," because it causes the saving appearance of Christ in the sacrament. Furthermore, the proclaimed word has an integrity in itself as a "ministry of the word" which illumines and stirs hearts to faith so that the "ministry of the sacrament" may be fruitful and complete.

"The word itself thus becomes a sacrament, namely in the seven sacraments which are an incarnation of the *verbum dei*. The word of God *in forma ecclesiae* is not an eighth sacrament, but it makes the seven sacraments sacraments and has, as the word of God, a distinctive meaning and a saving power—the power to arouse that obedience in faith which is the condition of the fruitful reception of any sacrament and the very pivot of Christian life."[201]

Because the Gospel was given to the community of believers as the testimony of the apostles' encounter with the historical Jesus and risen glorified Lord, "the place of the ministry of the word is, in principle, the assembled people of God, the faithful community which unites for the purpose of worshipping and praising God." Schillebeeckx insisted that "the word of God resounds in the community," and it is in this gathering that the obedience in faith that Jesus himself once accepted from his Father is made present to us and for us. In the community the Lord's grace-filled invitation is proclaimed, heard, and accepted as a response of faith. That proclamation is not only kerygmatic and instructional, but "can also be a 'word of prayer,' a 'word of hymn' or a song of divine praise, a doxology, an acclamation, or a priestly blessing."

In short, the Liturgy of the Word, in all its elements of gathering, proclaiming, testifying, and offering intercession, is an integrated

[199] Ibid., 45.
[200] Ibid., 46–8.
[201] Ibid., 47–8.

event of encounter with the "revelation-in-word" which "evokes our response in faith, strengthens it, and gives meaning to it."[202] Rather than a separate service or unrelated to what follows, the liturgical word "has to arouse in us a faith in the reality of what is about to take place." The response it evokes "flows over into praise, thanksgiving and rejoicing, into confession, and into acceptance into the demands of morality and religion and into supplication."[203] This "sacrificial disposition" revealed by the word becomes, in the Eucharist specifically, "something that enters into the full significance of the sacrifice through the active participation of the people."[204] Word and Sacrament, taken together, is part of the one proclamation of Christ's saving mystery in whose grace the Church lives.

"The word is not simply an interpretation of what takes place in the action. It forms a single liturgical whole with it, with the result that this proclamation even becomes the *forma* of the eucharist. . . . The whole celebration of the eucharist is thus a service of the word, and the whole eucharist is a sacramental event."[205]

The "sermon," for Schillebeeckx, is the moment of encounter when "the word of God sounds in the manner of the apostolic word of the Church."[206] It can then be called part of the "proper" of the Mass, even its *propriissimum*. Such preaching culminates in "what makes the eucharistic celebration the Eucharist—the *forma* of the whole liturgical event, the 'word of God'" and, as such, what patristics call the "mystagogical catechesis" which illumines the *mysterion*. This illumination is part of the unfolding "of the divine word addressed to us in the man Jesus" which captures hearts and changes "the things that surround us" into that visible presence of grace we call sacraments.[207] The proclamation of the word moves toward its fulfillment in "the pre-eminent word, the person of the living Christ." That is why the word continues to be fruitful after it is spoken in faith. "But it is here—that is, in the very core of the *anaphora*—that the word reveals its supreme saving power and, as it were, transcending itself,

---

[202] Ibid., 50–1.
[203] Ibid., 51–2.
[204] Ibid., 52.
[205] Ibid., 53.
[206] Ibid., 54.
[207] Ibid., 55–6.

becomes *compressed* into a personal reality, Christ himself in the form of the sacrificial bread and wine."[208]

In the final analysis, the manner of Christ's presence differentiates Word and Sacrament for Schillebeeckx. He asserted clearly and un-equivocally the sacramentality of the word as a constituent phase in God's proclamation of salvation to the world in Christ that enables the believing community to encounter Christ in the Eucharist; in-deed, this activity "penetrates to its very heart."[209] Even more, "Christ is personally present" in the interrelated elements which make up the Liturgy of the Word. Its ritual dynamic encompasses many voices as part of the dialogue and many modes of communica-tion to express the nature of this grace-filled encounter between God and the community. The energy of this encounter "flows over into praise, thanksgiving, and rejoicing," to conversion of heart and deeper faith, and a renewed sense of being in the world.[210]

The anthropological approach of Schillebeeckx, the importance he placed on the historical locus of revelation, and the distinction in the *manner* of Christ's presence in the proclaimed word as an *invitation to faith* underline again how that presence is neither static nor individ-ual. Christ acts in this dynamic word in an ecclesial context, in which the visible act of proclaiming and preaching is as important as the text itself. The result is a sacramentality of the word which is theo-logically congruent with the Roman Catholic sacramental and liturgi-cal tradition emerging at this time.

The theological framework for a sacramental presence of Christ in the word has taken shape around three complementary understand-ings of the Church and her sacramental worship: (1) an ecclesial par-ticipation in the redemptive dialogue of Christ, as Otto Semmelroth envisioned; (2) an uttered word of grace, part of a single proclama-tion of God's victory for us in Christ, as explored by Karl Rahner; and (3) a dynamic encounter between God and humankind, in which

---

[208] Ibid., 53–4. Schillebeeckx mentioned that he borrowed from Karl Rahner the image of the eucharistic words as the "*most compressed,* the most effective word spoken" in *Schriften zur Theologie,* I. In terms of all liturgical action lead-ing to and being fulfilled at the Table of the Eucharist, Rahner's image is im-mensely helpful. The four-fold presence of Christ is "compressed" into this eucharistic word and action as well, because food and word and assembly and priest effectively share in the holy communion in Christ's Body and Blood.

[209] Ibid., 48.

[210] Ibid., 51–2.

the revelatory word is heard and appropriated at both ambo and table, as Schillebeeckx declared. This framework provides a context now for exploring recent literary studies that consider a sacred text as a communal expression of meaning, one in which the hearers play a pivotal role. In addition, the use of literary theory can help clarify how the four-fold presence of Christ in the liturgy shares in the dynamics a sacred text engenders among a community of faith gathered to hear it.

PART II

3

The Dynamism of the Liturgy of the Word as a Sacramental Event: Insights from New Historicism on the Text and Its Context

LITURGICAL PROCLAMATION AS A COMPLEX INTERCHANGE OF GRACE

Sacred texts proclaimed in a liturgical gathering possess a shared meaning that involves the larger tradition and the particularities of the moment and place of ritual enactment. Building upon the ecclesial and dialogical character of the word, we will now explore how the scriptural proclamation interacts with *the liturgical and social contexts of worship* to announce the saving presence of Christ. Such interacting contexts appear on surface consideration to be unrelated to the weightier matters of feast and text. Recent literary and cultural studies suggest the opposite. They assert that the rich interplay of context, text, and intertext actually create the richest environment in which meaning takes place. Using what critic Brook Thomas calls "that favorite new historicist ploy—the anecdote, one that should help place me in relation to my subject matter,"[1] the following vignette, a historical memoir of a particular place and time, provides a setting for our consideration:

St. Francis Xavier Church in Portland, Oregon, is filled to capacity on this first night of the Easter Triduum, Holy Thursday. The altar is stark and bare, and the lights focus on its barrenness with intensity. The intentional lack reminds the congregation that this familiar table of celebration will soon be prepared and adorned with special solemnity on this night, as in years past. The gold, yellow, and white hangings that adorn the Church stand in vivid contrast to the purple and

---

[1] Brook Thomas, *The New Historicism and Other Old-Fashioned Topics* (Princeton, N.J.: Princeton University Press, 1991) xvi.

desert shades of the past forty days. The commentator quiets the crowd of worshipers, as the accustomed energy begins to heighten. The community expects something. It has gathered like this before, and part of the energy is a mixture of past grace and the possibility of new revelation. The candidates and catechumens to be initiated at the Easter Vigil are caught up in this intangible expectation, in which their own pasts and futures are gathered into this present.

The cantor invites the community into silence. The presiders, lectors, eucharistic ministers, and servers have paused to pray together in the narthex for a spirit of service and reverence. The community stands. As the familiar hymn begins, people strain to see the simple white and yellow banner move gracefully through the congregation. They smell the incense as the young server swings the thurible with practiced skill. Many in the congregation smile at him because they know him and his family, and they imagine how honored and nervous he is to be asked to perform this ritual action.

The lector holds the book of Scriptures as high as she can. She has practiced that Exodus reading for days. People know her as well. Even more, most of them remember that almost two years ago her daughter died unexpectedly and tragically, and they know that this memory and presence are very much a part of this event and this proclamation. She has only recently returned to the lector rotation.

After kissing the altar and going to the presider's chair, the pastor curtails the usual greeting and opening rites. Instead, his familiar voice prays solemnly and loudly: *"God our Father, we are gathered here to share this supper which your only Son left to his Church to reveal his love. He gave it to us as he was about to die and commanded us to celebrate it as the new and eternal sacrifice. We pray that in this Eucharist we may find fullness of love and life. We ask this through Christ our Lord."* And the people say, *"Amen."*

The congregation sits. They take a moment to settle, and an expectant quiet pervades the crowded assembly. The familiar lector bites her lip, takes a deep breath, and then begins to proclaim solemnly, *"A reading from the book of Exodus . . ."*

Most Roman Catholics, as well as most Christians from mainline liturgical traditions, do not find this anecdote unfamiliar. Indeed, churchgoers might identify similar experiences in their own worship, perhaps even remembering a time when they served or proclaimed the word on such a solemn occasion. Even experiences of past deaths and struggles or of moments of intimacy with God in the sacrament may all coalesce in the experience of reading this account of a Holy Thursday Evening Mass of the Lord's Supper. Some might then go to the book of Exodus to hear what the lector actually read and perhaps wonder a bit what that familiar pastor preached on that important night.

This interconnectedness of time and place and event, the complexity of shared texts and of people with a shared history, the ritual varieties of sights and smells, pauses and abrupt beginnings, even the differences in an established rubric that mark off an occasion for its specialness are all "strategies"[2] and complex interchanges of social energy. Together they effect what the congregation will soon hear and even how later readers receive that account. For example, during the scriptural proclamation and the homily which would follow in the vignette just presented, wandering minds in the pew may remember the woman whose faith is slowly healing her grief, or they may be musing on the barren altar and wondering what fare will be placed there shortly. Such apparent intrusions feed the interpretation of the text. Powerful, shared communication and a variety of meanings are not necessarily exclusive.

Part I of this book focused on the sacramentality of proclamation, within the context of the entire liturgical celebration, particularly of the Eucharist. The conclusions affirmed the intimate relationship between Word and Sacrament. They highlighted the sacramental dynamism of

[2] For an understanding of the "strategies" involved in ritualization, see Catherine Bell, *Ritual Theory, Ritual Practice* (New York: Oxford University Press, 1992), especially ch. 4, "Action and Practice," 69–93. Following the thought of Pierre Bourdieu (*Outline of a Theory of Practice,* trans. Richard Nice [Cambridge, Mass.: Harvard University Press, 1984] 3–9), Bell noted: "Practice, therefore, is a ceaseless play of situationally effective schemes, tactics, and strategies—'the intentionless invention of regulated improvisation' (Bourdieu, 79 and 96)."
Later, in her chapter on "The Ritual Body," Bell clarifies how ritual practice itself employs these strategies in a way that goes beyond the boundaries of the specific rite itself:
"Strategies, signification, and the experience of meaningfulness, are found in the endless circularity of the references mobilized, during the course of which certain differentiations come to dominate others. Ritual mastery is the ability— not equally shared, desired, or recognized—to (1) take and remake schemes from the shared culture that can strategically nuance, privilege, or transform, (2) deploy them in a formulation of a privileged ritual experience, which in turn (3) impresses them in a new form upon agents able to deploy them in a variety of circumstances beyond the circumference of the rite itself" (116).

a grace-filled word of God, revealed in the person of Jesus and embedded in the life of a community through its hearing and proclaiming it in faith. They acknowledged the sacredness of a shared, redemptive history and the saving death and victorious resurrection it commemorates within the faithful enactment of the Church's liturgy. Now, in Part II, the discussion broadens to examine how recent literary-critical theories about a classic text, the history of its reception, and the role of the community in its interpretation give a framework to this mysterious interplay of text and shared history. We will ask how the interaction between a biblical text, its public reader, and those who hear it affect the communication of God's word in a liturgical enactment. Following Karl Rahner, we assume at the outset "a reciprocal relationship of efficacious word of God and the effective hearing of the word effected by God himself." This means that the word uttered in both Scripture and Eucharist and the consequent hearing of that word are, in effect, inseparable components of the sacramental event in which Christ is present.[3]

In light of that argument, how does current literary and critical interest in the dynamism of a text and its context illuminate the theological and ritual claims that Rahner and others are making about the dynamics of liturgical proclamation? As these theories will suggest, a text is never just the words on the paper or in the author's creative mind. Rather, there is a rich interplay of social transactions, both immediate and historical, that go into any community's hearing of a literary artifact. Scripture and the liturgy, which is the setting of its proclamation, share that social richness. Sacramental and liturgical theology, therefore, can profit from discussions in related fields about the social dynamism of classic texts.

The arguments employed in Part II will use two strains of contemporary literary theory, New Historicism and Reader-Response Criticism, to assert that an appreciation of the active agency of the hearer of the text can illumine the theological mystery of graced communication taking place in liturgical proclamation. The sacramental theology that emerged at the time of the Constitution on the Scared Liturgy shares the concerns of these literary approaches that the reading of a biblical word in a communal context is a complex social event. Uncovering the nature of that complexity and appreciating its

[3] Karl Rahner, "The Word and the Eucharist," *Theological Investigations*, vol. IV (New York: Crossroad, 1982) 285; see Chapter 2 above.

power to convey truth provide a broader theological framework for a renewed look at preaching as a sacramental act in liturgical worship. Conclusions and suggestions regarding liturgical praxis can then be outlined in the final chapter.

NEW HISTORICISM: THE EVENT AS A SOCIAL TEXT AND THE LITERARY TEXT AS A SOCIAL EVENT

As far back as Aristotle in his *Poetics*,[4] literary criticism has raised the issue of the interrelationship between text and context, history and social practice. Current theory, while refusing to posit Aristotelian "concrete universals" over against the contingency of the present world, is still fascinated with the mimetic character of literary works.[5] The desire to encounter the mysterious complexity and fluidity of a text and its interpretation—one that is not limited by either linguistic rationality or a detached meaning—has resurfaced again since the 1980s with the popularity of what has been called "the New Historicism."[6] Literary texts, its proponents claim, are part of a social fabric whose dynamism shifts and changes, while simultaneously acquiring and expending "cultural energy"[7] whenever they encounter new audiences in different times and places. The shifting meanings and continuing power of such texts suggest, according to Stephen Greenblatt, "that cultural artifacts do not stay still, that they exist in time, and that they are bound up with personal and institutional conflicts, negotiations, and appropriations."[8]

[4] See Thomas, *The New Historicism and Other Old-Fashioned Topics*, 197. For a description of the similarities and differences between the Poetics and New Historicism's "contingent" slant on Aristotle, see especially ch. 7, "Stephen Greenblatt and the Limits of Mimesis," 179–218.

[5] The "mimetic character" of cultural productions is understood as that quality of enduring power in them "that produces, shapes, and organizes the very network that governs its very circulation," as Brook Thomas notes (*The New Historicism and Other Old-Fashioned Topics*, 181). For an extended discussion of the differences between a classical Aristotelian, New Historicist, and a reader-response understanding of mimesis, see Thomas, *The New Historicism and Other Old-Fashioned Topics*, 197–211.

[6] Stephen Greenblatt, introduction to "The Forms of Power and the Power of Forms in the Renaissance," *Genre* 15 (1982).

[7] The phrase "cultural energy" is an important term for Stephen Greenblatt, the foremost proponent of New Historicism. He expands on his meaning of this term in the chapter entitled "Resonance and Wonder" in *Learning to Curse: Essays in Early Modern Culture* (New York: Routledge, 1990) 162.

[8] Ibid., 161.

In his seminal "Introduction" in *Genre* that marked the advent of the popular term "New Historicism" in literary studies, Greenblatt attempted to place this literary movement over against "the dominant historical scholarship of the past."[9] The older historicism, he said,

"is concerned with discovering a single political vision, usually identical to that said to be held by the entire literate world or indeed the entire population. . . . This vision, most often presumed to be internally coherent and consistent, though occasionally analyzed as the fusion of two or more elements, has the status of an historical fact."[10]

A monological perspective of theory shields the historical text, whether it is "history" per se or "literature," from attacks upon variant interpretations or conflicts of meaning. It allows one to look at a literary piece or a historical artifact and encounter it in the present "as a stable point of reference, beyond contingency, to which literary interpretation can securely refer."[11] The older historicism carefully guards a "stable core of meaning within the text, a core that unites disparate and even contradictory parts into an organic whole."[12] As a result, Greenblatt went on to say in his critique, "Literature is conceived to mirror the period's beliefs, but to mirror them, as it were, from a safe distance."[13]

New Historicists, on the other hand, do not ignore history or its lessons; in fact, they revel in them and in all the inconsistencies, human quirks, and the guided and misguided passions to which humankind is heir. If Elizabethan theater, for example, which is Greenblatt's primary field of scholarly interest, is to mirror honestly nature

[9] Greenblatt, introduction to "The Forms of Power," 5. In an essay entitled "Professing the Renaissance: The Poetics and Politics of Culture," in *The New Historicism,* ed. H. Aram Veeser (New York: Routledge, 1989) 17, Louis A. Montrose noted that Greenblatt has subsequently returned to a previous term, "Cultural Poetics," because it appears more accurate in describing the "critical project" in which he is involved. Montrose added in a footnote that the term "new historicism" seems to have been introduced into Renaissance studies (with reference to cultural semiotics) in Michael McCanles, "The Authentic Discourse of the Renaissance," *Diacritics* 10:1 (Spring 1980) 77–87, although popularized and focused upon by Greenblatt himself, particularly since the *Genre* 15 article in 1982.

[10] Greenblatt, introduction to "The Forms of Power," 5.

[11] Ibid.

[12] Ibid., 4.

[13] Ibid., 5.

and society, both in its own time until the present "reading," then it must be open to the ways history and human interaction have shaped them. The critic, the actors, and the audience can appreciate this rich dynamic when they acknowledge that the contingencies of life, chance events, "places of dissension and shifting interests, occasions for the jostling of orthodox and subversive impulses"[14] all go into the creation, presentation, and reception of a literary artifact. Such classic texts are necessarily "embedded" within the historical lives of real people, times, and events. In point of fact, Greenblatt believed that such "hidden places of negotiation and exchange,"[15] although born in the past, continue to be the source of energy and attraction to contemporary audiences in spite of static theories of interpretation.

New Historicism also attempts to move beyond a "formalist criticism" that focuses on the autonomy of the text and an identifiable common meaning, regardless of the historical context of its creation and reception. This New Criticism, which, Greenblatt added, "partially displaced" the older historicist methodology in late 1940s,[16] also appeared inadequate and one-sided to Greenblatt and his school. In its attempts to "conceive of the text as an iconic object whose meaning is perfectly contained within its own formal structure," the New Criticism removes texts entirely from their historical specificity so that their greatness and endurance is attributed to "the mature expression of a single artistic intention."[17] Such a formalist understanding of the "organic unity of literary works"[18] establishes literary artifacts as conceived and written in a privileged sphere, uncontaminated by the complexities and competing motivations that make up human events. This univocal perspective gives the dubious impression that, as historian Michael Warner asserts, "a text means what it means regardless of what your cultural situation is,"[19] a fact easily disputed if one only looks at the plethora of Shakespearean or biblical critiques published in any given period.

[14] Ibid., 6.
[15] Stephen Greenblatt, "Towards a Poetics of Culture," *Learning to Curse*, 159.
[16] Greenblatt, introduction to "The Forms of Power," 5.
[17] Greenblatt, "Resonance and Wonder," 168.
[18] Greenblatt, introduction to "The Forms of Power," 6.
[19] Michael Warner, "Literary Studies and the History of the Book," *The Book* 12 (1987) 5; quoted in Thomas, *The New Historicism and Other Old-Fashioned Topics*, 6.

There *is* an integrity to the text, New Historicists would argue, but not at the cost of what Frank Lentricchia describes in *After the New Criticism* as "a conception [of history or literary text] that leans on a temporally and uncontaminated ideal meaning situated at some primal origin, or at the end of things, or within temporality as its secret principle of coherence."[20] Despite the fact that critics like Brook Thomas disputed the simplicity at times of such New Historicist critiques of the formalist approach,[21] their underlying skepticism remains trenchant and unshakeable. They eschew any literary approach that focuses on some *static meaning* of a text and its claim of a *formal method* to search out that core truth contained in the work.

New Historicism, however, cannot be accused of rampant relativism. In contrast to deconstructionists like Derrida, who reject both shared meaning and historical context in a circular movement of language and endless interpretation, of spontaneous history and artistic convention, most New Historicists do not see the process as "locking us into a perpetual present."[22] The literary text and the "real" world do interact and influence one another, indeed, produce something, albeit revelatory of the contingent reality of history, as opposed to the transcendental authority of some universal truth.[23] As Brook Thomas noted in his essay "Greenblatt and the Limits of Mimesis," the energy exchanged between theatrical representations and social practices is not closed. Instead, the interaction

"generates a spiral rather than a circle. This production of difference makes possible social change. Represented in the theater, social practices are transformed and refashioned and then recirculated into the nontheatrical world as the aesthetic dimension of a social strategy, a recirculation that involves another transformation and refashioning, and so on. . . . The spiral it generates allows works from the past to 'convey lost life,' if in a disfigured state."[24]

[20] Frank Lentricchia, *After the New Criticism* (Chicago: University of Chicago Press, 1980) xiv. For a proviso and critique regarding Lentricchia's pragmatic/progressive approach, see Brook Thomas' essay "The Uses and Abuses of a Pragmatic Past," in *The New Historicism and Other Old-Fashioned Topics*, 79.

[21] Thomas, *The New Historicism and Other Old-Fashioned Topics*, 7–8.

[22] Stephen Greenblatt, *Shakespearean Negotiations: The Circulation of Social Energy in Renaissance England*, The New Historicism: Studies in Cultural Poetics 4 (Berkeley: University of California Press, 1988) 6.

[23] Thomas, *The New Historicism and Other Old-Fashioned Topics*, 198–9.

[24] Ibid., 184–5.

Greenblatt and his colleagues have obvious affinities with Derrida and Foucault, especially with the latter's concern for the marginalized and repressed voices in a culture.[25] New Historicism's distinctive nuance from these other postmodern approaches is that it opts for "textual traces" that endure, that in turn interact and influence the present. This possibility of something "originally encoded"[26] is a step deconstructionists and post-structuralists are unwilling to make. Theory and practice, New Historicists argue, are too intertwined to be separated and analyzed.

At the same time, the New Historicist project is not without its numerous critics.[27] New Historicists claim to welcome the dialogue and continue to resist hard and fast definitions, preferring to "situate it as a practice—a practice rather than a doctrine," as Greenblatt admitted in *Learning to Curse*, "since as far as I can tell (and I should be the one to know) it's no doctrine at all."[28]

---

[25] Ibid., 44–8.

[26] Ibid., 209.

[27] Many of these critiques have been progressively addressed and even formally embraced by Greenblatt and others as the scholarly interchange continues. Brook Thomas cited not only his own concern for what he calls New Historicism's tendency toward "simplistic idealistic criticism," but also the more extreme critiques held by people like Frederick Crews, Ihab Hassan, and Richard Poirier, whose widely published arguments against New Historicist political polemics created a simplisitic position as well. See Thomas, *The New Historicism and Other Old-Fashioned Topics*, ix–x, n. 5. In addition, Catherine Gallagher, in her essay in Veeser's *The New Historicism* (37–48), lists the political critiques leveled at New Historicism and attempts to answer them. Other helpful critiques are Gregory Jay, "Ideology and the New Historicism," *Arizona Quarterly* 49:1 (Spring 1993) 141–56; Howard Felperin, "Making It 'Neo': The New Historicism and Renaissance Literature," *Textual Practice* 3 (Winter 1987) 262–77; and David E. Johnson, "Voice, the New Historicism, and the Americas," *Arizona Quarterly* 48:2 (Summer 1992) 81–116.

[28] Greenblatt, "Towards a Poetics of Culture," 146. My attempt here is not an exhaustive critique of the literary movement Greenblatt has popularized. The present chapter poses points of similarity and departure raised by these practitioners of cultural poetics in ways that will help clarify the mysterious dynamic of proclamation and preaching within the Christian liturgy. New Historicism's appreciation for vibrant endurance of literary artifacts suggests that mere exegesis of texts and clever pastoral applications to contemporary life do not encompass the theological and ritual energy that sacramental proclamation evokes when an assembly gathers to worship. Ignoring the latter results in the current ambiguity and lack of life that characterizes many celebrations of the Liturgy of the Word.

How, then, might such a slippery and fluctuating movement be of help to sacramental and liturgical theology, especially regarding proclamation? The New Historicist fascination with the myriad "negotiations" of cultural exchange[29] taking place in the midst of any shared reading of a text treads familiar ground with liturgical worship. Furthermore, the literary respect for the vital role an audience plays in interpreting that text gives solid ground to the theological shift of the liturgical assembly from a passive recipient to an active agent. Both fields would concur that the liturgical "hearers of the word" possess lives, in turn, which shape the sacred text's reception and its capacity to reveal a mystery at work in the midst of the body as a whole. Both New Historicism and contemporary liturgical studies revel in the multivalent communication occurring when biblical texts are proclaimed in the context of a sacramental liturgy. This common discourse, therefore, will be explored in greater depth, because New Historicists' interest in the resonance of literary texts and the spirit of wonder they engender cannot help but inform a theological inquiry into any theology of proclamation that claims to be sacramental. The Scriptures convey the saving mystery at work in our midst, and they render Christ present when heard by a community whose memory and identity are fashioned by that sacred text and by the sacramental action which fulfills it.

Five points will guide our inquiry here: First, we include a proviso about the New Historicist disdain for transcendental truths and its relationship to a theological enterprise such as this. Second, New Historicist concern for the "circulation of social energy"[30] and the on-going exchange between text and "the institutions and practices of society"[31] provides key insights into the ritual dynamics of the grace-filled encounter of Word and Sacrament outlined in Part I. Third, Greenblatt's notion of a cultural poetics and the contingency of texts give a theoretical grounding to the specific claim that Scripture and the Church's liturgy are a shared ritual experience, expressive of a common faith. Fourth, the similarities of theater and liturgy as a cultural production present insights into a "presence fulfilled in our midst." Fifth, the "embeddedness"[32] of "social texts"[33] and their con-

[29] On "negotiation" and "cultural currency," see especially Greenblatt, *Shakespearean Negotiations*, 12–13.
[30] Ibid., 1–20.
[31] Greenblatt, "Towards a Poetics of Culture," 158.
[32] Greenblatt, "Resonance and Wonder," 164.
[33] Thomas, *The New Historicism and Other Old-Fashioned Topics*, 39.

sequent capacity to evoke both "resonance" and "wonder"[34] suggest a deeper understanding of God's continual encounter with humankind through the concrete event of liturgical proclamation.

An Uneasy Relationship: New Historicism's Disdain for Transcendental Truths and the Concerns of a Theological Enterprise

Because of the New Historicist fascination with a whole host of interchanges between society and history, text and context, individual and community, author and audience, the question of ultimate foundations and sources becomes problematic. Even its own proponents consider their literary practice as a project whose "mode of engagement may be called *detached immanence.*"[35] Greenblatt himself, in *Shakespearean Negotiations*, grounds his critique with the following repudiation: "There can be no appeals to genius as the sole origin of the energies of great art."[36] Most New Historicists question the relevance or need for a divine purpose or for a God, benign or not, at the heart of this complex human enterprise. For instance, in Walter Benn Michaels' *The Gold Standard and the Logic of Nationalism*, a volume in the series *The New Historicism: Studies in Cultural Poetics*,[37] he tacitly accepts that the historical context in which human persons find

[34] Greenblatt addressed these terms specifically in "Resonance and Wonder." The book *Learning to Curse* (1990) is a reworking of many ideas originally developed in the preceding decade.

[35] "Detached immanence" is a term used by Alan Liu, especially in "Local Transcendence: Cultural Criticism, Postmodernism, and the Romanticism of Detail," *Representations* 32 (Fall 1990) 77. Liu's argument is that "worlds of context" become themselves the "foundational" principles in which the critic immerses her/himself. In a project with "avowed philosophical antifoundationalism," such "immanence" is the foundation upon which the critic engages the text in what Liu later calls a "meta-way" (81). This will be explored more fully in the fifth point below, regarding the "embeddedness of social texts."

[36] Greenblatt, *Shakespearean Negotiations*, 12.

[37] Besides Michaels' and Greenblatt's books just mentioned, this University of California Press series in "Cultural Poetics" includes *Holy Feast and Holy Fast: The Religious Significance of Food to Medieval Women* by Caroline Walker Bynum, *Nationalism and Minor Literature: James Clarence Mangan and the Emergence of Irish Cultural Nationalism* by David Lloyd, and *The Mirror of Herodotus: The Representation of the Other in the Writing of History* by Francois Hartog, translated by Janet Lloyd. The titles themselves reflect both the diversity of interests and fields affected by New Historicism and the common concern for forgotten accounts and margins of society as a means of charting a literary or historical study.

themselves is complete and closed unto itself. The contingency of human interchange itself is the boundary of interpretation about what is important and meaningful. Michaels says,

"Although transcending your origins in order to evaluate them has been the opening move in cultural criticism at least since Jeremiah, it is surely a mistake to take this move at face value: not so much because you can't really transcend your culture but because, if you could, you wouldn't have any terms of evaluation left—except, perhaps, *theological* ones. It thus seems wrong to think of a culture you live in as the object of your affections: you don't like it or dislike it, you exist in it, and the things you like and dislike exist in it too."[38]

Michaels reduces theological concerns here to a descriptive aside. Indeed, most proponents of New Historicism pride themselves on treating "the events of history as that beyond which there was no recourse."[39] Their alternative emphasis, as theologian William Dean has noted, is "on the creativity of the interpretive imagination."[40] Its purpose is not mimetic in an older historicist sense of mirroring the transhistorical; rather, "its purpose is really to communicate with the past—not merely to reproduce but to interact, to initiate, to create, as one does in conversation."[41] This interpretive imagination looks at history and experience through the lens of what Dean described as (1) "a pluralism that is unlimited," (2) "an empiricism that is radical," and (3) "a pragmatism that arbitrates."[42]

If liturgical proclamation makes foundational claims about transhistorical truth that is revealed to men and women in history, then a tension exists between Christian foundations and a cultural criticism that stridently eschews them.[43] At the same time, New Historicist

---

[38] Walter Benn Michaels, *The Gold Standard and the Logic of Naturalism* (Berkeley: University of California Press, 1987) 18; my emphasis. Michaels' comments receive close attention in Brook Thomas' chapter entitled "Walter Benn Michaels and Cultural Poetics: Where's the Difference?" in *The New Historicism and Other Old-Fashioned Topics*, 125.

[39] William Dean, "The Challenge of the New Historicism," *The Journal of Religion* 66:3 (July 1986) 265.

[40] Ibid.

[41] Ibid., 264.

[42] Ibid., 266–7.

[43] This transhistorical truth, of course, is inseparable from the historical truth incarnated in the world through it.

concern for a contemporary interaction, engagement, and communication with the past through literary artifacts and dramatic events strikes a chord with the dynamic sacramentality outlined in Part I, especially in its relationship to proclamation and ritual enactment. A conversational dialogue between sacred text and liturgical assembly captures the heart of a unified proclamation within the communal celebration of Word and Sacrament. The pluralist, empiricist, and pragmatic lens of New Historicism deserves, therefore, a closer look. Exploring in greater depth the theological possibilities of such critical perspectives will illustrate that there is, in truth, an uneasy relationship between theology and the New Historicist project, but a real relationship nonetheless.

Unlimited Pluralism and the Christian Theological Project. Literary theory and contemporary theology share the current postmodern skepticism of monolithic interpretations and univocal worldviews. Consequently, Greenblatt's interest in historical oddities and marginal interpretations is not a mere intellectual curiosity, but an attempt to surface a wider hermeneutic and a richer variety of voices than those commonly accepted as standard in both history and its literary productions.[44] He approaches the issue of pluralism as a reaction to the totalizing perspective of the formalist approach to Renaissance literature he had received and to a univocal reading of the historical period out of which texts such as Shakespeare's dramas emerged. Common understanding imagined a sublime total artist confronting a totalizing world, Greenblatt noted, producing "a set of unique, inexhaustible, and supremely powerful works of art."[45]

Most contemporary readers tacitly accept this totalizing society and singular intention of the author as a given. Perhaps Renaissance writers and their audiences did as well. Yet, for Greenblatt, more voices seemed to be at work below the surface of Shakespeare's society that contradicted this placid worldview. Consequently it was the marginal texts, the traces and mundane accounts of Elizabethan life, that captured his interest in Renaissance life and literature. The often-subtle discontinuities between accepted historical accounts of

---

[44] The emphasis here is on Stephen Greenblatt, although there are numerous and growing New Historicist critics who would serve as well, including both Marxist and neo-conservative perspectives, whose work is catalogued in H. Aram Veeser's two volumes of essays, *The New Historicism* (New York: Routledge, 1989 and 1994).

[45] Greenblatt, *Shakespearean Negotiations*, 2.

events and their dramatic depiction and the recognition of certain shifts in meanings of words over the centuries suggested a *pluralism* at play within the text that transcends mere differences in critical interpretation. As Greenblatt explained:

"I grew increasingly uneasy with the monolithic entities that my work had posited. No individual, not even the most brilliant, seemed complete unto himself—my own study of Renaissance self-fashioning had already persuaded me of this—and Elizabethan and Jacobean visions of a hidden unity seemed like anxious rhetorical attempts to conceal cracks, conflict, and disarray."[46]

Despite the structural unity and stability of command commonly associated with monarchic power and law, and the artists' concomitant obeisance to persons and offices of power needed to survive and produce their works, Greenblatt remained skeptical of positing unrestricted control over literary works "constructed out of conflicting and ill-sorted motives." As a result, "Even those literary texts that sought most ardently to speak for a monolithic power could be shown to be the sites of institutional and ideological contestation."[47] Furthermore, any attempt to posit univocal meaning is continually reevaluated and altered over centuries of literary discourse. "This project, endlessly repeated," Greenblatt asserted, "repeatedly fails for one reason: there is no escape from contingency."[48] One cannot appeal, therefore, to a higher universal authority. The mimesis of art does not imitate the overarching truths that define the cosmos, as Aristotle would insist, but, rather, emulates the *activity of creation itself*, pluralistic and changing as history itself. In fact, these "half-hidden cultural transactions" empower great works of art.[49] The enduring force and pleasure of literary artifacts emanates from this interplay of creativity. A "plurality of particulars"[50] replaces foundational realities. Furthermore, the interpretive imagination mimes this shifting array of realities and acts, to echo Dean's words, "to communicate with the past—not merely to reproduce but to interact, to initiate, to create, as one does in a conversation."[51]

[46] Ibid.
[47] Ibid., 3.
[48] Ibid.
[49] Ibid., 4.
[50] Dean, "The Challenge of the New Historicism," 267.
[51] Ibid., 264.

The complexity of issues regarding a pluralist theology is the subject of much research and discussion in contemporary theology. Unstable foundations of authority appear antithetical to universal truth, and diverse sociocultural experiences render common faith affirmations difficult.[52] In light of this skepticism, the New Historicist insistence on the historical embeddedness of this interchange of creative energy shares a common ground with the dialogical nature of Semmelroth's sacramental schema and with Rahner's notion of God's graced-filled communication uttered in Christ within history. Nor is it completely at odds with Schillebeeckx's insistence on the specificity of God's human, personal encounter with humankind through the historical event of Christ's incarnation and death—a historical event continually made new through the proclamation handed down by believers in the power of the Spirit. Twentieth-century sacramental theology focuses on the primacy of the "historical community"[53] and its expression of faith over against an individual interpretation. Its event-full approach to liturgical proclamation respects the powerful communication of sacred texts which are continually refashioned, spoken, and heard in particular times and conditions.

---

[52] Just a few examples of current work in a theology of pluralism include *The Postmodern Turn: Essays in Postmodern Theory and Culture,* ed. David Ray Griffin and Ahab Hassan (Columbus: Ohio State University Press, 1987); Charlene Spretnak, *States of Grace: The Recovery of Meaning in the Postmodern Age* (New York: Harper Collins, 1991); David Tracy, *Blessed Rage for Order: The New Pluralism in Theology* (New York: Crossroad, 1975); Leonard Swidler, *After the Absolute: The Dialogical Future of Religious Reflection* (Minneapolis: Fortress Press, 1990); Paul F. Knitter, "Key Questions for a Theology of Religions," *Horizons* 17:1 (1990) 92–102. I am indebted to a colleague, Katherine McCarthy, for an insight into the breadth of current discussion in an unpublished piece entitled "The Case for the Theology of Pluralism as the Appropriate Successor to Exlusivist and Inclusivist Theologies of Religion."

Granted that universals do not speak for the experience of different peoples throughout the world at all times, each community of believers needs to have a common center out of which their experience of God or the spirit-world or the numinous radiates. Hence, the universality of truth is like a glass sphere, and all humanity shares the same center, but each community looks to that truth through the lens and perspective of its own central experience of encounter with this revelation. People who worship or pray without a center, in short, have no identity. Liturgies which are so inclusive about deity that there is no specificity to it often end up being expressions of the community's own image, that is, they reflect a community worshiping itself.

[53] Dean, "The Challenge of the New Historicism," 268.

As a result, any serious inquiry into the sacramental character of the word would be very interested in the point to which Greenblatt's unlimited pluralism has brought him: "I want to understand the negotiations through which works of art obtain and amplify such powerful energy."[54] There is an enduring life to these works, he adds, whose source is not in "a perpetual present,"[55] but circulating among human persons and empowering their works and creativity and social interactions. Sacramental theologians liken this activity to grace, and liturgical theologians in particular locate a powerful moment of such shared communication within the celebration of the liturgy itself. Oddly enough, the social moments and collective intentions that make up these powerful interactions in a literary production led Greenblatt, in his considerations, to footnote the following aside: "We may posit (and feel) the presence of a powerful and highly individuated creative intelligence, but that creativity does not lead us back to a moment of pure sublime invention, nor does it secure a formal textual autonomy."[56] This wistful speculation suggests that secular theory can profit as well from sacramental theology, because critics like Greenblatt appreciate the dynamic of the event-full character of the word. However, most still imagine theology as concerned with God as a static, autonomous Creator. Incarnation and redemption, as a shared belief irrespective of veracity, chronicles a past event.

For Greenblatt, though, *something* is happening: it resides in the text and in the communal hearing and communicates something fresh and new. However, the possibility of a rich conversation with theology breaks down here because of issues surrounding the objectivity of theory and the need for secular purity. As such, this textual liveliness, from a critical perspective, cannot be grounded in a gracious act of God, because God is somehow outside the particularity of human encounter. Sacramental theology in this century rejects the totalizing denial to which New Historicists as a group fall prey when faced with arguments about God or God's action in the world. And at the same time, liturgical sacramentality welcomes the mysterious encounter occurring in our midst which, Greenblatt says, we feel and for which he cannot account. Literary or sacramental absolutism, as well as both sides' own rigorous claims and denials about God and the nature of human activity, can do little to account for this mystery

[54] Greenblatt, *Shakespearean Negotiations*, 7.
[55] Ibid., 6.
[56] Ibid., 4–5; 165, n. 3.

taking place. Attempts to control the gracious encounter by means of mere rubrics or to ignore its dynamism on rational grounds both lead to the same confusing ends.[57] The recognition of a plurality of perspective in each other keeps that grace-filled encounter—that creative act about which Greenblatt wonders—honorably intact.

Radical Empiricism and Sacramental Experience. The second lens on history and experience in New Historicist criticism relevant to Christian theology is its empiricism and the consequent boundaries of imaginative possibilities. "The interpretive imagination is utterly historical," Dean notes regarding the New Historicist perspective on experience.[58] This assertion makes for an interesting slant upon both "the church and the tradition," one that Dean claims is conservative in the sense of its reverence for past histories,[59] and for the essential role they play in shaping the present. However, although there is a respect for the objective content of these histories, "the treatment of those objects may be highly interpretive."[60] As such, following William James, Dean notes that the *empiricism* of New Historicism is radical in the sense that it attempts to "de-authorize" the appeal to experience in Bacon and Descartes and to go beyond theory to "replace it with what people actually experience."[61] But that experience is not merely individual or purely subjective, because it relies on what Greenblatt calls the "collective exchange"[62] between persons and histories, both central and on the margins. The world "can be known";[63] however, it is more complex and meaningful when it is imaginatively interpreted within the contingencies of concrete living rather than by avoiding them. As a result, from the perspective of New Historicist radical empiricism, "If history is to be experienced, then all experience of history, the valuational as well as the factual,

[57] Dean, "The Challenge of the New Historicism," 278.

[58] Ibid., 265.

[59] Louis A. Montrose, in his essay "The Poetics and Politics of Culture," in *The New Historicism,* ed. Veeser, speaks of critic Frank Lentricchia's critique of "totalized History" and adds, "It seems to me that the various modes of what could be called post-structuralist historical criticism (including modes of revisionist or 'post' Marxism, as well as 'New Historicism' or 'Cultural Poetics') can be characterized by such a shift from History to histories" (20).

[60] Dean, "The Challenge of the New Historicism," 265.

[61] Ibid., 266. He refers to William James' *The Principles of Psychology* (New York: Dover Publications, 1980) 1:271.

[62] Greenblatt, *Shakespearean Negotiations,* 12.

[63] Dean, "The Challenge of the New Historicism," 277.

must be included, and all the faculties, the affective as well as the five-sensory, must be used."[64]

How might this respect for a collective contingency relate to a notion of sacramentality that takes historicity seriously and the personal encounter as central? Rejecting both "absolute truths independent of the contingencies of history and a meaningless relativity,"[65] New Historicism claims that the encounter between historical persons and social histories, demanding "a reciprocal concern with the historicity of texts and the textuality of history,"[66] renders all activity capable of participating in the vibrant life which a literary work exudes and communicates. "Overt facts"[67] are only a part of the multivalent communication circulating at a variety of levels of a person's interior and exterior experience. This conscious and unconscious interplay is precisely at issue when considering the enduring power of ritual practice and Christian sacramental activity in particular. An unfiltered text or sacramental gesture never passes purely from one generation to the next; indeed, from one liturgy to another, one day to the next, human experience is constantly interpreting—even *misinterpreting*—what is heard and enacted.

New Historicism's empirical approach to the experience of history maintains that the dynamism or life of literary works does not lie simply in the direct transmission of past experience to the present. In a similar vein, liturgical remembrance in Word and Sacrament asserts that the grace-filled relationship between assembly and sacred text is always being renewed in the ritual encounter.[68] As Greenblatt maintains, speaking of the continuing power of a dramatic piece like *King Lear*, "That play and the circumstances in which it was originally embedded have been continuously, often radically refigured." These refigurations are "signs of the inescapability of a historical process, a structured negotiation and exchange, already evident in the initial moments of empowerment." Contemporary sacramental theology

[64] Ibid., 267.
[65] Ibid., 278.
[66] Montrose, "The Poetics and Politics of Culture," 20.
[67] Dean, "The Challenge of the New Historicism," 278.
[68] On the understanding of liturgical anamnesis as a covenantal relationship continually being renewed, see David Power, *The Eucharistic Mystery: Revitalizing the Tradition* (New York: Crossroad, 1992) 46–57. A helpful earlier essay of Power's entitled "The Anamnesis: Remembering, We Offer" can be found in *New Eucharistic Prayers: An Ecumenical Study of Their Development and Structure*, ed. Frank C. Senn (New York: Paulist Press, 1987) 146–68.

would maintain that liturgical proclamation is an event of reading whose moment makes ritually present the saving truths it proclaims, that is, it "effects what it signifies." New Historicism helps us understand the theological claim when it insists that the life of enduring works like those of Shakespeare "is the historical consequence, however transformed and refashioned, of the social energy originally encoded in those works."[69] A radically empirical approach to text and context appeals to a sacramental sensibility in which the liturgical text is not a closed book, but part of a rich interweaving of ritual action and uttered scriptural texts that have been canonized by the tradition. In the liturgy, they are enriched with new life, a continually transformed and refashioned proclamation about God's saving acts in Jesus "originally encoded in those works." Roman Catholic theology has implicitly understood this dynamic in its traditional understanding of Christ's abiding sacramental presence in general. Just how that dynamic is operative in the actual proclamation and preaching of the Word has remained largely unfocused and unexplored. Sacramentality and literary theory can combine to enrich liturgical theology on the ritual dynamics at work "when the Holy Scriptures are read in the Church" (CSL 7). Their mutual concerns reinforce the argument for a greater intentionality regarding the particular liturgical celebration *within which* that sacred text is read and the homily is preached. That intentionality respects both the normativity of the text and the historical transmission of grace, because something treasured is being passed on in this liturgical moment that is shaped by the present hearing. That hearing, in turn, looks forward to the fulfillment of its promise in the age to come. "Clearly it is not the text alone . . . that bears the full significance of Shakespeare's play, or of any version of the story," Greenblatt notes concerning *Richard II.* "It is rather the story's full situation—the genre it is thought to embody, the circumstances of its performance, the imaginings of its audience—that governs its shifting meanings."[70] The *full situation* of the Liturgy of the Word, we can now add, communicates the grace and presence of Christ.

Pragmatism as an Arbiter of a Community's Shared Experience. The pragmatic lens of New Historicism is the final point regarding the interpretive imagination at work within a text and its relationship to

[69] Greenblatt, *Shakespearean Negotiations*, 6.
[70] Greenblatt, introduction to "The Forms of Power," 3.

the sacramentality of the word. Given that interpretations abound and a myriad of factors are circulating when one encounters a social text in a social event like liturgical proclamation, how do we keep intact the normative power of sacred Scripture as the focal point of an individual's or the community's self-identity? What constitutes a community's shared experience and truth over time if the values and interpretations remain necessarily contingent? These dangers, inherent in the New Historicism's radically empirical approach, are tempered by a *pragmatism* that, according to Dean, "provides a formal criterion that sticks with empirical techniques but arbitrates disputes by concentrating not on the origins of ideas but on historical consequences of ideas and by asking which ideas contribute more to history."[71] Brook Thomas fears that the rejection of foundational criteria or of appeals to the authority of past historical evidence, expressed in critics like Jean Tompkins and her "Against Theory" position, can ultimately collapse into a blind "How I learned to stop worrying about theory by forgetting it" position while at the same time arguing for "an assumed sense of progressive temporal continuity." That is, things move toward "social change" by the continual evaluation of "the constructed nature of historical knowledge."[72] The assumption implicit within such an evaluation, however, remains a foundational criteria, something that differing interpretations and voices only appear to dissolve. Furthermore, David E. Johnson, in an article entitled "Voice, New Historicism, and the Americas," criticized what he called this common New Historicist penchant toward "the hypostatization of the concept of history in their texts," which makes the "heterogeneity" they value "at best a fiction, or at worse a ruse."[73] The issue of a "shared concept of history" is important for liturgical proclamation and will be discussed more fully below, regarding "cultural poetics" and shared ritual experience.[74] These critiques, however, highlight the tendency to misinterpret the creative energy around sacred texts as a

[71] Dean, "The Challenge of the New Historicism," 267.

[72] Thomas, *The New Historicism and Other Old-Fashioned Topics*, 79–80.

[73] David E. Johnson, "Voice, the New Historicism, and the Americas," *Arizona Quarterly* 48:2 (Summer 1992) 84.

[74] In my opinion, the "shared concept of history" is New Historicism's most ambiguous link in its own "anti-totalizing" claims, but at the same time its most vulnerable openness to contemporary Roman Catholic theology's understanding of an ecclesial sacramentality already outlined. The shared tradition of "hearing" of Scripture and preaching is key to any liturgical enactment in which Christ is present.

reductionist exercise in selective, historical interpretation. The proclamation of the saving word of God cannot succumb to such a fluid standard of normativity. The authenticity of the proclaimed word, however, *can* be measured by the "historical consequences" of the lived experience of Christians practicing what they preach. An appeal to pragmatism maintains that how the community values the Scriptures as a normative guide ultimately expresses itself in the way they use them and the vehicles with which they choose to communicate their importance. The liturgical enactment embodies these historical consequences, and the normative power of the Scriptures does not rest in the biblical text alone, regardless of how they are employed. As a result, the liturgical proclamation of Scripture communicates something very different from televangelistic preaching. The shared history of the word, rooted in a faithful Christian tradition, also tempers current nuances.

The proponents of New Historicism as a secular and cultural theory, admittedly, have also left themselves open to the charge of "arbitrary connectedness"[75] and positing "the equal significance of all social practices."[76] They look *preferentially* to the margins of historical accounts and pay special attention to the insignificant details and transactions that lurk behind the scenes of literary works and social interactions. This is where an arbitrary pragmatism answers that critique, albeit somewhat confusedly, since any theoretical appeal to some transhistorical value would be inconsistent and "totalizing." The source of creativity, the "interpretive imagination," uses the stuff of past exchanges and transforms and refashions them, as we mentioned earlier. A focal text or a revered dramatic production is the product of the past, and its present reception, therefore, remains somehow shaped by the original work and its creative energy. But the manner in which a past work circulates this social energy "originally encoded in it" into the present is not an isolated event of individual genius or insight. "In other words," as Dean explains, "no individual's interpretation is individual; it is what it is because the

[75] Walter Cohen, as quoted in Thomas, *The New Historicism and Other Old-Fashioned Topics,* 40.

[76] Thomas, *The New Historicism and Other Old-Fashioned Topics,* 43. The popularity of non-canonical texts and gnostic interpretations provide excellent biblical examples. When they enter the liturgical arena, which is a corporate public act, the issues of meaning and truth become more crucial to communal identity.

individual lives within and is profoundly affected by a historical community."[77] This is important for any consideration of a shared text that purports to remember the past, transform the present, and orient that historical community toward the future. As Jeffrey Stout maintains in *The Flight from Authority*, outlining a New Historicist perspective in postmodern philosophy: "Beyond deconstruction lies a self whose character is not 'divorced from the traits that constitute it,' whose freedom does not consist in decisions taken apart from all desires, habits and dispositions, and whose history is inextricably intertwined with the histories of other selves."[78] As a result, Stout goes on, "Moral and theoretical decisions are alike constrained by the values and norms of a living inheritance within which even the changes we call revolutionary leave nearly everything in place."[79] Possibilities are sifted into probabilities, and the probabilities reflect the community's experience of what is important and enduring. Religious belief and liturgical practice are part of the cultural sifting that takes place. Belief and practice inhabit the arena in which Christians, over time, identify themselves as the body of Christ in which they were claimed by their baptism. Christian tradition understands the importance of belief, but it has not always valued the importance of the *ritual medium* through which the message of sacred texts reveal themselves. The medium is the *full situation* of the Liturgy of the Word, described above, and its ritual boundaries arbitrate the communal value to which they speak.

New Historicism's concern for a communal experience of valued texts and the pragmatic appeals to the event itself are shared by theories which shift the focus from the text to the reading event itself, as we will see in detail in the next chapter. Stanley Fish's notion of "communities of interpretation," which grew out of his investigation of the "reader reading,"[80] reflected a similar interest in the pragmatist

---

[77] Dean, "The Challenge of the New Historicism," 267–8.

[78] Jeffrey Stout, *The Flight from Authority: Religion, Morality, and the Quest for Autonomy* (Notre Dame, Ind.: University of Notre Dame Press, 1981) 261. The points on deconstruction he is refuting here are from Donald Davidson, "On the Very Idea of a Conceptual Scheme," *Proceedings and Addresses of the American Philosophical Association* 47 (1973–1974) 7. Stout's own influences in this area are Stanley Hauerwas and Iris Murdoch.

[79] Ibid., 261.

[80] Vincent B. Leitch, "Reader Response Criticism," *American Literary Criticism from the 30's to the 80's* (New York: Columbia University Press, 1988) 217. See also Fish's article "Interpreting the *Variorum*," *Critical Inquiry* 2 (Spring

bent of Charles Sanders Peirce. Peirce posited the *community of interpretation* as the foundation of what endures and of what is important in a culture's texts and practices, instead of some elusive position or system endlessly deconstructed. The hermeneutics of the community is informed by its reality as a living, interacting subject. Acknowledging this dynamic intersubjectivity, New Historicists like Greenblatt speak of the "life" of a literary artifact that testifies to its enduring power, a social energy which circulates with renewed vigor within a historical community.

Christian theologians, in the same vein, find such life embedded within a historical moment of grace, but acknowledge as well a position which New Historicists would avoid: that such enlivening action within history is a sacramental expression of what Rahner calls the "inner word of grace." The enduring life Christians experience in the sacramentality of the word participates in the action of God creating, loving, encountering, and saving the world into which Jesus was uttered as a sign and reality of that grace. These transcendental and historical expressions of this one grace spoken in the individual heart and in the historical community are, as Rahner said, "mutually complementary moments of the one word of God to [humankind]" and are the foundation for the fruitfulness of its promise.[81] From a Christian liturgical perspective, therefore, the pragmatic arbiters of that grace—those who hold the center—are the concrete communities of believers, whose proclamation and worship express and enact that shared, sacred history that Christ's paschal drama makes possible.[82]

1976) 465–85. For an extended discussion of Fish's notion of "interpretive communities" see Chapter 4 below.

[81] Rahner, "The Word and the Eucharist," 258–9. This point of the role of proclamation as part of a process of the "one whole word of God" is discussed in Chapter 2. In *Revelation and Theology* ([London: Sheed and Ward, 1966] 26ff.) Schillebeeckx speaks of the "horizontal and vertical" nature of the relationship between the saving activity of Christ the Lord and the kerygma of the apostles handed down through the Church's preaching tradition and sacramental life.

[82] Even struggles between different communities of interpretation, seen in bold relief in the contemporary Church, are an essential element of that shared history. The fruit of such struggles is what we might accurately call the "tradition." As Jaroslav Pelikan remarks concerning Cardinal Newman and his similarity to patristic notions of ecclesial faith: "Tradition for Newman was, therefore, a profoundly democratic concept, which did not trickle down from theologians, popes, and councils to the people, but filtered up

Although the ends and boundaries of interpretation differ between the New Historicist project and Christian sacramental concerns, they share a mutual respect for the dynamism of the community's active participation in what Greenblatt and others call "the event as a social text and the literary text as a social event."[83] Liturgical studies, heretofore, has avoided discussion of the particularly ritual aspects surrounding the proclamation of biblical texts, confining itself to the more obvious performance aspects of rubrical, sacramental gesture and its symbolic meaning. New Historicism provides a conversation partner and a fruitful way of unraveling the mysterious power possible in the social event of liturgical proclamation. The interchange of social energy between texts and events gives a theoretical language and a broader perspective in which to appreciate the Liturgy of the Word as a constituent part of a sacramental *encounter,* while still maintaining the integrity of the biblical text as a literary artifact.[84] If sacraments at root are not *things* but *events,* then the same is true for the liturgical procla-

---

from the faithful (who are the church) to become the subject matter for the speculations, controversies, and systems of the dogmatic theologians." See Jaroslav Pelikan, *The Vindication of Tradition* (New Haven, Conn.: Yale University Press, 1984) 30. Pelikan notes further that, contrary to the Church Fathers' assertion of some "single and total entity" called "the tradition," what one usually confronts in these sources "is usually what Newman calls 'local tradition, which each separate Christian community already possessed'" (36).

[83] Thomas, *The New Historicism and Other Old-Fashioned Topics,* 39.

[84] The sacramental quality of this interchange argues implicitly for the integrity of the lectionary and the liturgical year as a vital part of a common liturgical tradition. The proclamation of a biblical text is not just subsumed under a general rubric of a written word that is manipulated to explain the sacramental action to follow. If the entire ritual action "acts" as if this manipulation is the purpose of the proclaimed texts, then requests to find a passage to fit a theme or for poets and writings of dubious literary quality are legitimate and understandable. One reason a biblical text is affirmed as "sacred" stems from the grace revealed throughout the history of the Church whenever it is proclaimed in its integrity: the encounter with the Scriptures has transformed the community and the hearts of its members in a way that engenders ultimate commitment and faith. The evidence of conversion and the appeal to shared identity are more convincing testimony than endless arguments appealing to authority or taste. There are, of course, complex issues of biblical hermeneutics here that are left unaddressed. What I am attempting here is to limit the discussion to a liturgical and pastoral perspective that takes the experiences of worshipers seriously and locates them within the context of a shared, liturgical tradition. This discussion will continue in the next two chapters.

mation of the Scriptures as well. Having explored the interpretive imagination through which New Historicism looks at history and experience, the final four points concerning its contribution to liturgical proclamation can now be explored in more specific depth.

The "Circulation of Social Energy" and the Sacramental Encounter with Grace

Greenblatt, in his important and formative essay "Towards a Poetics of Culture," spoke of "currency" being exchanged whenever a work of art is created, performed, and experienced. It is not a "pure flame" with a neatly packaged commodity, whose pleasure and interest is set in stone by a single author or by a particular period's critical assessment. As Greenblatt said, those who read or hear the text also shape its life:

"The work of art is itself the product of a set of manipulations, some of them our own (most striking in the case of works that were not originally conceived as 'art' at all but rather as something else— votive objects, propaganda, prayer, and so on), many others undertaken in the construction of the original work. That is, the work of art is the product of a negotiation between a creator or a class of creators, equipped with a complex, communally shared repertoire of conventions, and the institutions and practices of society. In order to achieve the negotiation, artists need to create a currency that is valid for a meaningful, mutually profitable exchange. It is important to emphasize that the process involves not simply appropriation but exchange, since the existence of art always implies a return normally measured in pleasure and interest."[85]

The economic world of market exchange seems the last place to look for a richer insight into the grace-filled encounter that Christian liturgy purports to be. However, the "unsettling circulation of materials and discourses" with which Greenblatt is concerned provides a helpful working image to clarify the distinctive qualities of liturgical proclamation. Recognition of its lively circulation highlights a key ritual element in a sacramental approach which situates grace within the mysterious interaction of a loving God, an assembly of believers, texts, shared and personal history, and ritualized enactment. The temptation to view sacraments and homilies as *things* whose energy is self-enclosed is still a tremendous draw in experience and practice,

[85] Greenblatt, "Towards a Poetics of Culture," 158.

perhaps because of the security of such an exchange of commodities. Greenblatt's notions of the "circulation of social energy" and the empowerment that results from the transactions inherent in proclaiming an enduring text like Scripture help to disengage liturgical proclamation, particularly, from *talking about* God to *revealing* God in our midst. Rahner, for example, refers to this energetic understanding of proclamation "as the word in which the reality itself draws nigh and announces itself and constitutes itself present," as opposed to the more commonly employed didactic word, that is, "the word which makes a statement about something."[86]

It is important at this point to recall briefly some key insights about the changing notion of sacramentality that emerged in the decades before Vatican II. There are strong affinities between the sacramental theologies outlined in Part I and the dialogic, interactive communication Greenblatt and others assert is taking place in the "life" of a literary artifact. Hearing them again with some knowledge of the New Historicist critique clarifies how sacramentality is expressed when Scriptures are read in the assembly.

Semmelroth, for example, insisted that the Church was not a "warehouse" storing sacramental objects dispensed from her coffers.[87] The Church is, more accurately, an arena of encounter, a basic sacrament in which the Holy Spirit gives life to the Church. The individual's engagement with the Church, in turn, "is at the same time an immersion into the living union with God, that is, into grace."[88] This "redemptive dialogue" is part of the "single work" of Word and Sacrament, the "word" and "answer" of Christ's incarnation and redemption, in which believers are invited to share.[89]

In a similar vein, Rahner spoke of the Church who hears, affirms, and preaches this word as both sign and reality of the grace of God's irrevocable mercy in Christ—the "well-spring" of sacramental life in the Church.[90] This "self-communication" of God must be "proclaimed and accepted" because Christ's relationship with the Church

[86] Rahner, "The Word and the Eucharist," 255.
[87] See Otto Semmelroth, *Church and Sacrament* (Notre Dame, Ind.: Fides Publishers, 1965) 82 and his second point in Chapter 2 above.
[88] Ibid., 86; see his second point in Chapter 2 above.
[89] Otto Semmelroth, *The Preaching Word: On the Theology of Proclamation* (New York: Herder and Herder, 1965) 230–2.
[90] Kenan Osborne, *Sacramental Theology: A General Introduction* (Mahwah, N.J.: Paulist Press, 1988) 91; see also Rahner's second point in Chapter 2 above.

is immanent and dynamic at each moment in history, in the power of the Spirit. As such, the text and the proclamation of the word in the liturgy are never static and generic, but specific, personal, and participatory; they are part of the "one whole word" and the "historically real and actual presence of the eschatologically victorious mercy of God that abides in the Church."[91]

Schillebeeckx's sacramentality of revelatory encounter, rooted in the historical contingencies of human life in this world, understood both preaching and sacramental life as the "burning focal points" of the whole "visible presence of grace in the world which is the Church."[92] The dynamism of the immanent Trinity is lived out in the saving events of Jesus, an "offer of grace" bestowed now on all who share in her sacramental life.[93]

How might these notions of grace-filled power, communicated between God and human persons—through the vehicle of the social community of the Church and her ritual expressions of communal identity—share a mutuality with the concerns of Greenblatt and his New Historicist colleagues? At first consideration, the primacy of the Bible as the definitive revealed word of God would appear problematic to a critical project whose "practitioners," Catherine Gallagher asserts, "generally posit no fixed hierarchy of cause and effect as they trace the connections among texts, discourses, power, and the constitution of subjectivity."[94] Yet, as critic Howard Felperin has noted concerning the radical contextualization of a New Historicist approach, the "context" always engages a "text." There is, after all, a work called *The Tempest*, or one of John Donne's metaphysical poems, or, in this case, the Christian Scriptures that are proclaimed in the assembly. As Felperin goes on to say, uncovering "background" or repressed voices or different cultural interpretations to reveal a new hearing or reading makes such contextualization "subject to the same indeterminacy and ultimate 'undecideability' that conditions the 'text.'"[95] As a result,

[91] Karl Rahner, *The Church and the Sacraments* (New York: Herder and Herder, 1964) 14; see his fourth point in Chapter 2 above.

[92] Edward Schillebeeckx, *Christ the Sacrament of the Encounter with God* (Kansas City, Mo.: Sheed, Andrews and McMeel, 1953) 216; see his fourth point in Chapter 2 above.

[93] Ibid., 51; see Schillebeeckx's third point in Chapter 2 above.

[94] Catherine Gallagher, "Marxism and the New Historicism," *The New Historicism*, ed. Veeser, 37.

[95] Howard Felperin, "Canonical Texts and Non-Canonical Interpretations: The Neohistoricist Rereading of Donne," *Southern Review* 18:3 (November 1985) 247.

"from a methodological point of view it is the text that still calls the shots, that determines, in fact over-determines, the question of which of the many available or constructible contexts it can be inserted into at any given moment to produce *new and unforeseen meaning.*"[96]

For the Christian sacramental tradition, the word of God in the canonical Scriptures is surely "the text that still calls the shots." However, to consider the sacred quality of the biblical word as simply consisting of a compilation of canonical "books," or *ipsissima verba* of Christ, or even accurate historical accounts of foundational events is clearly inadequate. The saving word embraces a much broader dynamic, not only from the perspective of biblical hermeneutics, but from the nature of a sacramental theology which takes the encounter and the faith response of the believing community as a necessary component to the truth of its proclamation. God's grace communicates a "new and unforeseen meaning" whenever the Scriptures are proclaimed *in our midst,* and the enduring power within that text to bring about that conversion and transformation situates itself in the context itself. The sacramental encounter, in which the *reality and sign* of Christ's abiding presence in the Church is expressed, necessarily includes a proclamation which is intrinsically dependent upon its being heard. As Rahner explains:

"For the Church is a community of believers to the end, and as a whole it is subjectively holy, and hence truly believing. In this reciprocal relationship of efficacious word of God and the effective hearing of the word effected by God himself, both realities are ordained to each other in such a way that one may safely say: if one did not exist, the other could not exist, that is, be what it is."[97]

This ecclesial context for the enduring, perennial truth of the revealed word of God is not simply a theological construct; a shared truth that is passed down from generation to generation through a common ritual has *liturgical* implications as well. What happens during the Liturgy of the Word, investigated from the perspective of a literary artifact's "life," uncovers a vibrant "circulation of social energy," embedded, flowing, and at work "to produce new and unforeseen meaning." Greenblatt's intellectual curiosity resonates with our

[96] Felperin, 246; my emphasis.
[97] Rahner, "The Word and the Eucharist," 285; see his fourth point in Chapter 2 above.

94

exploration into the dynamics of liturgical proclamation as a moment of Christ's sacramental presence: "I want to understand," he said, "the negotiations through which works of art obtain and amplify such powerful energy."[98] In our turn, we want to understand how Christ is speaking "when the holy Scriptures are read in the Church," and how it is that assemblies hear this proclamation as central to their communal identity *per ipsum, et cum ipso, et in ipso.*

Greenblatt uses the root image of a "mirror" to describe the dynamism of a dramatic production and its power to endure and to "refigure" itself in successive presentations and different contexts. The purpose of the play's action, Hamlet says in Act Three, is "to hold as 'twere the mirror up to nature: to show virtue her feature, scorn her own image, and the very age and body of the time his form and pressure."[99] The static sense of "form" is familiar to us, but Shakespeare's curious use of the term "pressure" suggested for Greenblatt "an impression, as with a signet or a ring."[100] This tactile image reflects the prevalent understanding in Renaissance culture that a mirror does more than passively reflect what is placed in front of it. Greenblatt, with typical New Historicist concern for these peripheral historical oddities, reports on his study of mirrors at the time of Shakespeare:

"Both optics and mirror lore in the period suggested that something was actively passing back and forth in the production of mirror images, that accurate representation depended upon material emanation and exchange. Only if we reinvest the mirror image with a sense of pressure as well as form can it convey something of its original strangeness and magic. And only with the recovery of this strangeness can we glimpse a whole spectrum of representational exchanges where we had once seen simple reflection alone."[101]

What is "passing back and forth" during the play's performance, in Greenblatt's schema, corresponds to what the Aristotelian rhetorical tradition called "a stir to the mind" or *"energia."*[102] This energy does

[98] Greenblatt, *Shakespearean Negotiations*, 7.

[99] Hamlet, 3.2.21–24.

[100] Greenblatt, *Shakespearean Negotiations*, 8.

[101] Ibid. The reference he uses concerning mirror lore of the period is Jurgis Baltrusaitis, *Le Miroir: Essai sur une légende scientifique: Révélations, science fiction, et fallacies* (Paris: Elmayan, 1978).

[102] Ibid., 6. The reference to *"energia"* is taken, as he mentions in a footnote, from Aristotle's *Rhetoric* (33.2.2), "as interpreted especially by Quintilian

not reside in the language alone, but flows "from the network of practices that governs the circulation of social energy"[103] and, therefore, "its significance is social and historical."[104]

Greenblatt preferred the term *energy* instead of *power,* because such a stir is embedded in the whole fabric of the culture, not merely in those who officially control the reins of authority or create its literary works. This communal location of energy has interesting implications for appreciating the power that liturgical proclamation possesses to move a congregation on many levels, both collectively and personally, at the same time.[105] The Scriptures and the homily, in the end, are not in the hands of the preacher or the lector alone; indeed, the argument will be made shortly that such power is not even *primarily* located within an individual. The proclamatory energy—what sacramentality calls the "dynamism of grace"—circulates throughout the shared tradition of the Church, the concrete lives of believers who have passed it on in faith, and the social context of a particular time and congregation that gathers to hear this proclamation in new and unforeseen ways. This hermeneutical perspective reinforces what most congregations already instinctively sense: that exegesis alone, or a powerful canonical position or rhetorical style, or even an elegant application to the lives of the assembly, does not necessarily ensure a powerful hearing of God's saving word. Rather, the sacred text is recognized as alive and immanent because of the social energy circulating there. That multifaceted circulation is the locus for the "dynamism of grace" taking place in the encounter between God and the assembled community of faith that hears that word. Something is "passing back and forth," as Greenblatt contends, rather than emanating from a message contained within a static text or an authoritative speaker and then handed over to a passive congregation of listeners. And all

---

(*Institutio* 8.3.89) and Scaliger (*Poetics* 3.27)"; see *Shakespearean Negotiations,* 165, n. 5.

[103] Ibid., 18.

[104] Ibid., 6.

[105] The issue of ritual power being located in the ritualized body is discussed in detail in Catherine Bell's *Ritual Theory, Ritual Practice,* especially in the chapters entitled "The Ritual Body" and "The Power of Ritualization." She expanded her study in *Ritual: Perspectives and Dimensions* (New York: Oxford University Press, 1997), especially in sections entitled "Rites: The Spectrum of Ritual Activities" and "Contexts: The Fabric of Ritual Life." Bell's work has important ramifications for the study of the role worshiping assemblies play in the authority of the preacher's role.

of the strangeness and magic in the Scripture's proclamation is present, and can even be appreciated and exploited in its richest and most positive sense, "where we had once seen simple reflection alone."[106] Cooperating with this grace incarnates that Word more authentically in our midst.

This social energy for Greenblatt is not measurable but recognized "only indirectly, by its effects."[107] Because there is no "originary moment" in Greenblatt's theory, he is forced to rely on something less transcendental: "a subtle elusive set of exchanges, a network of trades and trade-offs, a jostling of competing representations, a negotiation between joint-stock companies."[108] They make themselves known "in the capacity of certain verbal, aural, and visual traces to produce, shape, and organize collective physical and mental experiences."[109] What is more, this social energy, as a collective experience, "must have a minimal *predictability*—enough to make simple repetitions possible—and a minimal *range:* enough to reach out beyond a single creator or consumer to some community, however constricted."[110]

Note the similarities between the qualities of this collective experience and the liturgical concerns being addressed here. The ritual repetitiveness of the liturgy and the communality of the address in which the proclamation is uttered make up the arena of encounter for the bestowal of sacramental grace in the Church. The locus of this grace is not *out there* but *here* in the liturgical gathering, although, at the same time, Christian theology would argue for an originating moment out of which this communication flows. Sacramentality maintains that the originating grace is enfleshed within the ritual enactment of the liturgy itself, through the *predictability* of what Rahner called "intrinsically real symbols . . . the spatio-temporal, historical

[106] A parallel example regarding the immanence of such powerful energy circulating among a group of people as a shared experience is the live performance of music, in which the shared energy literally pulls an audience to its feet in appreciation as much as it hushes that same gathering in a communal silence. And all of this takes place without a sign flashing to direct such joint response. That same sense of shared experience happens even in a solitary gazing at a masterpiece of visual art. The dynamic, immediate character of graced activity can, however, be ignored ritually and, sadly, often is. Bell's notion of "ritualized bodies" as primary actors documents this.
[107] Greenblatt, *Shakespearean Negotiations*, 6.
[108] Ibid., 7.
[109] Ibid., 6.
[110] Ibid.; my emphasis.

phenomenon, the visible and tangible form in which something that appears, notifies its presence, and by so doing, makes itself present, bodying forth this manifestation really distinct from itself."[111] And the *range* of this social energy for the Christian understanding of proclamation extends not to a word addressed primarily to individuals, but as Greenblatt maintains, to a *people*—a community that provides the shades and contours of this historical proclamation. Even more, in the transaction, the community who hears the word becomes shaped by its saving proclamation. As Schillebeeckx insisted:

"The place of the ministry of the word is, in principle, the assembled people of God, the faithful community which unites for the purpose of worshipping and praising God. *The assembled people of God is thus the inward situation in which the word of God resounds.* But the form of God's word is influenced by this situation and many different aspects of this one service of the word are thus brought out."[112]

The ongoing exchange between texts and "the institutions and practices of society" is not something that happens all at once. Greenblatt argues for a circulation that empowers over time, drawing from the past, communicating to the present moment, and re-orienting and transforming the future: "Each individual play may be said to make a small contribution to the general store of social energy possessed by the theater and hence to the sustained claim that the theater can make on its real and potential audience." As a result, the energy passes back and forth repeatedly between the enactment and the people who attend its performance. "Through its representational means," Greenblatt goes on, "each play carries charges of social energy onto the stage; the stage in its turn revises that energy and returns it to the audience."[113]

---

[111] Rahner, "The Church and the Eucharist," 37.

[112] Schillebeeckx, *Revelation and Theology*, 50. At the same time, the opposite effect can take place: where the word does not resound, energy is fragmented and displaced. This fragmentation can be expressed in a variety of ways: through the assembly's disengagment from the preacher's message due to a perceived lack of connectedness to the Scriptures or to the concrete circumstances of the lives of its members, through the confused ritual symbols and unspoken messages being communicated during the Liturgy of the Word and the celebration as a whole, and even through unrelated circumstances taking place simultaneously that pull the energy of the worshipers elsewhere.

[113] Greenblatt, *Shakespearean Negotiations*, 14.

The dynamism of circulation characterizes well the grace-filled encounter of liturgical proclamation, because its enduring power to transform the heart of a community does not rest in singular, stellar performances or exceptionally alert listeners or even the choicest set of Scripture readings. The proclaimed word—that which Rahner calls part of the "one whole word of God"[114]—reveals and transforms over time. It follows, therefore, that the privileged arena is the sacramental and ecclesial one: in the repetitive activity of worship week after week, to a gathered community who themselves know the paschal trials and joys of other pilgrims like themselves. The worshiping assembly embodies the expressive representation of this social and historical circulation of grace.

New Historicists clearly agree that tracking all these hidden places for valued "currency" is worth the effort. The rich interplay of "negotiation and exchange," the life of a work which has been "transformed and refashioned" over time and cultures and performances, yields a corpus of Shakespeare which, according to critic Richard Halpern, "is both guide and quarry."[115] The Scriptures in the Christian liturgical assembly are certainly that: both *guide* and well-spring of faith and, at the same time, revelatory of the *treasure* worshipers seek, "the light of the knowledge of the glory of God in the face of Jesus Christ" (2 Cor 4:6). God's definitive Word in Jesus, the *Ursakrament* of human salvation, shares that same immanent and powerful dynamism of being both the sign and the reality—"guide and quarry" we might say—of this gracious offer of God to all women and men. As Schillebeeckx reminds us again:

"Christ's present speaking in the church's preaching of the word on the one hand and inwardly in our hearts through grace on the other is not a double address, but one and the same address, in which what was said at an earlier time is really included in what is said here and now. Christ's power as Lord is revealed first and foremost in the Church and her preaching."[116]

---

[114] Rahner, "The Word and the Eucharist," 279; see his fourth point in Chapter 2 above.

[115] Richard Halpern, "Shakespeare in the Tropics: From High Modernism to New Historicism," *Representations* 45 (Winter 1994) 21.

[116] Schillebeeckx, *Revelation and Theology*, 31.

These "textual traces," Greenblatt suggests, mysteriously carry about them "so much life."[117]

Common Faith and the Contingency of Cultural Practices:
Liturgical Proclamation and Cultural Poetics

The "cultural poetics" that critics like Greenblatt hope to realize in their distinctive way of reading social events and texts is eminently tied to "the interpretive constructions the members of a society apply to their experiences."[118] Greenblatt, early on in his work (1980), called this "a more cultural or anthropological criticism" whose difficult-to-realize goal suggests an approach whose "central concerns prevent it from permanently sealing off one type of discourse from another or of decisively separating works of art from the minds and lives of their creators and their audiences."[119]

A multiplicity of discourses encompasses any sacramental celebration: the gathering of a liturgical assembly in a common faith, symbolic gestures and actions, and a shared word and proclamation that is both sign and reality of the presence of Christ that binds them. Indeed, the particularly sacramental and ritual milieu in which proclamation and preaching take place begins from a starting point that is ecclesial: what is done in this gathering is corporate; the communication God initiates is first and foremost to the Church. Texts and contexts, according to Greenblatt, "are themselves always embedded in systems of public signification."[120] Religious rituals and sacred texts are immersed in such a collective interchange. Consequently, one who preaches as if the texts were static and fixed, and whose words and actions appear oblivious of the congregation, acts against the ritual dynamic taking place. The proclamation of texts that are read as if the richness resides merely in the words on the page, rather than in the present hearing, flies in the face of these New Historicist concerns. Such ritual dissonance and disrespect for what is taking place can account for the seeming absence of life in the ritual celebration of the word experienced by so many worshipers today.[121] A critical pro-

[117] Greenblatt, *Shakespearean Negotiations*, 2.
[118] Stephen Greenblatt, *Renaissance Self-Fashioning: From More to Shakespeare* (Chicago: University of Chicago Press, 1980) 4.
[119] Ibid., 4–5.
[120] Ibid., 5.
[121] Mary Catherine Hilkert has noted a study by Dean R. Hoge, Jackson W. Carroll, and Francis K. Sheets entitled *Patterns of Parish Leadership: Cost and Ef-*

ject whose goal is a cultural poetics shares, therefore, in liturgical theology's inquiry into a sacramental foundation for preaching which moves a congregation and radiates life. New Historicism creatively wonders how a treasured text takes part in a circulating energy that communicates mystery and energy and, in this sacramental context, dynamic grace.

The multivalent contingency of New Historicism's cultural poetics illumines for liturgical theology the complex dynamics and negotiated energy involved in liturgical proclamation. As we said, there is a specific text at the core of Christian ritual activity: the canonical Scriptures in the lectionary, themselves the production of a complex interchange of interpretations, manipulations, and refigurations. Understanding the historical complexity of this text, however, is not enough for a sacramentality of the word that asserts that the saving action these texts portray represent an instance of God's contemporary communication with a believing community.[122] In this sense, what critic Jean Howard calls "the crux of any 'new' historical criti-

---

fectiveness in Four Denominations (Kansas City, Mo.: Sheed and Ward, 1988) where preaching was listed as the first priority among all mainline congregations regarding "their highest hopes and expectations." It was also one of the most significant disappointments in their worship experience. See "Bearing Wisdom: The Vocation of the Preacher," *Spirituality Today* 44:2 (Summer 1992) 143–4. We could add that the more disjointed and confused the ritual itself becomes—for example, through excessive didacticism and "peeking around the rite," or through liturgical actions that are ritually dissonant, or in rudderless celebrations that lack a foundational *ordo*—the more the homily alone bears the burden of meaning. In such liturgies, the shared experience seems to be manufactured by a group of "planners" or professionals, and the resulting experience de-energizes the worshiping assembly. Catherine Bell makes a helpful point on how even the dissonance is an active "strategy" taking place in ritual practice. In *Ritual Theory, Ritual Change,* Bell remarks:

"The dynamic interaction of texts and rites, reading and chanting, the word fixed and the word preached are *practices,* not social developments of a fixed nature and significance. As practices, they continually play off each other to renegotiate tradition, authority, and the hegemonic order. As practices, they *invite* and *expect* the strategic counterplay" (140; my emphasis).

[122] The complementary field of biblical hermeneutics is another investigation entirely. However, for an important corollary to the New Historicist criticism related to biblical hermeneutics, see Sandra M. Schneiders, *The Revelatory Text: Interpreting the New Testament as Sacred Scripture* (San Francisco: Harper, 1991) especially ch. 6, "The World Before the Text: Witness, Language, and the Revelatory Text," 132–56.

cism" is the contention that history does not exist in some realm of retrievable fact, but instead is "a *construct* made up of textualized traces assembled in various configurations by the historian/interpreter."[123] In terms of the Liturgy of the Word, these traces present themselves in the choice and form of the canonical texts selected for a given day or feast, the prayers in the proper that surround them, and the insights of biblical experts who inform the preacher's exegesis. Furthermore, in light of Greenblatt's "circulation of social energy" we have been discussing, the assembly of hearers is itself a part of the hermeneutic at play in the proclamation event. Despite the insistence on this inescapable interplay between texts and hearers and social situation, though, the central texts do not become arbitrary or revisionist in the interchange.

If the heart of liturgical proclamation rests in the power of the word to transform current assemblies and to imagine new ways of appropriating the liberating message of the Gospel, then contingent lives and social events, contemporary worldviews and discontinuities with past interpretations cannot be ignored. These various configurations are all crucial to the new hearing of a "fresh word" that grace-filled communication with God suggests.[124] Greenblatt noted in *Renaissance Self-Fashioning* the contingent and communal nature of this dynamic representation of resonant texts: "Language, like other sign systems, is a collective construction; our interpretive task must be to grasp more sensitively the consequences of this fact by investigating both the social presence to the world of the literary text and the social presence of the world in the literary text."[125] He reiterated that the *literary text* is the focus of his interest here and not simply an anthropological study of cultures because "great art is an extraordinarily sensitive register of the complex struggles and harmonies of culture." This highly contingent status of texts draws the preacher and the congregation into the relevant particularities of one's own situation. Greenblatt himself acknowledged "that the questions I ask of my material [his Renaissance studies] and indeed the very nature

[123] Jean E. Howard, "The New Historicism in Renaissance Studies," *English Literary Renaissance* 16:1 (Winter 1986) 23–4.

[124] For a rich discussion of a new hearing or a "fresh word," see Mary Catherine Hilkert, "Naming Grace: A Theology of Proclamation," *Worship* 60 (1986) 434–49 and *Naming Grace: Preaching and the Sacramental Imagination* (New York: Continuum, 1997).

[125] Greenblatt, *Renaissance Self-Fashioning*, 5.

of this material are shaped by the questions I ask of myself."[126] Both preacher and assembly, therefore, cannot escape the facticity of their own lives and questions and hopes if they want to encounter the enduring life of these biblical accounts. The intersection of word and the human situation represents a precise instance of God's grace, communicated in the saving events of Jesus, drawn into the present by a sacramental enactment whose historicity makes that word *for us* in this time and place.

Honoring this contingency, therefore, need not signal an endless relativism or a slippery foundation of truth that leaves a particular community marooned from the lives of faithful believers before and around them. Rather, because we cannot escape our own historicity,[127] we are already embedded in the powerful life of these sacred texts and of the faith that rendered them as central to the ecclesial tradition's own self-fashioning. The shared faith and experience which the community sees reflected in these scriptural texts selects and canonizes the biblical accounts because, as Greenblatt would say, we find "resonance and centrality in them."[128] The cultural energy originally encoded in them is exchanged with the present lives and stories of those assembled; even the *resistance* to certain texts expresses this interrelationship. And the communication "passing back and forth" is called, in sacramental terms, a word uttered and heard or an encounter realized or a dialogue initiated that is, to echo Semmelroth, both *"Wort und Antwort."* A relationship is forged between the contingency of texts and a "power at once localized in particular institutions [i.e., the church] . . . and diffused in ideological structures of meaning, characteristic modes of expression, recurrent narrative patterns," Greenblatt asserts. He posits a sense of shared identity and focus that galvanizes around these common texts *along* with the patterned, communal structures that communicate them:

"It is not surprising that we engage in a similar narrative selection when we reflect upon our shared origins. . . . So from the thousands, we seize upon a handful of arresting figures who seem to contain within themselves much of what we need, who both reward

---

[126] Ibid.

[127] See Louis Montrose, "Professing the Renaissance: The Poetics and Politics of Culture," *The New Historicism,* ed. Veeser, 20; and Howard, "The New Historicism in Renaissance Studies," 20–3.

[128] Greenblatt, *Renaissance Self-Fashioning*, 6.

intense, individual attention and promise access to larger cultural patterns."[129]

The shared event, mysteriously, feeds both the body of believers and the individual hungers of the heart, which Christian liturgy and its sacramental understanding of God's personal communication of grace express and bring about in its ritual enactment.

To summarize, a cultural poetics as a way of reading literary texts honors, even exploits, the enduring energy which is real and active for those who encounter them. The life that emanates from these focal texts reaches directly into the present, into every aspect of the individual and shared life of a community seeking identity in them. The privileged text and the liturgical context dynamically express the self-identity of the community, and, at the same time, actually re-present it as the body of Christ that word effects. Greenblatt hinted at this mysterious self-fashioning when he noted:

"We respond to a quality, in the figures themselves, who are, we assume by analogy to ourselves, engaged in their own acts of selection and shaping and who seem to drive themselves toward the most sensitive regions of their culture, to express and even, by design, to embody its dominant satisfactions and anxieties."[130]

Sacramental theology and the liturgical proclamation outlined here assert that a community responds on an identifying level to the transformation explicit in the Scriptures and the tradition which compiled them. This response is itself a grace from God, a living sacrifice of praise and thanks, which renders the community vulnerable to be "embodied" in Christ.

The Similarities of Theater and Liturgy as a Cultural Production:
Insights into a Presence Fulfilled in Our Midst
     The field of Renaissance literary studies was the birthplace of New Historicism, although recent years have seen an increased broadening of that perspective.[131] The movement's selective fascination with

---

[129] Ibid.
[130] Ibid., 6–7.
[131] Examples of current broadened interests in New Historicism include American colonial literature and the emerging interests in feminist and multicultural studies. See Liu and Halpern for a sampling of current works in this area. The two collections of essays edited by H. Aram Veeser (1989, 1994) pro-

the literature of this period, particularly Shakespearean drama, has been critiqued as a new "romanticism of detail" and a "fragmentary atomism of cultural critical-detail [which] harbors a huge error or trope: 'microcosm' in the old sense."[132] Part of this critique unmasks an inconsistency in late-twentieth-century cultural criticism in general. On the one hand, its proponents reject absolutes, transcendental truths, or transhistorical realities beyond the contingency of the historical locus. On the other, they simultaneously opt for something *more*, as if such criticism reluctantly lingers, as Liu phrases it, on "the 'threshold' of transcendence," in search of some "moment of sublimity."[133] Stage drama as a focal cultural production of the Renaissance provides a particularly fertile site for this interplay of tension between the historical contingency of texts and their mysteriously enduring capacity to move contemporary audiences.

New Historicism highlights such theoretical confusion and the widespread, furtive lingering with transcendence. In terms of the present discussion, that "threshold of transcendence" will be exploited in order to illustrate how the proclamation of scriptural texts *as a cultural production* in the liturgy shares this liminal, mysterious dynamic. Liturgical theology implicitly recognizes this dynamism as

---

vide an additional example of the widening perspective in current New Historicist research, as well as the journal *Representations* (University of California, Berkeley).

[132] Liu, "Local Transcendence," 86. Earlier in his argument about the New Historicist passion for hidden detail, Liu calls this tendency in cultural criticism "a symbolics or iconic metaphorics putting the part for the cultural whole" (86). Liu makes frequent reference to the importance of Naomi Schor's *Reading in Detail: Aesthetics and the Feminine* (New York: Methuen, 1987) on synecdoche and detail. Schor, in this study of what Liu calls "the genealogy of detailism," speaks of this "pervasive valorization of the minute, the partial, and the marginal" (3). Liu also notes Theodore Adorno on "fragmented transcendence" (*Aesthetic Theory*, ed. Gretel Adorno and Rolf Tidermann, trans. C. Lenhardt [London: Routledge & Kegan Paul, 1984] 184). The relationship of all this detailism to the theater and the liturgy will be clarified below. The arena of negotiation and exchange of conflicting details is highlighted by the role drama played in the shifting social scene of Shakespeare's time. One final note on Liu: the generous detailism of his own endnotes makes this article especially helpful for an overview of contemporary cultural criticism. See especially pp. 101–2, n. 17, which provides an overview of "high cultural criticism" and its influences in the last decade. Other critiques, such as Johnson and Halpern, note the similarities to a modernist project and a metaphysical formalism which New Historicists claim to have eschewed.

[133] Ibid., 92.

the event of God's self-communication with a worshiping community. Consequently, the ambiguous tension lurking within a literary project that claims to have no room for universal absolutes can actually illumine the sacramentality of the word that most contemporary Roman Catholic theology wants to affirm, but for which it has yet to find the appropriate analytical tools to express.[134] Christian worship possesses few imaginative constructs to answer the theological question: "How is Christ present in the word"? The same lack of imagination does not exist surrounding the eucharistic elements.

A closer look at that lingering confusion, therefore, is in order. Despite all the anti-foundationalist rhetoric in New Historicism, its proponents still appeal to the life of a literary artifact like Renaissance drama; *something* endures there, although always being re-fashioned; that literary artifact transmits and exchanges energy or power with present-day cultural "products, practices, [and] discourses."[135] As a result, New Historicist enchantment with detail suggests "a world within a world" that is handed down from previous generations to the present. The critique of their clinging to some microcosm, therefore, is a fair one. Yet, *what* actually endures is itself *creative* and *relational.* The cultural production acts over time to "convey lost life"[136]

[134] The working assumption here is that the Constitution on the Sacred Liturgy's claim that Christ "is present in his word, since it is he himself who speaks when the holy scriptures are read in the Church" (no. 7), follows upon the revolution in sacramental theology by such people as Semmelroth, Rahner, and Schillebeeckx (outlined in Part I), but what that means and how the liturgical enactment plays a role in that presence has been largely unexplored. As was noted earlier, Rahner himself referred to this issue of the relationship between Word and Sacrament in Roman Catholic theology as one in which "a unanimous answer is still lacking" ("The Word and the Eucharist," 253). The discussion becomes even more intriguing when Paul VI's *Mysterium Fidei* nuances the presence of Christ just two years after *SC* with the statement: "There is another way in which he is very truly present in his Church; when she is engaged in preaching" (no. 36). I am not aware of significant work done on this topic from a particularly sacramental perspective in the intervening years since the council. This present study attempts to do so.

[135] Greenblatt, *Shakespearean Negotiations,* 13. A colleague of mine, John Markey, O.P., has maintained the interesting thesis that "culture" in current critical theory is not that dissimilar with the notion of "nature" in classic Christian theology. This has interesting implications, I think, for a contemporary theological discussion of the relationship between nature and grace and the presuppositions of an anti-foundationalist cultural criticism. Recent works, such as Stephen Duffy's *The Graced Horizon: Nature and Grace in Catholic Thought* (Collegeville: The Liturgical Press, 1994), address these issues.

so that the contemporary representation is refashioned by that activity and social change can occur. A particular community, in turn, encounters the refashioned production and is itself transformed and refashioned by it.[137] The life that passes back and forth between a literary production, its audience, and its social setting gathers fuel in the myriad details of culture, historical setting, and the shifting nuances of linguistic expression. The interactive contingency of these negotiations and exchanges provides the friction for the energy that binds these multivalent levels of social texts and events into a creative moment of encounter.[138] This social moment evolves from the time of its creation to each succeeding production and expresses a larger vision that embraces past, present, and future.[139] The event of its reading enables a community, as Greenblatt stated, "to embody [their culture's] dominant satisfactions and anxieties."[140]

New Historicism, therefore, embraces what Liu calls this microcosm, but understands it differently from common parlance. The "world within a world" encompasses an arena of dynamic interchange and not a passive expression of reality hardened into unassailable fact. "Greenblatt," remarks Brook Thomas, "demonstrates how the boundary between literary text or performance and other social practices is not a fixed and stable one but one in a constant process of negotiation and reconstitution."[141]

These interactive dynamics of theater as a cultural production suggest helpful parallels to the singularly ritual aspects of liturgical proclamation in contemporary sacramentality. Two theatrical points of contact with liturgical ritual illustrate these parallels: (1) the Renaissance period as a bridge between changing worldviews and sensibilities and the role drama plays in a period of social tension, and (2) the communal nature of drama as a social text and event and its widespread popularity in this period, as opposed to the individualistic experience of the private reader so prevalent in the enlightenment period which follows the Renaissance.

---

[136] Greenblatt, *Shakespearean Negotiations*, 3.

[137] Thomas, *The New Historicism and Other Old-Fashioned Topics*, 184–5. It is perhaps clearer, after all this discussion, what Thomas meant when he commented that this refashioning "generates a spiral rather than a circle."

[138] Veeser, *The New Historicism*, xiv.

[139] Greenblatt, *Shakespearean Negotiations*, 5.

[140] Greenblatt, *Renaissance Self-Fashioning*, 6.

[141] Thomas, *The New Historicism and Other Old-Fashioned Topics*, 39.

(1) The first point we consider is the focal position of the Renaissance and its *cultural productions as a bridge between radically different worldviews.* Contemporary liturgical enactment, as a cultural production, shares a similarly privileged place in a period of immense ecclesial change. The Renaissance period as a whole speaks to the contemporary world's "exhilaration and fearfulness of living inside a gap in history," as Jean Howard calls it.[142] This situational position responds comfortably to a literary critique that pays attention to the "manipulation and adjustment"[143] of social texts and events. Renaissance drama in an age of transition portrayed a world of collective unity and order, reflective of a medieval sensibility that preceded it; yet, this transitional world did not share the certainty of structures and systems of belief that underpinned the medieval worldview. This continuity/discontinuity dynamic in dramatic production becomes a privileged arena of this collective struggle for a culture's identity that will eventually seek refuge in the autonomous, reasoning self in later periods.

Current liturgical experience provides the stage for a similar socio-religious shift: the Christian community versus the autonomous self, the struggle for a meaningful communal identity amid conflicting desires for personal transcendence. This polarization in liturgical sensibilities, especially observable in the North American church in recent years, expresses the widening chasm between two competing desires: the personal quest for transcendence and the formation of communities that bind people together in a shared identity.[144] The reformed liturgy after Vatican II articulated the radical ecclesial shifts enunciated by the council. Contemporary sacramental and liturgical theology, therefore, appreciates the role a dramatic production plays as a cultural vehicle for the expression of the shifting social constructs, such as occurred in Renaissance life and culture. As current worship experience makes evident, the ritual rubrics alone do not tell the complete tale. Transactions and exchanges, both traditional and subversive, abound whenever the Church gathers to pray. They are all being played out within a liturgical ritual which, to appropriate Greenblatt here, attempts "to express and even, by design, to embody

[142] Howard, "The New Historicism in Renaissance Studies," 17.

[143] Greenblatt, "Towards a Poetics of Culture," 158.

[144] Richard R. Gaillardetz, "North American Culture and the Liturgical Life of the Church: The Separation of the Quests for Transcendence and Community," *Worship* 68:5 (September 1994) 404.

its dominant satisfactions and anxieties."[145] If liturgy as a whole expresses this shift in ecclesial self-identity, then what is happening in the proclamation event shares that embodied struggle taking place in the community as a whole. As such, well-meaning attempts at sophisticated exegesis or a familial style of delivery do not begin to get at the heart of what is clearly more than a gap in rhetorical communication. Proclaiming the word in truth cannot ignore this reality. Authentic proclamation demands a reverence toward all the shifting transactions taking place throughout the whole liturgy and in the assembly that gathers. Even more, it dares to claim that grace is located in the midst of that tension.

From a New Historicist perspective, the presence of this tension and struggle in any bridge period of history reflects the exhilaration and fearfulness of living in a time when the dominant paradigms are shifting. The intensity of this age of transition has been recognized in both Renaissance studies and twentieth-century theology for some time. What New Historicism adds to this recognition, however, is a chance to look at alternative aspects of this shift. As Jean Howard notes regarding Renaissance studies in general:

"Previous critical emphasis was on continuity—on the way the period linked to the past or anticipated the future. Now the emphasis is on discontinuity, seen most clearly in [Jonathan] Dollimore's insistence on the early seventeenth century as a kind of interperiod standing free of the orthodoxies of the Middle Ages and the Enlightenment. But the difference between prior and past conceptions of the Renaissance is also clear in the way the new historical critics so often make the period intelligible by narratives of rupture, tension, and contradiction. . . . These narratives of continuity and contradiction are narratives which owe much to the way late twentieth-century man construes his own historical condition."[146]

The historical condition of the Church after Vatican II can be understood in the same manner. Continuity in the Church's tradition

---

[145] Greenblatt, *Renaissance Self-Fashioning*, 6–7.

[146] Howard, "The New Historicism in Renaissance Studies," 17. The author's reference to Dollimore is from his book *Radical Tragedy: Religion, Ideology and Power in the Drama of Shakespeare and His Contemporaries* (Chicago: University of Chicago Press, 1984), esp. ch. 10, "Subjectivity and Social Process," 153–81. The notes in this whole article are of particular help regarding New Historical bibliography.

remains an important value for contemporary theology in general, and sacramentality in particular, and this methodology is helpful. But the New Historicist shift to an alternative focus on the *"dis*continuity" provides a new lens upon which to look at liturgical enactment and the role of proclamation in passing on that tradition. The discontinuity lens focuses on exposing the gap between the *ideology* of conciliar understandings of the "people of God" and "the priesthood of all believers," for example, and the *actuality* of authority structures and liturgical enactments that appear to be in conflict with this more horizontal social configuration. To recognize the tension and to honor its presence as a preacher or a worshiping assembly allows participants to be vulnerable to the transformation of the message and of the body of believers hearing its Good News. Too often, instead, the presider or lector ignores the discontinuity and acts as if it is not there; or, at the other extreme, those in charge simply substitute the text and mollify its challenge. Both responses thwart the fullest possibilities in this graced exchange.

A similar case can be made for the specifically ecclesial and communal focus and language in recent sacramental theology. Ideally, the grace of the sacrament is imaged as the visible expression of the Church herself, as the grace of God embodied in the world through Christ. In reality, however, many worshipers simply do not experience the liturgy as reflecting that communal reality. Consequently, the ritual both contradicts and reinforces both paradigms at once. The biblical texts read in the midst of such contemporary assemblies often jar sensibilities that have been shaped by a nuanced, individualistic, less-hierarchical world. And yet the unity, the hope, and the mysterious passion expressed in those Scriptures still give voice to a great desire and hope among the people. New Historicism's interest in precisely those narratives of rupture, tension, and contradiction suggests to us that if energy circulates *there,* amid the ritual confusion, then a powerful life is also being communicated. This grace of conversion and transformation courses through both the institutional structures of rubrical enactment and through the underlying circulation of dissonance. The shared tradition, in fact, can be enhanced through this dynamic interchange in an age of transition.

The playing out of cultural struggle and refiguration thrives on a cultural practice that engages the world and still is not synonymous with it. Dramatic production as a cultural practice held a privileged place in the Renaissance for dealing with this shift in paradigms.

Greenblatt's insights into the role that boundaries play between the theater and the world may deepen our appreciation of liturgical proclamation's prophetic role in an analogous shift in ecclesial self-identity in the post–Vatican II Church.

New Historicism acknowledges the fluid interchange between social event and historical text. Louis Montrose emphasizes its attempt "to resituate canonical literary texts among the multiple forms of writing, and in relation to the non-discursive practices and institutions."[147] At the same time, Greenblatt asserts that such interchange does not dissolve the boundaries between the theater and the world. This liminal space provides a necessary separation that allows the dramatic production to "make up" different possibilities of social construction, rather than to be totally immersed in the culture itself.[148] The separation is never complete. In fact, this incompleteness provides its chief transformative attribute. Greenblatt employs two metaphors to describe this permeable boundary: first, "the erection of a gate through which some people and objects will be allowed to pass and others prohibited"; second, "the establishment, as in a children's game, of ritualized formulas that can be endlessly repeated."[149]

[147] Louis Montrose, "Renaissance Literary Studies and the Subject of History," *English Literary Renaissance* 16 (1986) 6.

[148] Jean Howard mentions in "The New Historicism in Renaissance Studies" (35–6) that Louis Montrose highlights the role of literature and dramatic texts in doing "social *work*." In this sense, the work of these texts is not merely to support an economic or power structure in place in a society. Rather, as she quotes Montrose, "Culture is represented as at once more autonomous in its processes and more material in its means and relations of production." This, as was mentioned earlier, is New Historicism's most inconsistent position: insisting on the continual blurring of boundaries while still positing the centrality of cultural productions. Positing their relative autonomy affirms a sacramental view of privileged texts and arenas of grace such as the liturgy. But New Historicists are not prepared to accept a transcendental structure outside of the history. It is the contemporary problem of abandoning any form of metaphysics, even though it is ultimately realized in the context of historically contingent events and persons.

[149] Greenblatt, *Shakespearean Negotiations,* 13. The reliance of Greenblatt and most New Historicists on Victor Turner and Clifford Geertz is obvious here. They frequently refer to issues of structure and anti-structure so familiar in Turner's work and images such as Geertz's "ethnographic thickness" to describe the multivalent interchanges of cultural energy taking place. See Victor Turner, *The Ritual Process: Structure and Anti-Structure,* 6th ed. (Ithaca, N.Y.: Cornell University Press, 1989); Clifford Geertz, "Thick Description: Toward an Interpretive Theory of Culture," *The Interpretation of Cultures* (New York:

Public dramatic production in the Renaissance literalized these metaphors and created a space and a system where these permeable boundaries could be explored.[150] Greenblatt's examples include the physical building, the admission charge, the script, the theater company, the government regulations that controlled public behavior, and the usual passivity of the audience, to name a few. As he goes on:

"This literalization and institutionalization of the place of art makes the Renaissance theater particularly useful for an analysis of the cultural circulation of social energy, and the stakes of the analysis are heightened by the direct integration of Shakespeare's plays—easily the most powerful, successful, and enduring artistic expressions of the English language—with this particular mode of artistic production and consumption. We are not, that is, dealing with texts written outside the institution and subsequently attached to it or with encysted productions staged in a long-established and ideologically dormant setting but with literary creations designed in intimate and living relation to an emergent commercial practice."[151]

Shakespeare's company, therefore, is dependent upon the survival of the system of transactions that keep it in operation. But the boundaries, as was noted, are permeable. The audience can reject what is portrayed, the government can question certain allusions, and the legitimacy it seeks to uphold circulates between stage and audience and suggests, often in a subversive and subtle manner, that things could possibly be different than they are. Because of the boundary between the theater and the world, such possibilities can safely be said to be, like Prospero's magic, merely illusionary. But they strike a chord in that circulation between audience, stage, culture, and authorities, which allows them the freedom to resist and suggest other ways of envisioning the world and the relationships that make it up. The possibilities interact in the safety of this creative arena, and the social context embraces those discontinuities and makes them part of the fabric of that culture's life. As Greenblatt explains, concerning

---

Basic Books, Inc., 1973); and Clifford Geertz, *Local Knowledge: Further Essays in Interpretive Anthropology* (New York: Basic Books, 1983).

[150] For the image of a "semipermeable boundary" I am indebted to Richard Halpern, *The Poetics of Primitive Accumulation: English Renaissance Culture and the Genealogy of Capital* (Ithaca, N.Y.: Cornell University Press, 1991) 14.

[151] Greenblatt, *Shakespearean Negotiations*, 13.

this confusing and subtle interchange between the theater and the world:

"Thus the conventional distinction between the theater and the world, however firmly grasped at any given moment, was not one that went without saying; on the contrary, it was constantly said. This 'saying' did not necessarily subvert the distinction; often, in fact, it had the opposite effect, shoring up and insisting upon the boundaries within which the public theater existed. . . . But the consciousness in the sixteenth century, *as now*, of other ways to construe the relation between the theater and the world heightened awareness of the theater as a contingent practice, with a set of institutional interests, motives, and constraints *and with the concomitant possibility of inadvertently or deliberately violating these very interests*. This possibility, even if never put into practice, affected the relation of the theater both to social and political authorities and to its own sense of itself."[152]

Playwrights themselves, in succeeding productions, were affected by these interactions. Slowly, cultural refashioning reaches wider and wider circles. In the same vein, ecclesial authority, liturgical presiders, and official liturgical commissions that formulate rites are affected in this organic manner as well. Over time, amid the safety and embrace of the accepted rubric, different social constructions gradually emerge in ritual enactment. The changing theological and cultural horizon and the faith of the community acts upon these repetitive forms, through a dynamic exchange akin to what happens to a Shakespearean play produced in ensuing generations. As Greenblatt asserted, "Plays are made up of multiple exchanges, and the exchanges are multiplied over time, since to the transactions through which the work first acquired social energy are added supplementary transactions through which the work renews its power in changed circumstances."[153]

This dynamic helps to explain why the reform of the liturgy and the renewed interest in the homily as a barometer for a meaningful celebration have emerged as such lightening rods for the ferment happening in the Church as a whole. As in the privileged arena of the dramatic production, so too in the liminal space of ritual enactment, discontinuities provide a *necessary* adjunct to the continuities in the

[152] Ibid., 15–16; my emphasis.
[153] Ibid., 20.

113

system, and both are inherent in a shift from one paradigm to another. The particularities of this shift in horizon have an arena in the liturgy where these emerging possibilities can be tested, played out, affirmed, or rejected. This exchange of energy in altered circumstances renews the shared tradition, still held to be sacred and inviolable. The change in practice results from far more than official ritual changes handed down from above. We find ourselves doing things differently, rather than simply responding to planned changes in official liturgical texts.

Proclamation represents a central ritual strategy in a liturgical renewal that is biblically based and vernacular in expression. The Liturgy of the Word renders a privileged opportunity to renew the central story whose utterance calls the community into existence. In previous decades, when the self-identity of the Christian assembly was easier to articulate and the paradigms of authority and social organization clearly reflected the self-understanding of the community, the liturgy seemed to be a commonly accepted presupposition, or at most an afterthought, in theological and communal reflection.[154] The quality and content of proclamation now, in an age of dissonance, take on a sharpened focus. The solidity of the pulpit and the normativity of the book within the liturgical celebration furnish an acceptable boundary to play with new configurations of ecclesial structure and meaning. And the more the negotiations and exchanges occur, the more the identity of the community is illuminated, even if that identity itself is in a state of flux. The great desire on the part of people for powerful preaching today, as well as their regretful disappointment, does not stem from mere whims of a restless assembly or the pressured directives of liturgical professionals. The desire springs from a renewed self-identity in the Church as a whole, being explored within the boundary of this liturgical space. In the context of this transitional moment and social context, people hunger more and more for the liberating word of God and for the paschal meal as its natural fulfillment. The role that liturgical proclamation plays in this transition allows *both* the continuities and discontinuities of that tradition to be expressed as a fresh word, a newness of life, and a call to

---

[154] Indeed, it was somewhat of a novel concept in the Constitution on the Sacred Liturgy to insist that "the study of liturgy is to be ranked among the compulsory and major courses in seminaries and religious houses of studies; in theological faculties it is to rank among the principal subjects. It is to be taught under its theological, historical, pastoral, and juridical aspects" (CSL 16).

conversion and transformation in this historical time and place. This renewed expression is, again, what sacramentality affirms as the grace of God present *in our midst.*

(a) The second point concerning the *interactive dynamics of theater as a cultural production* and the *specifically communal enactment of liturgy* as a sacramental presence fulfilled in our midst follows from the first point on the role drama plays in a period of social tension. The design of the liturgy does not read as a private text (as in, for example, the archaic term "to read a Mass"), no matter how often that tendency has seeped into sacramental practice. The Liturgical Movement of the early part of the twentieth century emerged as a pastoral response to the concrete experience of worshipers and their growing estrangement between ritual practices and their everyday lives. Pastoral analysis does not negate the role of scholarship and critical theological reflection as *an agent of ritual change.* Rather, as Kevin Irwin and others have shown,[155] the interrelation between *lex orandi* and *lex credendi* fluctuates and interacts to transform the community of believers and to enrich the faith that binds them into God's people. Serious analysis about what is taking place in the social event of contemporary liturgy, particularly regarding the sacramentality of the word, hastens the pastoral response.

---

[155] Cf. Kevin Irwin, *Context and Text: Method in Liturgical Theology* (Collegeville: The Liturgical Press, 1991). Irwin notes how this interactive dynamic has expanded the *lex orandi/lex credendi* dialogue to include the critical function of liturgiology, the *lex agendi,* which includes a reflection of the rites as "enacted" and on the implications of a sacramental life on the spirituality of the community. For a brief and clear discussion of this, see also Irwin's essay "Liturgical Theology," *The New Dictionary of Sacramental Worship,* ed. Peter E. Fink (Collegeville: The Liturgical Press, 1990) 721–33. Other helpful works are Mary Collins, "Liturgical Methodology and the Cultural Evolution of Worship in the United States," *Worship* 49 (February 1975) 85–102; Albert Houssiau, "The Rediscovery of Liturgy by Sacramental Theology," *Studia Liturgica* 15 (1982–83) 158–77; Aidan Kavanagh, *On Liturgical Theology* (New York: Pueblo, 1984); and David N. Power, "Cult to Culture: The Liturgical Foundation of Theology," *Worship* 54 (November 1980) 482–95. All are cited by Irwin. Another brilliant example of the fluid interaction of dogmatic reflection and ritual worship is Gordon W. Lathrop's *Holy Things: A Liturgical Theology* (Minneapolis: Fortress Press, 1993) and its sequel, *Holy People* (Minneapolis: Fortress Press, 1999). Geoffrey Wainwright's *Doxology: The Praise of God in Worship, Doctrine, and Life* (New York: Oxford University Press, 1980) remains the standard text in ecumenical studies on the topic.

The social nature of liturgy provides a litmus text for the Church's self-identity in any given period. It bears certain important parallels to the collective nature of Renaissance drama as a privileged medium for the social transformation occurring in sixteenth- and seventeenth-century European culture. Greenblatt has noted that the search "to locate the power of art in a permanently novel, untranslatable formal perfection will always end in a blind alley,"[156] and the study of Shakespearean drama is especially illustrative of that futility to isolate an individual genius at work. This attempt is destined for failure because of the specifically *communal* nature of drama as a form of artistic practice, both in its creation as a social text and its *production* as a social event. These two aspects of communality will be explored here with more detail, because they have rich insights for liturgical proclamation.

As a social text, Greenblatt notes, "the theater is manifestly the product of collective intentions," by which he goes on to assert that the actual writing of a script does not appear to be the heart of the mystery of its creation.[157] Shakespeare, for example, was indebted to historical events, literary sources, and "collective genres, narrative patterns, and linguistic conventions."[158] Novels, poetry, painting styles, and the like all share this indebtedness to multivalent influences. But in the creation of Renaissance plays, playwrights rarely composed out of context from the company they directed, the theater space at hand, or the expectations of those who would fund the production. Because of this, Greenblatt calls the apparently solitary, artistic moment as "itself a social moment."[159]

Liturgical proclamation and the entire liturgy share that same position of being an enactment prepared in the midst of "collective intentions." The faith of the Church, the liturgical cycle of feasts and biblical readings, the communal life of the assembly (the neglect of which enhances ritual dissonance), and the rubrical progression of proclamation/intercessions/sharing of the paschal feast are all a part of that shared cultural storehouse. This richness represents the "collective genres, narrative patterns, and linguistic conventions" that embrace liturgy's social moment. Even the preaching is not the isolated utterance of an individual, but part of a shared ritual action, in

[156] Greenblatt, *Shakespearean Negotiations,* 4.
[157] Ibid., 4–5.
[158] Ibid., 5.
[159] Ibid.

which layers of simultaneous interactions are taking place. Even in the seemingly isolated work of homiletic *preparation*, one cannot ignore this communal character of liturgical proclamation. Even more, preachers can adopt positive strategies for liturgical preparation, homiletic construction, and delivery to enhance the ecclesial nature of this "heart of the mystery." In short, the collective intentions of liturgical proclamation, as for theater, reach back to the creative moment itself.

Greenblatt posits the participatory role of the playgoers as the second reason that the power of art resides in the communal exchange of energy and eludes a fixed point of location. He wrote:

"the theater manifestly addresses its audience as a collectivity. The model is not, as with the nineteenth century novel, the individual reader who withdraws from the public world of affairs to the privacy of the hearth but the crowd that *gathers together in a public play space.* The Shakespearean theater depends upon *a felt community:* there is no dimming of lights, no attempt to isolate and awaken the sensibilities of each member of the audience, no sense of the disappearance of the crowd."[160]

The felt community requires that the illusions and patterns of speech, the dramatic gestures, and the immediacy of the collective event be articulated with some shared language and experience, or else communication is severely hampered. New Historicist critic John D. Schaeffer roots such metaphoric and imaginative communication in what philosopher Giambattista Vico called the *sensus communis.*[161] This standard of practical judgment or shared imagination and ideals grounds itself in a rhetoric that taps into a people's common wisdom. The interplay between shared ideal and common metaphorical language "generates the possibility of other figures, connotations, and allusions, some shared by the entire language community, some by a part of the community, and some peculiar to each individual and derived from his own experiences."[162] A communal sense of language and meaning is the foundation of a person's sense of self, which allows

[160] Ibid.; my emphasis.
[161] John D. Schaeffer, "The Use and Misuse of Giambattista Vico: Rhetoric, Orality, and Theories of Discourse," *The New Historicism,* ed. Veeser, 95.
[162] Ibid., 97.

the dramatic production the further possibility of speaking to personal experiences and individual situations. If that were not true, such productions would resemble communally controlled propaganda machines. The source of the dramatic energy, therefore, remains always a *sensus communis* and not an actor or an orator's personal eloquence. The apparently individual act of proclaiming the word also locates the *sensus communis* as the source of its grace.

What is interesting here from a theological perspective is that, according to Vico, "The *sensus communis* is the *sensus numinous*."[163] Poetic discourse and logic is rooted in a religious event, something that Schaeffer notes is inimical to much post-structural, Enlightenment-based thought. Yet, in the typical New Historicist mode of uncovering the repressed and marginal voices, Schaeffer makes a powerful point on the role of participants in cultural productions like drama or liturgy. As he said:

"The orality of Vico's paradigm allows it to be holistic in its account of the 'power' and the 'play' that constitutes the interaction of discourse and history, while the Enlightenment paradigm divorced power from play and concealed behind it a tone of ironic objectivity, a tone available exclusively to writers."[164]

The communal nature of the social text in public productions, as emphasized by Greenblatt and Schaeffer, expresses precisely the quality of communication in liturgical proclamation that often is ignored in much current homiletics. Reading biblical texts and preaching embody "the social instrumentality of writing and playing."[165] Because of the immediacy of the ritual assembly's presence—much like the setting of a live stage production—language which moves and transforms must ground itself in a sense of the hearers as a social body.[166]

[163] Ibid., 98.
[164] Ibid., 99.
[165] Montrose, "The Poetics and Politics of Culture," *The New Historicism*, ed. Veeser, 23, 30.
[166] David Buttrick attempts this in *Homiletic: Moves and Structures* (Philadelphia: Fortress Press, 1987) but falls short, I believe, in yoking this communal hearing to a religious one, as Schaeffer does, or to the dynamics of proclamation as conveying what Vico calls, according to Schaeffer, "the meaning which inheres in language and community, the *sensus communis*" whose shared nature "remains at base a religious meaning" (Schaeffer, "Rhetoric, Orality, and Theories of Discourse," *The New Historicism*, ed. Veeser, 98).

And that social body's shared language itself is recognized as "numinous." It conveys a communal religious sensibility which then interacts with the text and helps to circulate the energy and grace-filled life present in both the word and those who hear it.

This shared wisdom of the assembly, therefore, holds a central place for the effective communication of grace in the proclamation of the word. Minute exegesis that merely attempts to fix the meaning of a passage and which ignores the *present* communication of religious meaning, the *sensus communis,* can silence a graced hearing of the word. Similarly, homiletic praxis cannot assume that language that speaks of God and God's actions is most precise when it employs, to use Schaeffer's critique again, "a tone of ironic objectivity, a tone exclusively available to writers." Rhetorical objectivity in liturgical proclamation, which shuns the language of poetic logic, metaphor, and passion, dilutes the most powerful event of grace that sacramentality claims. Graced communication occurs first and foremost with a people; the nature of religious ritual itself is communal; and the immediacy of the assembly and the rhetorical moment of communication all interact and exchange energy to allow a powerful proclamation to be heard in our midst.

The "Embeddedness" of Texts as a Vehicle for God's Encounter with the Church in Liturgical Proclamation: "Resonance and Wonder"

New Historicism pays particular attention to "the embeddedness of cultural objects in the contingencies of history."[167] Sacred texts, dramatic productions, and great works of art do not exist in a vacuum. The environment out of which they emerged allows them to communicate the unique life of people, events, and beliefs that surrounded their making. In addition, a contemporary encounter with these artifacts in the midst of the present historical and cultural milieu sets up the possibilities for a fertile dialogue in which texts and artifacts come alive in a strange and powerful way. Over-zealous interpretations of this embeddedness, however, can lead to assumptions that history itself becomes a steamroller over which humankind has no control, that contingency renders all value judgments by literary critics anathema, and that a historic past or tradition is always *the* inviolable element in understanding a literary work. Greenblatt, in response to many similar critiques, asserted in his later series of essays

---

[167] Greenblatt, "Resonance and Wonder," 164.

Learning to Curse (1990) that "most of the writing labelled new historicist, and certainly my own work, has set itself resolutely against each of these positions."[168]

This clarification replies to a measured concern on the part of critics that a "practiced detachment," as Liu calls it, pervades among New Historicists that looks upon the struggles in a society and its culture as if they were "faceless, anonymous."[169] Others claim that New Historicism's distaste for "ideology" obscures the important role that foundational values play in holding communities and their critics responsible "both for the way ideas are organized together (in texts and institutions) and for the work such organization does in societies."[170] Consequently, in response to his focus on the particularities of time and place and text, Greenblatt asked "what is at stake in the shift from one zone of social practice to another?"[171] What does that shift evoke in the community that interacts with such an energy exchange? It is in the context of such questions that he coined the phrase "resonance and wonder" as a way to describe the effect such "embeddedness of cultural objects" has on those who encounter them.

Attention to the shared values inherent in focal texts, which help to shape the lives of a *felt community*, is important when considering the dynamism at work in liturgical proclamation. The reading of the word and the preaching, for example, announces and calls the assembly to *something*. It is not a rhetorical interlude before the matters of real importance at the table commence. The fact that the Scriptures took shape because of the lives of specific people and communities of faith in dialogue with God makes them embedded in a sacred history. The path this history weaves now leads to the particular gathering present at the liturgy. Communities must value and highlight this historical connectedness for the fullest contemporary appropriation to take place. Honoring and noting a sacred tradition embedded in a text exemplifies the quality of Greenblatt's "resonance and wonder," and these terms can help us to illuminate a sacramental understanding of grace that is actually fulfilled in our hearing.

[168] Ibid.

[169] Liu, "Local Transcendence," 97.

[170] Gregory Jay, "Ideology and the New Historicism," *Arizona Quarterly* 49:1 (Spring 1993) 153–4. Although Jay's article was written shortly after Greenblatt's *Learning to Curse*, its arguments are similar to many critiques about New Historicism that led to Greenblatt's 1990 book.

[171] Greenblatt, "Resonance and Wonder," 163.

The appreciation of a text's resonance and its ability to evoke wonder anchors itself in "the cultural specificity, the social embedment, of all modes of writing."[172] This understanding shares much in common with Karl Rahner's efforts in 1960 to articulate a specifically ecclesial theology of the word. Rahner attempted to elucidate how the word of God is embedded *in* the Church and, hence, is indispensable to its sacramental nature.

"The word of God is uttered by the Church, where it is preserved inviolate in its entirety, and necessarily so, in its character of the word of *God*. This statement should be clear. To deny it would be to deny the essence of the Church, in which and through which (and not passing by it) Christ makes his message contemporary to all ages as the word of God, the Church through which he is present to us in his own mission."[173]

Rahner's insistence here is the theological predecessor to Greenblatt's simple declaration, "Agency is virtually inescapable."[174] Agency demands continual engagement in the embeddedness of these texts within the social climate and interactions of their creation. As a result, value judgments implicate themselves that reach from the historical situation into present social constructs and negotiations. Rather than dispassionately retreating from these values, Greenblatt finds their engagement pervasive on many levels: "in the textual traces I choose to analyze, in the stories I choose to tell, in the cultural conjunctions I attempt to make, in my syntax, adjectives, pronouns."[175]

Homilists at once recognize here valued criteria for effective preaching: how do we read the lections so that a meaningful dialogue between tradition and present faith occurs? Powerful texts like Scripture do not, as Rahner says, "pass by" the real lives and stories and struggles of the contemporary community. Instead, in refashioned form, their pervasive values embed themselves in its communal identity. The assumption these values make generates a faith in the truth of what is being proclaimed and makes a claim upon this

[172] Louis Montrose, "The Elizabethan Subject and the Spenserian Text," *Literary Theory/Renaissance Texts*, ed. Patricia Parker and David Quint (Baltimore: Johns Hopkins University Press, 1986) 305.
[173] Rahner, "The Word and the Eucharist," 257.
[174] Greenblatt, "Resonance and Wonder," 164.
[175] Ibid., 167.

community's life. Such a ritual hearing, therefore, is essential for the life of the world.

Greenblatt's focused attention on "what is at stake in the shift from one zone of social practice to another" situates the issue regarding the proper reverence for the mystery at the heart of liturgical proclamation. Shakespearean drama shares the same "air of veneration"[176] as most of the biblical stories that shape the liturgical lectionary. In addition, Shakespearean productions over time suffered from a similar malaise that afflicts much contemporary liturgical proclamation. Traditional formalism and historicism, according to Greenblatt, had so enshrined Shakespearean drama in a vision of the world and the way things supposedly *were* that the imaginative possibilities became capsulated and constrained. In words that might serve as a hearty reminder to liturgists and homilists in the contemporary Church, Greenblatt charts the result of such a lack of imagination and engagement with the dynamism of life embedded in these texts: "A criticism that never encounters obstacles, that celebrates predictable heroines and rounds up the usual suspects, that finds confirmation of its values everywhere it turns, is quite simply boring."[177] From a theological perspective, such an attitude toward Scripture and the liturgical enactment indicates something more than boredom: a spiritual resistance or even a crisis of faith. To engage the text and the rite honestly and imaginatively always risks the possibility that nothing new or life-giving will be found there.

A similar risk in Shakespearean studies led Greenblatt to the "points at which one cultural practice intersects with another." What he found hidden beneath all the apparent aesthetic and cultural uniformity was a "psychic, social, and material resistance, a stubborn, unassailable otherness, a sense of distance and difference," which became for him an avenue *into* the vitality these dramas contained.[178] This recovery of the real contingencies of past lives, he concluded, reveals how "cultural structures" become embedded in our own. Our own narrow world broadens when we venture an engagement with the life that energizes these texts. *Resonance* emanates from the forces and energies that surround them, and the attention one pays to the dynamic life embedded there evokes a contemplative appreciation

[176] Ibid., 168.
[177] Ibid.
[178] Ibid., 169.

Greenblatt called *wonder*. He articulated these descriptive terms using the media of visual art and museum exhibition, as a more accessible way of uncovering these subtle dynamics at work in a rhetorical/linguistic text. Galleries and museums as repositories of "surviving visual traces" help us to imagine the "textual traces" of a shared literary tradition such as Scripture:

"By *resonance* I mean the power of the object displayed to reach out beyond its formal boundaries to a larger world, to evoke in the viewer the complex, dynamic cultural forces from which it has emerged and for which as metaphor or more simply as metonymy it may be taken by a viewer to stand. By *wonder* I mean the power of the object displayed to stop the viewer in his tracks, to convey an arresting sense of uniqueness, to evoke exalted attention."[179]

The notion of resonance outlines descriptively what Montrose has called "the historicity of texts and the textuality of history," because it gives proper focus to what Greenblatt calls a "dense network of evolving and often contradictory forces . . . operative in a culture at any given moment in both its history and our own."[180] It is not "a collapse of the distinction between art and non-art," but "an awakening" that leads one to move beyond the isolation of the artifact to the complex arrangement of "only half visible relationships and questions" that adhere around the piece.[181] The meaning, therefore, is multivalent and interactive.

Liturgical proclamation, it can be asserted, shares these same ends. The privileged arena of the liturgical space and the ritual enactment provides the broader context that allows the resonance in sacred texts to become embedded in the life of the assembly. The Liturgy of the Word provides the *sacred distance* so that the "stubborn, unassailable otherness" of the Gospel imperatives may break through and interact with the community in need of such grace and life circulating there. Resonant biblical texts, according to Greenblatt's schema, are not collapsed vignettes of contemporary struggles, which modern homiletic

[179] Ibid., 170; my emphasis. In a similar vein, Doris Grumbach, in her literary journal *Extra Innings: A Memoir* (New York: W. W. Norton and Company, 1993), describes the "continued existence in the creative world" that a past author still conveys as "revenance" (20).

[180] Ibid.

[181] Ibid, 172–3.

contextualization often assumes. Instead, they open up a wider boundary where the "half-visible relationships and questions," the stuff of real conversion and transformation, can be encountered by the attentive hearers and blessed with the nourishment that sacramental life offers to the world.[182] These texts display an "openness and precariousness" when resonance is allowed its play. This "vulnerable text," as Thomas Greene calls it, radiates "power and fecun-

[182] Some years back, the *New York Times Book Review* noted a similar insight by Jacque Barzun in his book *Begin Here: The Forgotten Conditions of Teaching and Learning* (Chicago: University of Chicago Press, 1992). The sacramental claims concerning a grace-filled proclamation are apparent in his description of a literary classic:

"Because a classic is thick and full, and because it rose out of a past situation, it is hard to read. The mental attitude and attention that are good enough for reading the newspaper and most books will not work. . . . But why, after all, learn to read differently by tackling the classics? The answer is simple: in order to live in a wider world. . . . Wider than the one that comes through the routine of our material lives and through the paper and factual magazines . . . wider also than friends' and neighbors' plans and gossip; wider especially than one's business or profession. For nothing is more narrowing that one's own shop. . . . If one reads them with concentration . . . the effort gives us possession of a vast store of vicarious experience; we come face to face with the whole range of perception that [humankind] has attained and that is denied by our unavoidably artificial existence. Through this experience we escape from the prison cell, professional or business or suburban. It is like gaining a second life."

Author David Leavitt poses another helpful reflection on the creative process as a communal gift to the wider world in "Two Dead Writers" (*Southwest Review* 79, nos. 2–3), 313–5. David Tracy's reflections on the "public status of all classics, including religious classics, as *cultural classics*" in *The Analogical Imagination: Christian Theology and the Culture of Pluralism* (New York: Crossroad, 1981) are a lasting contribution to hermeneutical theology. As Tracy said concerning the capacity of "cultural classics" to broaden religious horizons, "they interpret us as much as we interpret them" (134). In his chapter on "Interpreting the Religious Classic," Tracy adds this life-giving dimension to the humble recognition of our humanness and the depth of its religious possibilities:

"To enter the world of a major classic the interpreter must be prepared to be caught up in the back-and-forth movement of disclosure and concealment of a truth about life itself, to be carried along by the intensification process of the mode of being in the world disclosed by the text" (154).

For the role of the assembly as a "co-creator of the work" and as an "interpretive community" from a reader-response critical perspective, see Chapter 4 that follows.

dity," rooted in its human, historical, and complex circumstances "that enabled [the work] to come into being in the first place."[183]

Greenblatt's use of the museum image casts important light on the liturgy's greatest focal purpose, because the museum as a cultural institution forms "a memorial complex" whose "atmosphere has a peculiar effect on the act of viewing."[184] Liturgy invites such a memorial complex of word and action that has this peculiar effect as well: an atmosphere of openness and vulnerability which contemporary sacramentality insists is the locus of grace. It invites the assembly into the vulnerable mystery it announces, "into the symbolic wounding to which [Scripture] is prone."[185] Such is the power of Christ's presence in the word and these are the stakes involved when we choose to take our nourishment there.

This atmosphere of expectation and risk leads to the notion of *wonder,* in many ways the very context in which resonant life and meaning are evoked. The presence of awe represents the contemplative side of encountering literary artifacts and texts. This attitude demands "a certain kind of looking" whose ultimate use is not so much for the "knowledge" of the work itself or the culture from which it came, "but it is vitally important in the attempt to understand our own."[186]

The contemplative locus enhances the arena of mystery, which is shaky ground for post-structural literary critics, but familiar ground for liturgical and sacramental theology. Greenblatt calls the activity "enchanting looking . . . when the act of attention draws a circle around itself."[187] He insists that this wonderful capacity is as true for textual artifacts as for visual ones. From the perspective of liturgical theology, the worshiping assembly and its ministers, in powerful moments of graced communication, reverence and gaze and stay silent

[183] Greenblatt, "Resonance and Wonder," 170–1. Greenblatt's reference is to Thomas Greene, *The Vulnerable Text: Essays on Renaissance Literature* (New York: Columbia University Press, 1986) 100.

[184] Greenblatt, "Resonance and Wonder," 173.

[185] Ibid., 171. Greenblatt is referring to great literature here. The sacrificial character of such wounding, in a liturgical sense, embraces Christ's self-offering in which the community is invited to share. As David Power says in *The Eucharistic Mystery,* "The suffering of Christ and the love of Christ do not transform the world by the mere fact of having occurred. They are salvific in being brought to expression within an already existing narrative tradition, changing this tradition from within" (308).

[186] Greenblatt, "Resonance and Wonder," 180.

[187] Ibid., 176.

and muse, rather than grasp and tame. The contemplative way of looking literally transforms the work itself. As Greenblatt concluded:

"The object exists not principally to be owned but to be viewed. Even the *fantasy* of possession is no longer central to the museum-gaze, or rather it has been inverted, so that the object in its essence seems not to be a possession but rather to be itself the possessor of what is most valuable and enduring."[188]

Sacramental language calls this symbolic transformation the "sign and reality" which inheres in the word and action of the rite. Conversely, preaching and proclamation that make the text or the constituent sacramental activity too mundane or overly down-to-earth disperse this attention from the power at work at "the heart of the mystery."[189] Liturgy's patterned ritual and recurrent texts, and the expressive gestures, rich sights, smells, and sounds, all transform the sign and the reality, an awesome Presence that announces that we do not possess the word, but that it possesses us. Ritual enactment creates the space for metaphors to explode and the boundaries to be widened. We can then explore the "half-visible relationships and questions" embedded there. The event becomes a proclamation "fulfilled in our midst."

Surprisingly enough for a contemporary literary critic, Greenblatt cites Albert the Great here about the role of wonder ("something like fear in its effect on the heart"). St. Albert states, "This effect of wonder, then, this constriction and systole of the heart, spring from an unfulfilled but felt desire to know. . . ."[190] Greenblatt shares this wondrous search to the heart of things with the Christian quest for the origins of life in God. However, New Historicists feel obliged to make a departure from theological conjecture here, but one which sacramental theology, in response, would not find that hard to bridge in order to maintain the dialogue. Commenting on this "remarkable passage" of Albert, Greenblatt articulated the philosophical departure and said: "Such too, from the perspective of the new historicism,

---

[188] Ibid., 178.

[189] Ibid.

[190] Ibid., 181. The quote is from Albert the Great's *Commentary on the Metaphysics of Aristotle,* which Greenblatt discovered in J. V. Cunningham, *Woe or Wonder: The Emotional Effect of Shakespearean Tragedy,* trans. M.R.B. Shaw (Harmondsworth: Penguin, 1963) 315.

is the origin of a meaningful desire for cultural resonance. But while philosophy would seek to supplant wonder with secure knowledge, it is the function of the new historicism continually to renew the marvelous at the heart of the resonant."[191] Had contemporary criticism a more in-depth knowledge of the tradition of philosophical theology and the mystery of the spiritual journey, "secure knowledge" would not be the word most descriptive of a life of faith. Even more, New Historicism's glimpse "at the heart of the mystery" would be, from the perspective of people like Semmelroth, Rahner, and Schillebeeckx, precisely the openness and vulnerability that allows the "power and fecundity" of the sacred text to be revealed as an encounter with grace.

[191] Ibid.

4

Reader-Response Criticism and the Liturgical Assembly as *Communitas Verbi*

THE SHIFT FROM A DYNAMIC TEXT TO THE READING PROCESS AS A WAY OF UNDERSTANDING THE SACRAMENTAL CHARACTERISTICS OF PROCLAMATION

Because sacraments are events and not things, interrelated actions combine to express the grace-filled encounter with God. The Liturgy of the Word, with all its ritual components and participating actors, differs from the activity of reading a novel or a poem. However, both events involve a direct interaction between a focal text and the persons who "make sense"[1] out of the words and ideas that comprise that text. Consequently, a literary theory that shifts the critical focus from a *text which is read* to the *readers who actively encounter the text* involves strategies of investigation that are central to a study of the sacramental event of proclamation taking place within the liturgy. This chapter attempts to broaden the conversation between these similar, text-centered activities.

The dynamic quality of sacramentality proposed in Part I grounds its effectiveness in the ecclesial nature of its expression and the revelatory resonance of its ritual words and actions. Reader-response

---

[1] Stanley Fish, a key spokesperson for the American movement called "reader-response criticism," maintains that the primary mode of experiencing *meaning* in the act of reading consists in making sense out of the utterances in a document. The activity of *making sense,* "rather than any reportable 'content,' will be its *meaning,*" Fish asserts. See especially the essay "Literature in the Reader: Affective Stylistics," in his *Is There a Text in This Class? The Authority of Interpretive Communities* (Cambridge, Mass.: Harvard University Press, 1980) 21–67. This essay first appeared in *New Literary History* 2:1 (Fall 1970) 123–62. It is a classic statement of the concerns of reader-response critics in the first years of the movement.

criticism[2] provides a helpful dialogue partner for contemporary sacramental theology, because its motivating focus in studying literary texts remains the activity of reading and the dynamism surrounding the person who reads. Reading must be understood imaginatively as an *event*, first and foremost as something people *do*. Our sacramental understanding finds an easy conversational entrée in that simple, underlying assumption. In the Christian celebration of worship, the gathered assembly's communal hearing of the *kerygma* possesses an event-full character. The proclamation of the Scriptures, the hearing of that word by all assembled, the preaching of the homily, and the intercessions that follow form a contiguous whole in the Liturgy of the Word.[3] This ritual activity "participates in the nature of the Church," according to Rahner, and is thus a constitutive "act of its self-*realization*."[4] The *enactment* of these liturgical actions,

---

[2] Reader-response criticism, as will be more fully illustrated below, is the overarching term for a variety of critical perspectives which, as Peter Rabinowitz says, "take the existence of the reader as a decisive component of any literary analysis." Its roots, of course, can be traced back to Aristotle and Plato, because they "based their critical arguments at least partly on literature's effect on the reader." See Peter J. Rabinowitz, "Reader-Response Theory and Criticism," *The Johns Hopkins Guide to Literary Theory and Criticism,* ed. Michael Groden and Martin Kreiswith (Baltimore: Johns Hopkins University Press, 1994) 606. See also Jane Tompkins, "The Reader in History: The Changing Shape of Literary Response," *Reader-Response Criticism: From Formalism to Post-Structuralism,* ed. Jane P. Tompkins (Baltimore: Johns Hopkins University Press, 1980) 201–32. Tompkins' compilation is also classic in North American criticism.

[3] The first part of this book outlined the inseparable relationship between the proclamatory aspects of the Liturgy of the Word and the Liturgy of the Eucharist from the perspectives of Semmelroth, Rahner, and Schillebeeckx. The same unity obviously holds true for the other sacramental rites as well. Our emphasis on the contiguous nature of the liturgical rite is often ignored in the all-important *doing* of liturgy. To fracture that connection is to stifle the power of the sacramental proclamation taking place in the assembly's hearing.

[4] Karl Rahner, "The Word and the Eucharist," *Theological Investigations,* vol. IV (New York: Crossroad, 1982) 274. He referred to these events as "basic acts of the Church" and expressive of the notion of *opus operatum* from the perspective of an activity of the "society" of the Church, rather than "something static and substance-like, less dependent on the act being done." Earlier in the essay, Rahner called the appropriation of the Church's self-identity as *communitas verbi* to be an essential task even of "those to whom the word has been entrusted for preaching." Therefore, to speak of "hearers of the word" also, by necessity, includes those who preach that word by virtue of their calling. Simply understood, one cannot preach what one has not *"heard* and *believed"* (253).

therefore, brings to symbolic expression the dynamic nature of the Church as "the final, irrevocable, eschatologically permanent word of salvation to the world."[5]

Following the sacramental paradigms outlined by Semmelroth, Rahner, and Schillebeeckx, the audible event of "the ministry of the word"[6] and the transformation it enacts upon the community of believers are efficacious acts of a proclamation imbued with the very presence of Christ *in the sacred texts read and pondered.* The sign and the reality it signifies co-inhere. Furthermore, because of the rootedness of this sacramental *kerygma* in the Church as *Ursakrament,* the assembly itself embodies this saving presence, in virtue of its ecclesial identity as the body of Christ. The Church, Semmelroth argued, comprises "a community of those who, as true believers, accept God's revelation, but is also part of the content of that revelation."[7] The assembly as active participant rests at the heart of the theological understanding of the liturgical reform.

Most Roman Catholic liturgical theology, however, has ignored the explicit ritual *activity* of reading or hearing as itself event-full, as a vital bearer of that immanent presence and reality which is the essence of sacramental life and worship. The following discussion broadens the horizons concerning the dynamism of text and context begun in the previous chapter on New Historicism by shifting the focus of concern from the energy circulating around the text to the *community who hears* and the *preacher who preaches.* Specifically, our intent is to show how these persons and their activities actually shape the mystery of God's self-communication in and through the word. Recent literary studies investigating the "role actual readers play"[8] in the shaping of texts and their meaning provide a theoretical perspective in this shift from the sacred text to the hearers of that liberating message.

---

[5] Rahner, "The Word and the Eucharist," 274.

[6] Schillebeeckx used this term in reference to Acts 6:2-4 and to the Church's mission of carrying on of that mission "in its specifically ecclesial acts, which are all visible signs of grace." See Edward Schillebeeckx, *Revelation and Theology,* vol. 1 (London: Sheed and Ward, 1987) 43–4.

[7] Otto Semmelroth, *Church and Sacrament* (Notre Dame, Ind.: Fides Publishers, 1965) 11.

[8] Jane P. Tompkins, "An Introduction to Reader-Response Criticism," *Reader-Response Criticism,* ix.

THE READER "READING" AS THE CHOSEN FOCUS
IN THE INTERRELATIONSHIP BETWEEN TEXT, READER,
AND CONTEXT

Since the 1970s, the reader-response school of criticism has sig-naled a major movement away from a text whose power and mean-ing are enclosed within the confines of its printed pages to the dynamics taking place in the reader. The reader participates in the creative act of bringing those pages to life in the complex act of read-ing. Something happens in that activity that is personal, new, and dy-namic. The seemingly arrested movement of a novel's plot or a poetic rhyme comes alive within the imaginative processes of the mind and emotions of the person who encounters that text.

Whereas New Historicism explores that dynamism from the per-spective of the interplay between literature and history and between text and context,[9] reader-response criticism focuses more narrowly on the *person acting* in concert with a dynamic, culturally-contingent lit-erary work. The reader reading, both individually and as a commu-nity of interpreters, employs strategies in that event which shape the text and even writes it anew. Here "meaning" happens, rather than being understood as something extracted out of the container of a static text.[10]

What critic Robert Fowler calls "the mysterious merger of text, reader, and context"[11] has been addressed extensively in the previous chapter through the literary tools of New Historicism, whose develop-ment evolved perhaps a decade behind that of reader-response in the United States. The different foci of these two theories lead to op-posing emphases on what is important in the efficacy of a literary ar-tifact. For example, New Historicists insist that the text itself has a

[9] Louis Montrose, "Professing the Renaissance: The Poetics and Politics of Culture," *The New Historicism*, ed. H. Aram Veeser (New York: Routledge, 1989) 16.

[10] See Fish, *Is There a Text in This Class?*

[11] Robert M. Fowler, "Who Is 'The Reader' in Reader Response Criticism?" *Semeia* 31 (1985) 15. Fowler's concern for the ambiguity surrounding the na-ture of the reader led him to articulate the importance of "text, reader, and context." Although writing here in 1985, he appeared unaware of New His-toricism's similar work in this area. For some unexplainable reason, aside from Stanley Fish and William Benn Michaels, as will be shown below, adher-ents of both schools largely ignore the insights and approaches of one an-other. Fowler's emphasis on the "temporal experience" of reading brings important focus to the ritual act of proclamation.

life in the form of a dynamic social energy, a position that is largely rejected or ignored by most reader-response critics even today. At the same time, the concerns of New Historicism, while taking the reader or audience's role seriously, deliberately moved to a wider socio-historical setting. Beyond the individual and the basic act of reading, New Historicist critics claim to "contest the validity of disciplinary boundaries themselves" and to restore a "preeminently thick descrip-tion" in reading texts.[12] This divergent lens, which explores the "rest-less energies, disorderly desires, [and] aspiration"[13] that characterize human discourse and relationships, was influenced by the emerging cultural critiques surfacing in the later seventies.[14] Yet reader-response criticism, with its tighter focus on the immediate act, represents the older cousin who is still a significant literary partner in this cultural critique. Fowler's "mysterious merger of text, reader, and content," which posits a kinetic relationship among things previously consid-ered static and unrelated, translates into the reader-response concerns for *"the reader, the reading process,* and *response."* These focal concerns theoretically opposed earlier New Critical critiques such as Wimsatt and Beardsley in "The Affective Fallacy" (1949), a literary sophistry rooted in "a confusion between the poem and its results. . . . It begins by trying to derive the standard of criticism from the psychological effects of a poem and ends in impressionism and relativism."[15] That argument still continues in literary circles forty years later, but the participants in the discussion have widened to include feminist, multicultural, and a host of other post-structural voices.

Reader-response criticism, therefore, although roughly ten years older than New Historicism, embodies a parallel but distinctive movement. Its concerns share in New Historicism's reaction to the formalist text of New Criticism, and reader-oriented theory represents

[12] Elizabeth Fox-Genovese, "Literary Criticism and the Politics of New His-toricism," *The New Historicism,* ed. Veeser, 215.

[13] Jonathan Goldberg, "The Politics of Renaissance Literature: A Review Essay," *ELH* 49 (1982) 527.

[14] Clifford Geertz's later work, *Local Knowledge* (New York: Basic Books, 1983), and the works of J. Derrida, M. Bakhtin, and M. Foucault are the most frequently mentioned in this wider cultural dialogue.

[15] Jane Tompkins notes these terms and the critique by Wimsatt and Beard-sley in "The Affective Fallacy" (1949) in *Reader-Response Criticism,* ed. Tomp-kins, ix. See also W. K. Wimsatt and Monroe C. Beardsley, "The Affective Fallacy," reprinted in *Critical Theory Since Plato,* rev. ed., ed. Hazard Adams (Fort Worth: Harcourt Brace Jovanovich, 1992) 945–51.

the initial change of direction that New Historicism and others would follow. However, its preferred focus remains on the reader and the community of readers who make up an essential factor in the confluence of "text, reader, and context." Contemporary sacramental theology struggles with similar boundaries of concern surrounding liturgical enactment as a local event and as a cultural expression of a wider historic community and tradition.

No attempt can be made here to cover all the aspects of reader, the reading process, and response that Jane Tompkins uses as the umbrella over a widely divergent set of critical concerns covering the evolving field of reader-response criticism. "Reception theory" in the Constance School in Germany, for example, through the works of people like Hans Robert Jauss, is often considered an influential European counterpart to the American movement. Our present discussion leaves out this important school of German theory, because this European approach considers itself a much more radically based cultural-political movement, as opposed to the more "immanent" and textually-based concerns of American reader-response.[16] In addition, Susan Suleiman, in her classic and respected introduction to *The Reader and the Text*, identifies no less than five diverse strains of reader oriented criticism itself, each with its own nuance and concerns.[17] Our comparison with the act of liturgical reading necessarily limits itself to the broader, general category of response theory.

Sacramental theology can employ reader-response criticism to move the conversation regarding liturgical proclamation from the richness of the dynamic text to the person in the pew, to the preacher in the pulpit, and to the congregation that shares the moment of hearing the sacred word in the context of worship. We consider three points to aid this shift in liturgical perspective: First, the argument

[16] For a detailed account of the American disinterest or ignorance concerning reception theory in Germany and Europe, and the counter claim that reader-response criticism is only formalism in a contemporary guise, see Robert C. Holub, *Crossing Borders: Reception Theory, Poststructuralism, Deconstruction* (Madison: University of Wisconsin Press, 1992), especially Part I entitled "German Theory in the United States: The American Reception of Reception Theory," 3–38.

[17] Susan Suleiman, "Introduction: Varieties of Audience-Oriented Criticism," *The Reader in the Text: Essay on Audience and Interpretation*, ed. Susan R. Suleiman and Inge Crosman (Princeton, N.J.: Princeton University Press, 1980) 3–45. The varieties of reader-oriented criticism she notes are rhetorical, structural/semiotic, phenomenological, sociohistorical, and hermeneutical.

engages Wolfgang Iser's contention that "the reader must act as a co-creator of the work,"[18] and acknowledges with Stanley Fish that a "set of interpretive strategies"[19] by that reader brings forth something new in that process. Christ's presence in the word, therefore, embraces the creative role of hearer and reader within the liturgy. Second, Fish's notion of "interpretive communities"[20] provides a way to account for both different *individual* responses to a single text and for similar *shared* responses among diverse readers. A liturgical assembly can share in the same event of proclamation on a variety of levels. Third, reader-response criticism insists that the "informed" or "implied" reader[21] possesses both an attentive responsibility and a hermeneutic "competence" that generates a text's meaning and efficacy. This responsibility places the preacher—a minister of the four-fold presence of Christ in the liturgy—as both the hearer of a saving message and a bearer to the gathered assembly of a word that is "really effective of redemption and salvation."[22] Furthermore, the preacher's voice embeds itself within the members of the assembly as the hearers of the word and the communal reader of the sacred text.[23]

The Reader as "Co-Creator" of the Work: Imagining the Assembly's Active Role in Sacramental Proclamation

Stanley Fish speaks of "the explanatory power of a method of analysis which takes the reader, as an actively mediating presence, fully into

[18] Tompkins, *Reader-Response Criticism*, xv.

[19] Stanley Fish, "Interpreting the *Variorum*," *Is There a Text in This Class?* 168.

[20] Stanley Fish popularized the term "interpretive communities" in the widely-circulated article "Interpreting the *Variorum*." However, versions of the notion are employed by a number of others in the reader-response school, such as Jonathan Culler in his *Structuralist Poetics* (Ithaca, N.Y.: Cornell University Press, 1975) and David Bleich in "Epistemological Assumptions in the Study of Response," *Reader-Response Criticism*, ed. Tompkins, 134–63.

[21] Fish, "Literature in the Reader," esp. 48–9. Jonathan Culler noted why such hermeneutic competence is important for literature in ch. 6 of *Structuralist Poetics*, 113–30. The concept of the "implied reader" is discussed extensively in Wolfgang Iser's *The Act of Reading: A Theory of Aesthetic Response* (Baltimore: Johns Hopkins University Press, 1978) 32–8.

[22] William Hill, "Preaching as a 'Moment' in Theology," *Search for the Absent God: Tradition and Modernity in Religious Understanding*, ed. Mary Catherine Hilkert (New York: Crossroad, 1992) 179.

[23] For a detailed discussion of the role of the minister acting *in persona Christi* and its foundational relationship to the notion of *in persona ecclesiae*, see Susan K. Wood, "Priestly Identity: Sacrament of the Ecclesial Community," *Worship* 69:2 (March 1995) 109–27.

account."[24] Spotlighting the reader's activity suggested to Fish a host of issues concerning the objectivity of the text, the meaning inherent in that transaction between text and reader, and the creative role the reader plays in shaping the meaning which results from that activity.

Fish's method raises interesting parallels for liturgical proclamation as well. An assembly of believers sitting in the pews during a liturgy share similar qualities of "an actively mediating presence" of the sacred word. In addition, worshipers listen to a homily, another text-of-sorts,[25] which ideally flows from the Scriptures just proclaimed.[26] Imagining worshipers as "readers," therefore, gives an illuminating perspective to common actions often taken for granted in the liturgical gathering.

An assembly understood as primarily *doing something* draws them directly into the arena of interaction between the text being read, the temporal nature of that activity, and the multi-levels of interpretation going on as that enactment takes place. Applicable questions surface immediately, given Fish's understanding of readers as this actively mediating presence. For example, can the person in the pews, or the assembly as a body of shared faith and life, shape in any way—by their sheer presence as worshipers—the *content* of the proclamation that centers around the biblical Scriptures and the preaching that follows? Does the creative act of these "readers" mean that the Scriptures become a servant to individual or prevailing group interpretations? And finally, how does the assembly's role as hearers and readers change the *meaning* of that grace-filled proclamation as it takes place within this ritual action? These questions illuminate the theological claim that the Scriptures, proclaimed in the context of liturgical action, are "fulfilled in our hearing" in an immanent way.

Reader-response criticism shares the timbre of these concerns, and its approach to these issues sheds important light on the vital role

[24] See *New Literary History* 2:1 (Fall 1970) 123–62. It is reprinted in *Reader-Response Criticism*, ed. Tompkins, 70–100.

[25] This raises the concerns of Speech-Act Theory, rhetoric, and various strands of what are called "performance studies." All of these are relevant, but beyond the bounds of this short chapter. See Stanley Fish's "How To Do Things with Austin and Searle: Speech-Act Theory and Literary Criticism," *Is There a Text in This Class?* 197–245; on performance studies see Lawrence E. Sullivan, "Sound and Senses: Toward a Hermeneutics of Performance," *History of Religions* 26:1 (August 1986) 2–14.

[26] See Constitution on the Sacred Liturgy (CSL) 52 and the Bishops' Committee on Priestly Life and Ministry document, *Fulfilled In Your Hearing: The Homily in the Sunday Assembly* (Washington, D.C.: USCC, 1982) 17.

that worshipers play in shaping the sacramental presence of Christ in the word. In their role as "hearers of the word," worshipers are like bread and wine placed on the "table of God's Word."[27] Without these people, there is no presence.

The Assembly as "Co-Creator" with the Kerygmatic Tradition. The "reader" in the context of this argument is understood as both the individual and the community of worshipers gathered for a communal hearing of the word.[28] Wolfgang Iser considered a literary work as having two poles (the *artistic* and the *aesthetic*), which he defined as the text created by the author and "the realization accomplished by the reader." The literary work that we engage and in which we take pleasure "in fact must lie halfway between the two."[29] Consequently, an interaction takes place that cannot be limited to the words on the page, but is dependent on its realization that occurs in the reading activity. "Thus, reading causes the literary work to unfold its inherently dynamic character." The creative realization, furthermore, is itself dependent on "the individual dispositions of the reader." This meeting of the artistic pole and the aesthetic pole takes place amid the creative interplay that Iser calls "the virtuality of the work." As Iser explained:

"The convergence of text and reader brings the literary work into existence, and this convergence can never be precisely pinpointed, but must always remain virtual, as it is not to be identified either with the reality of the text or with the individual disposition of the reader.

"It is the virtuality of the work that gives rise to its dynamic nature, and this in turn is the precondition for the effects that the work calls forth. . . . A literary text must therefore be conceived in such a way that it will engage the reader's imagination in working things out for himself."[30]

---

[27] "Lectionary for Mass: Introduction" (par. 10), *The Liturgy Documents: A Parish Resource,* 2d rev. ed. (Chicago: Liturgy Training Publications, 1985) 138. The document cites references to the nourishment provided at "the Table of the Word" in a number of previous documents, including CSL 51, *Dei Verbum* 21 (Vatican II's Dogmatic Constitution on Divine Revelation), and *Presbyterorum Ordinis* 18 (Vatican II's Decrees on the Ministry and Life of Priests).

[28] The specifically communal nature of the hearing will be explored more extensively in the second point below on "interpretive communities."

[29] Wolfgang Iser, "The Reading Process: A Phenomenological Approach," *Reader-Response Criticism,* ed. Tompkins, 50.

[30] Ibid., 50–1.

For Iser, the "virtuality of the work" is neither in the mind of the reader nor in the written text; its illusive power locates itself in the dynamic interchange. The reader uses "the various perspectives offered him by the text" and, in *doing* this, "sets the work in motion, and this very process results ultimately in the awakening of responses within himself." The engendered responses, moreover, are not the same as the dynamic act of relating "the patterns and 'schematized views' to one another."[31] The reader engages the text as both a source of its creativity and an expression of its effects, much like the liturgy expresses itself as source and summit of Christian life. The "virtuality of the work," therefore, affords a useful way to speak about the grace-filled energy at work in a kerygmatic tradition[32] and about the role the assembly plays in shaping the content of what is *being proclaimed* in their midst. The community's participation involves more than an interpretive response to what Iser calls the *artistic* pole in this "convergence of text and reader." The participative act of ritual engagement itself is something the assembly *does*; it is a creative act which "sets the work in motion" and is distinct from the hermeneutical dispositions which flow from it.

According to Iser, this virtuality occurs because of "gaps" or "blanks" that interrupt the flow of "connectability" conditioned by expectations about the direction the narrative is taking. The open-endedness of liturgical proclamation, embedded in a ritual which includes biblical texts and the homily which follows, illustrates those creative spaces of which Iser speaks. Concerning these "blanks," Iser said: "As an empty space they are nothing in themselves, and yet as a 'nothing' they are a vital propellant for initiating communication." This interaction between the orderly construction of the segments of the text and the "suspension of connectibility" of these empty spaces "make[s] it possible for the 'object' or world of the text to be constituted."[33] The liturgical cycle or the homily never tell the story "in its entirety," and in these gaps "the opportunity is given to us to bring

---

[31] Ibid., 51.

[32] The *kerygma* is understood here to be "both the act and the message," signifying "in a specifically biblical way a central reality of Christianity." See Eberhard Simons, "Kerygma," *The Concise* Sacramentum Mundi (New York: Seabury Press, 1975) 797.

[33] Wolfgang Iser, *The Act of Reading: A Theory of Aesthetic Response* (Baltimore: Johns Hopkins University Press, 1978) 195.

into play our own faculty for establishing connections—for filling in the gaps left by the text itself."[34] This creative intervention is the source of the claim for the reader as co-creator of the text.[35]

Iser and Fish are not in agreement here concerning the relative content a text possesses, although both posit the creative role of the reader as essential to the reading process. Iser's understanding of the interaction between text and reader differs from the creative act of ordering our experience that Fish calls "making sense." The author's text, for Fish, consists of little more than words on page and a sequence of words that await their reality when the reader *does* the act of reading. In this act, the reader is creating "sense" by ordering experience temporally and spatially in such a way that she or he easily comprehends it: "and *that*," Fish says, "rather than any reportable 'content,' will be its *meaning*."[36] The possibility of a textual tradition, like the Scriptures, as a partner in that interaction is a moot question for him:

"What I am suggesting is that there is no direct relationship between the meaning of a sentence (paragraph, novel, poem) and what its words mean. Or, to put the matter less provocatively, the information an utterance gives, its message, is a constituent of, but certainly not to be identified with, its meaning. It is the experience of an utterance—*all* of it and not anything that could be said about it, including anything I could say—that *is* its meaning."[37]

Fish's experience—roughly akin to Iser's "realization"—makes up the "response," and it develops as the activity of reading progresses. This reading activity, he asserts, is the sole bearer of the riches; the text is servant of the interpretation. In short, for Fish, what is read "is no longer an object, a thing-in-itself, but an *event*, something that *happens* to, and with the participation of, the reader."[38] The "utterance," along with the "consciousness" that receives it, cannot be separated. "The objectivity of the text is an illusion," Fish said boldly, "and, moreover, a dangerous illusion, because it is so physically convincing."[39]

[34] Iser, "The Reading Process," 54–5.
[35] Ibid., 54.
[36] Fish, "Literature in the Reader," 29.
[37] Ibid., 32.
[38] Ibid., 25.
[39] Ibid., 43.

Fish and Iser's debate about the autonomy of the text, the subject/ object dichotomy, and the meaning of experience achieved notoriety in literary studies. What is important in their disagreement rests in their highly public debate over this issue in the post-structuralist journal *Diacritics* in 1981,[40] which highlighted the role of a focal text. In that dialogue, Iser insisted that the act of creativity on the part of the reader does not negate the integrity of the work in its own right. Nor does it relegate the reader's creativity to an "interpretive strategy" in the act of reading that itself could be considered accurate or inaccurate, relevant or tangential to the creative experience taking place. As such, he replied to Fish on the important role of the preexistent text as a partner in the creative process:

"Interpretation is always informed by a set of assumptions or conventions, but these are also acted upon by what they intend to tackle. Hence the 'something' which is to be mediated exists prior to interpretation, acts as a constraint on interpretation, has repercussions on the anticipations operative in interpretation, and thus contributes to a hermeneutical process."[41]

Iser's clarification militates against a theological rejection of a reader-response approach as inherently narcissistic and relative. The subjectivity of the reader for Fish, which admittedly includes "a community's codes and conventions," always interprets perception. Iser, on the other hand, argued for an author's *text* that exists prior to interpretation and whose *artistic* pole shares the act of creativity and plays a role in shaping the reading response. The meaning, therefore, involves more than "the immediate and spontaneous reaction of individual readers," as Fish's critics generally describe his position.[42] Iser would add the effect of the creative "convergence of text and reader," who together create a literary work that is meaningful.

By observing the internecine battles within the field of reader-response, we can isolate some key issues surrounding a liturgical as-

[40] The details are reported in Vincent B. Leitch's *American Literary Criticism from the Thirties to the Eighties* (New York: Columbia University Press, 1988) 233.

[41] Iser, as quoted in Leitch, *American Literary Criticism*, 233.

[42] For example, see Jonathan Culler, *Structuralist Poetics* (Ithaca, N.Y.: Cornell University Press, 1975) 124. In *Blindness and Insight: Essays in the Rhetoric of Contemporary Fiction* (Minneapolis: University of Minnesota Press, 1983), Paul de Man likewise criticized Fish's notion of meaning as "regressive, unmediated experience" (189).

sembly's presence and role in the ritual act of reading a sacred text together. The biblical tradition is not created anew in the mind of the hearers, as Fish's extreme position would assert, nor is it merely one "interpretive strategy" among many that "makes" the text itself.[43] Rather, Christian revelation grounds itself in a historically situated experience of God "passed on," as Schillebeeckx reminded us, through "the *kerygma* of the apostles" in relation to the saving "activity of Christ as Lord."[44] That kerygmatic tradition creatively engages the ongoing faith of the assembly, whose faith experience shapes the present context of that proclamation by actively "recreating the world [the literary text] presents,"[45] or, even more accurately, *re-presents* it. The "gaps" between the faith tradition's experience and their present experience within the Christian community sets this interaction in motion. The preaching which follows takes this dynamism even further, since this creative "new hearing" is engaged again by those who listen to the homily. The lived faith tradition continues to grow.

Theologian William Hill called this activity in preaching "kerygmatic reinterpretation," in which, out of the questions raised by the historical context in which the preacher speaks, "something genuinely new comes to light." This "fresh word" is not the subjective whim of the preacher, but emerges from the text itself, out of the richness of God's word in its "*sensus plenior,* a sense that God himself intends beyond the explicit sense of the words." This *sensus plenior,* Hill said, provides a hearing whose purpose is unequivocal: to arouse faith.[46]

The Assembly as "Servant to the Text." Considering the dynamics of the reader put forth by reader-response criticism, the specifically *sacramental* aspects of the encounter between the sacred word and the ecclesial assembly in liturgical proclamation take sharper focus. We

[43] Fish's position is quite clear concerning the absolute dependence of the text on the reader's interpretation of it. As he says in "Interpreting the *Variorum*":

"Interpretive strategies are not put into execution after reading (the pure act of perception in which I do not believe); they are the shape of reading, and because they are the shape of reading, they give texts their shape, *making them rather than, as is usually assumed, arising from them*" (168; my emphasis).

[44] Schillebeeckx, *Revelation and Theology,* 26.

[45] Iser, "The Reading Process," 54.

[46] Hill, *Search for the Absent God,* 171. The term *sensus plenior* was deliberately employed by Hill, Congar, de Lubac, and others in order to retrieve it from the purely "spiritual meaning" assigned to it in the scholastic manuals. It is in that wider and richer sense that Hill described above that I use the term.

imagine a liturgical assembly in the role of a reader reading the sacred texts that shape its tradition. The assembly's activity converges with the biblical text within the temporal enactment of the liturgy and co-creates a dynamic proclamation that is "fulfilled in our hearing," that is, a kerygmatic reinterpretation.

Furthermore, that act of creativity makes the reader—in this case the assembly—a "servant to the text" rather than its "judge and master."[47] Instead of "reifying" the text, as a critic might do in establishing critical distance, the reader "tries to eliminate the distance between himself and the text."[48] In the meeting of text and reader, the latter discovers what George Steiner remarkably labeled a *real presence* and, in the richness of the creative act, becomes in a very real way the *one being read*.[49] Noting the difference between a reader's activity and the critic's "exercise of delineation and judgment," Steiner observed this curious sacramental quality to the encounter: "The 'reader,' by contrast, inhabits the provisional—in which manifold term he recognizes as relevant the notions of 'gift,' of 'that which serves vision,' and of that which 'nourishes' indispensably."[50] In its creative act, therefore, the community of worshipers does not make biblical revelation a servant to individual or prevailing group interpretations. Such relativism, according to the dynamic outlined so far, would be a far greater temptation when the liturgical assembly has not creatively engaged the text in the way Iser outlined, or in what Steiner called reading's "plenitude."[51] The Christian *kerygma* is always, first and foremost, a response to Christ, not to words on a page. The creativity of *kerygmatic interpretation* does not admit of such a dismissal of the sacred text's "*artistic* pole" that manipulation and relativism require.

The freshness of the word, however, remains a dialogical process. The *meaning* of the text—in the context of its hearing—changes in the process because in the creative interaction with the *kerygma,* as Hill has noted, "Something genuinely new comes to light, and granting that this occurs only within human subjectivity, it is not subjectivistic because it comes from the text itself, which (in this case) is God's own

[47] George Steiner, "'Critic'/'Reader,'" *New Literary History* 10:3 (Spring 1979) 423–52. This distinction between the reader as "servant to the text" and the critic as "judge and master of the text" is found on p. 449.

[48] Fowler commented on Steiner's approach in his article, "Who Is 'The Reader' in Reader Response Criticism?" 6.

[49] Steiner, "'Critic'/'Reader,'" 439–40.

[50] Ibid., 439.

[51] Ibid.

objective Word."[52] The grace-filled meaning remains immanently linked to the word "addressed to us . . . which Christ himself speaks in us and through us" to employ Rahner's notion of a *sacramental word*, "the word which renders present what it proclaims."[53] In truth, the *meaning* of the text as something genuinely new is not a solipsistic expression of individual or prevailing group concerns, but a sacramental expression of the community's encounter with the word in which its identity as Church is nourished and deepened.[54]

Finally, within the homily itself, the individual preacher engages in this "kerygmatic reinterpretation" as well, a point that will be taken up in more detail in the third point below. However, the creative process of "filling in the gaps" and creating "expectations" for the Good News that such an activity entails does not rest in the preacher's words alone. This personal, sacramental voice must be considered as one pole in a larger three-fold dialogue occurring among sacred text, assembly, and those who read and break open the text. The participative activity and presence of all these "actors" shapes the content of the word just heard and affects the preaching, which is a constituent part of its proclamation. This grace-filled interchange occurs, following the schema of reader-response criticism, within the complex liturgical action of "reading" the texts: in this "event," the *kerygma* truly is "fulfilled in our hearing."

Having employed the notion of "reading" as a way to understand the activity of the liturgical assembly in the proclamatory event, the discussion now moves to the second point concerning the assembly as a collection of readers. This specific reading assembly encompasses a community of shared identity and faith who come to hear the word together. We will employ reader-response criticism's notion of "interpretive communities" to look more closely at how this gathering of worshipers can be said to share the same "event" on a variety of levels.

"Interpretive Communities" and the Unity and Diversity which Characterize Liturgical Proclamation

The reading activity outlined so far, when applied to the notion of the liturgical assembly, required that we bracket the individuals that

---

[52] Hill, *Search for the Absent God*, 171.
[53] Rahner, "The Word and the Eucharist," 254.
[54] This is another way of expressing the point made by Semmelroth in Part I concerning the Church "as a 'sign' of the divine encounter." See his first point in Chapter 2 above.

make up that assembly and to imagine them as one "reader reading." Now we will investigate the dynamic that takes place when that imaginative vacuum is removed, and the complex interchange of a variety of peoples, concerns, and points of view intersect in the liturgical gathering. Unity and diversity within the assembly present complex challenges for worshiping communities. Reader-response criticism faced similar issues, because its approach developed initially from a fascination with the dynamics of the individual's private act of reading and grew to a broader discussion of how such experiences and interpretations relate to the wider context of the society and culture in which the reader lives.

Stanley Fish developed the notion of "interpretive communities" to accommodate a growing shift in his own critical position about the dynamics of the reading activity. In his earlier explorations, the literary work itself seemed to direct the successive responses taking place within the reader's mind and imagination. Consequently, Fish interested himself in the "response [that] includes any and all of the activities provoked by a string of words,"[55] so that one ascertains a literary work's meaning by "the rigorous and disinterested asking of the question, what does this word, phrase, sentence, paragraph, chapter, novel, play, poem *do*?"[56] In succeeding theoretical adaptations, however, Fish blurred what a literary work does with the emerging priority of what the reader does.[57] In trying to pin Fish down on this shift in perspective, Fowler contended that for Fish at this later stage "the text is invented in the process of being read—the text and all its features are only defined and therefore brought into existence by the reader's interpretive strategies."[58]

The direction Fish's thought was taking centered on the dilemma of positing a notion of interpretation distinct from the facts contained in the text. Critical questions surfaced regarding the relationship between text, reader, and context. For example, if *meaning* is totally in the experience of reading, as he staunchly maintained, does the text

[55] Fish, "Literature in the Reader," 26.

[56] Ibid., 26–7.

[57] Fish described the development of this shift, and his eventual turn to "interpretive communities" in the introduction to *Is There a Text in This Class?* (see esp. pp. 3–11). On the dichotomy between interpretation and facts see also "What Is Stylistics and Why Are They Saying Such Terrible Things About It?" (1973), reprinted in *Is There a Text in This Class?* 68–96.

[58] Fowler, "Who Is 'The Reader' in Reader Response Criticism?" 14.

itself play no role in determining what that meaning is? Why is it that people gather critically or pleasurably around certain texts? Why do individuals have varied reading tastes?[59] Are there standards of interpretation shaping the text that are separate from the experience of reading itself? Confident that his hunches were correct that "the reader's activities *are* interpretive,"[60] Fish began to look at what he saw as "my unthinking acceptance of another formalist assumption, the assumption that subjectivity is an ever-present danger and that any critical procedure must include a mechanism for holding it in check."[61] Investigating the activity of shared, communal reading allowed Fish's critical focus to remain on the reader, instead of on some standards or criteria divorced from the reading activity.

Fish came to assert, in the end, that the interpretive activity of reading is not only an individual's domain; rather, those strategies occur in communities as well. A community "makes" a text together by endowing it with the conventional category of "literature." This affirms the obvious presence of a text outside an individual person's experience, therefore, but not in the formalist sense of an objective source of meaning in and of itself. And, as Fish concluded further,

"What will, at any time, be recognized as literature is a function of a communal decision as to what will count as literature. . . . In other words, it is not that literature exhibits certain formal properties that compel a certain kind of attention; rather, paying a certain kind of attention (as defined by what literature is understood to be) results in the emergence into noticeability of the properties we know in advance to be literary."[62]

"Interpretive communities" represent the wider context within which the individual reader "reads" and they can account for the differing strategies that an individual and a community use to read different texts. An individual acts "as an extension of"[63] the community, and any strategic agreements or disagreements occur within that interdependency. At the same time, the community is not a hard and fast entity. Shifts in possible interpretations occur because *persons*

[59] See Fish, "Interpreting the *Variorum*," 167–8.
[60] Fish, *Is There a Text in This Class?* 9.
[61] Ibid.
[62] Ibid., 10–11.
[63] Ibid., 14.

within the community change and challenge and respond differently in different contexts and with different kinds of texts.

Fish posited the ideal or informed reader as the communal context within which this conversation takes place. The stability is not in the text, but in "the makeup of interpretive communities and therefore in the opposing positions they make possible."[64] The "subject-object dichotomy" disappears, because individuals that comprise the community "do not stand apart" from the source of their thinking and strategizing:

"To put it another way, the claims of objectivity and subjectivity can no longer be debated because the authorizing agency, the center of interpretive authority, *is at once both and neither.* An interpretive community is not objective because as a bundle of interests, of particular purposes and goals, its perspective is interested rather than neutral; but by the very same reasoning, the meanings and texts produced by an interpretive community are not subjective because they do not proceed from an isolated individual but from a public and conventional point of view."[65]

In a later essay, Fish went even further in explaining that disagreements are not stifled by the presence of interpretive communities and the ideal reader. Hermeneutical conflicts are the sign of the dynamism of the community itself:

"Disagreements are not settled by facts, but are the means by which such facts are settled. Of course, no such settling is final, and in the (almost certain) event that the dispute is opened again, the category of facts 'as they really are' will be reconstituted in still another shape."[66]

[64] Ibid., 15.
[65] Ibid., 14.
[66] Stanley Fish, "What Makes an Interpretation Acceptable?" *Is There a Text in This Class?* 338–9. In the end, Fish claims, "the truth about a work will be what penetrates to the essence of its literary value" (351). Sacramental theologians should find reader-response critics' appeals to "value" interesting, especially since such critics eschew any form of metaphysics. Yet they continue to make foundational truths a part of the discussion despite themselves. As a Christian community that constitutes the presence of the risen Lord as the dynamic Word that shapes its identity, that coherence of truth and value is not a critical ambiguity for ecclesial worship as it is for the "interpretive community" of postmodern critical scholars. See the discussion which follows on "negotiation" within the community, according to David Bleich.

146

Fowler noted that the protean slipperiness of Fish's critical evolution "has helpfully highlighted, if idiosyncratically, what must be simultaneous foci for reader-response criticism."[67] A critical tension must remain that respects the focal text, the integrity of the individual reader, and the community from which that reader finds her/his identity. As Fowler described it, "The issue is not about a two-sided relationship between text and reader, nor about the over-arching pre-eminence of interpretive communities, but a matter of *text* and *reader* meeting *in the context of the critical community.*"[68]

In terms of this present discussion, these simultaneous foci provide a critical framework for distinguishing the kerygmatic quality of liturgical proclamation (both lection and homily) from very different activities such as "reading the Bible" as a devotional exercise or using the Scriptures to engage in a particular polemic. The "mysterious merger of text, reader, and context" that occurs in the liturgy ensures interpretive constraints on the extreme abuse of any of these poles at the expense of another. Taken together, they articulate the liturgical expression of the Church as the fundamental sacrament of an encounter in which the sacred word, the tradition of faith, and the contemporary community intersect in the grace-filled event of Word and Sacrament. Simply put, the Church embodies the dynamic place of meeting between God, an individual, and the local assembly. The liturgy provides the expression of that sacramental encounter.

Fish himself talked about the stability that comes from having such a meeting place, although the communities themselves may change and evolve. The importance lies, first and foremost, in the *meeting*:

"The notion of interpretive communities thus stands between an impossible ideal and the fear which leads so many to maintain it. The ideal is of perfect agreement and it would require texts to have a status independent of interpretation. The fear is of interpretive anarchy, but it would only be realized if interpretation (text making) were completely random. It is the fragile but real consolidation of interpretive communities that allows us to talk to one another, but with no hope or fear of ever being able to stop."[69]

---

[67] Fowler, "Who Is 'The Reader' in Reader Response Criticism?" 14.
[68] Ibid.
[69] Fish, "Interpreting the *Variorum*," 172.

David Bleich elaborated upon Fish's notion that such communities are composed of "people who already agree with one another."[70] The community maintains its existence, Bleich qualified, because those who make up the community share similar "concerns" which must be "negotiated." Agreement, from this nuanced perspective, consists of more than mutual toleration or friendly camaraderie; it focuses fundamentally and intentionally on what is crucial to the community's self-identity. As Bleich says: "If this [agreement on *concerns*] is not obvious, it is always negotiated until it is; if the negotiation is unsuccessful, the community dissolves. Conversely, the sheer continuance of the community means that negotiations have thus far been successful."[71] Bleich's nuanced understanding of interpretive communities and the bond that identifies them raises the stakes beyond personal interaction or like-mindedness. If liturgical communities claim to be about matters of ultimate concern, then the mission of being rooted in God's love and being sent by Jesus into the world (John 17:18, 26) necessarily involves grappling with ongoing issues of changing identity and the role of foundational values. Furthermore, if liturgical enactment builds and expresses that identity, then radical disagreement in truth dissolves that union in Christ. Finally, if communal disagreements remain merely on the surface of minor rubrics, the assembly of believers can eventually forget the concerns that bind them as a community and the same dissolution results, through an anemic sense of self-identity. The great sacramental meeting in which the grace of Christ's presence is offered may actually dissolve into little actual encounter at all.[72] The grace of an "interpretive community" like a Christian assembly, as Fish has demonstrated, is that its "fragile but real consolidation . . . allows us to talk to one another with no hope or fear of being able to stop."

Other reader-response perspectives on the relationship between the individual and the community branch off in different directions and end up in a surprising array of conclusions. Jonathan Culler, in his

[70] David Bleich, "Epistemological Concerns in the Study of Response," *Reader-Response Criticism*, ed. Tompkins, 152. Fish described this "agreement" in "Interpreting the *Variorum*."

[71] Ibid.

[72] The importance of what is at stake in sharing communal identity perhaps explains why people expect so much from preaching, and why they are also sorely aware of its absence. The encounter, we could say, simply is not taking place. For some ways to bring unity to the ritual celebration that respects the integrity of proclamation, see the final chapter of this book.

Structuralist Poetics, focused much more than Fish on acknowledging the presence of prevailing institutional and semiotic structures within communities before they can be effectively employed. This demands, he said, a blunt recognition that a literary work "has meaning only with respect to a system of conventions which the reader has assimilated."[73] This internalized grammar or system of rules is embedded within the community and provides the way to read the text. Tompkins concluded that "his position pushes both text *and* reader into the background . . . and trains its sights instead on a literary discourse implicit in any and all acts of textual interpretation."[74] The implicitly dialogic nature of liturgical proclamation welcomes a focus on discourse, because the particular presence of Christ in the word relies on this interaction.

At first glance, Culler's *semiotic approach* appears on many levels to be less personal and more mechanistic than Fish's. Yet a moral dimension clings to his conclusions about communities of interpretation, which aid the present discussion regarding unity and diversity within a liturgical community. The explicit honesty of the structuralist approach regarding the dependency on such conventions and the underlying values to which they speak helps a community claim its shared identity and the cost of what it chooses. In this sense, sharing texts does mold the community and, consequently, "reading is not an innocent activity." It creates a set of expectations that shapes the response of the readers.[75] In terms of liturgical proclamation, such radical honesty can be translated, first of all, into awe for the grace-filled power at work when "reading" the word in the context of a worshiping assembly. Furthermore, Scripture *can* and *does* call the assembly to conversion and to the end of oppression; in hearing it with all its multivalent power, the community places itself at the service of its transforming mission. The acknowledgment of this possibility fuels the expectation, and those who minister and preach serve its mystery.

Even more, Culler insisted that "a willingness to think of literature as an institution composed of a variety of interpretive operations makes one more open to the more challenging and innovatory texts." The confrontation with stubborn texts and hard critiques invites a challenge to prevailing assumptions and a "questioning of self and of ordinary social modes of understanding which has always been the

---

[73] Culler, "Literary Competence," *Structuralist Poetics,* 116.
[74] Tompkins, *Reader-Response Criticism,* xviii.
[75] Culler, "Literary Competence," 129.

result of the greatest literature."[76] The mind and heart exceed their
often narrow boundaries and the experience "allows us, painfully or
joyfully, to accede to an expansion of self."[77] In these experiences, the
sensus plenior in the word reveals itself precisely because of the community's confrontation with the realities of its prevailing structures
and ethos, set against the liberating summons to which the Gospel
gives utterance. An expansion of the community's identity results,
which may have narrowed or become solipsistic over time, especially
when the ambiguity surrounding that identity was never called into
question. The act of preaching, particularly, profits from this perspective Culler provides. Difficult texts and unbearable pronouncements
have been the spur for more than one encounter with the depth and
power of grace at work within a community that is honest enough to
struggle with them.

The *psychological approach* to interpretive communities provides another variation on the communal theme in reader-response theory.
For critics like Norman N. Holland, the identity a person acquires in
the act of reading enables one to shatter the barriers between the self
and others. The dynamic of shared text and committed community
shift the social dynamic from isolationism to "ingathering and inmix-
ing of self and other." The individual self participates in the symbol
making, a creative act that calls one into the life the text expresses
and identifies the boundaries of relation between human persons
with shared beliefs and values.[78] Such nuanced perspectives around
the activity of reading testify to the variety of possibilities that a life
surrounding a text affords. As Susan Suleiman has noted concerning
the difference in viewpoints between people like Culler and Holland
(and, by extension, Fish and Iser and Bleich), "Reading is far too rich
and many-faceted an activity to be exhausted by a single theory."[79]

Sacramental theology needs the open-endedness of such theoretical
creativity because confusion around liturgical proclamation as a
sacramental act rests largely in a passive, one-dimensional under-

[76] Ibid.

[77] Ibid., 130.

[78] See Norman N. Holland, "Unity Identity Text Self," *Reader-Response Criticism*, ed. Tompkins, 130–1.

[79] Suleiman, "Introduction: Varieties of Audience-Oriented Criticism," 31.
Suleiman commented that each of the five varieties of reader-response criticism (see n. 17 above) employs its own lens in order to focus on the topic of
the dynamism of reading and of the reader.

standing about the nature of the ritual act taking place and the sacredness of the dialogue that nurtures it. In the end, whether one agrees with the specific dynamics of interpretive communities as Fish or other reader-response critics have outlined them, they do provide the believing community the access to the richness of meaning and perspectives the biblical texts contain.[80] As R. B. Gill noted concerning the self-identity that is formed when shared communities express a common vision:

"Interpretive communities, then, mediate between individuals and a meaningless world by giving them the patterned and purposive categories and slots into which they can place their experience. These communities rescue individuals from the radical isolationism of subjectivism by giving them not only fellowship but, more basically, a common epistemology that allows them to understand experience in similar ways and thus to share a common sense of purpose. 'We preach Christ crucified,' Paul writes to the Church at Corinth, 'a stumbling block to Jews and folly to Gentiles, but to those that are called, both Jews and Greeks, Christ the power of God and the wisdom of God' (1 Corinthians 1.23-24)."[81]

The community encompasses the meeting place where that common identity is experienced, and through which the sacred text and the believer make sense together in the course of the sacramental encounter. The concurrence of thought with sacramental theology heightens the importance of the conversation. What remains for us to explore are the specifics of the preaching person and his or her individual voice within the communal context. The final point in this chapter, therefore, will investigate the preacher's privileged role as one who mediates this encounter in a particularly focused manner. Situated in a charismatic office in service of the assembly, the preacher acts as both a hearer of the word and the bearer to the gathered assembly of the riches that unfold in the liturgical event of proclamation.

[80] See Stanley E. Porter, "Reader-Response Criticism and New Testament Study: A Response to A. C. Thiselton's New Horizons in Hermeneutics," *Journal of Literature and Theology* 8:1 (March 1994) 99; and R. B. Gill, "The Moral Implications of Interpretive Communities," *Christianity and Literature* 33:1 (Fall 1983) 55–8.
[81] Gill, "The Moral Implications of Interpretive Communities," 57.

The "Informed Reader" in Reader-Response Criticism and the Perspective of the Preacher as the Bearer of Good News

Dominican William Hill spoke of the engagement of the preacher in the process of mediating God's meaning to a community that gathers to hear its saving message:

"The [preacher] does not merely transport mechanically a meaning from the New Testament to the congregation. Preachers let the text come to meaning in their own intentionality on which basis they are formally constituted as those who are now enabled to announce the message of Christ. This meaning, precisely as it occurs, constitutes the revelatory and saving act of God. At the same time, it constitutes the preacher as 'one who saves'—in however deficient and instrumental a way. Thus as meanings alter in the one who speaks, so does the very reality of the speaker."[82]

This intentionality of the preacher places him or her in a unique position within the body of Christ. The *New Code of Canon Law* (1983) labeled preaching as an office in the Church (c. 756, 1).[83] Whatever legal technicalities the discipline stipulates about the office of preaching, the important point remains that official preaching, as opposed to an individualized notion of charismatic preaching, embodies a role within the Church community that carries with it both rights and responsibilities. The United States Bishops' 1982 document on preaching, *Fulfilled in Your Hearing: The Homily in the Sunday Assembly*, clearly stated the fundamental, ecclesial nature of that role. Speaking of the presbyter as the normative preacher, the document stated: "We think of the priest as the representative of Christ. This way of thinking is true, as long as we remember that one represents Christ by representing the church, for

---

[82] Hill, *Search for the Absent God*, 181.

[83] Canon 764 stipulates that by ecclesiastical law that office is a sharing in the bishop's office and is normally reserved for priests and deacons. This, of course, is a Roman Catholic discipline. In fact, exceptions to this rule are occurring unofficially throughout the world and some dioceses are even making guidelines to that effect. "Exception," however, is misleading, because the bishop can be said to exercise faithfully his proper ministry of the word by delegating lay preachers. The official status expresses the ecclesial tradition, which may continue to broaden in order to be faithful to the Gospel entrusted to the Church. All of this does not negate the fact that official preaching expresses a sacramental charism in virtue of its corporate, liturgical context.

the church is the fundamental sacrament of Christ."[84] This perspective clearly represents the sacramentality outlined in Part I of this book, and its focus is crucial in trying to situate the authority of the preacher within a liturgical assembly which constitutes the fundamental sacrament of the eschatological grace of Christ.[85]

The privileged role of articulating "the riches of [Christ's] glorious inheritance among the saints" (Eph 1:18) raises the question of how that office actually is expressed in the concrete moment of preaching called the homily. Hill suggested that a concomitant intentionality goes hand in hand with that office. The preacher must cooperate in "doing what the Church intends" in participating in the grace-filled action of Word and Sacrament, which Semmelroth called a single work bestowing grace.[86] The activity of preaching cannot be divorced from all the ecclesial responsibilities that embody one's identity as a believer and as a minister of the Gospel. Rather, all these expressions of the Church's life and mission call forth the activity of preaching; this call results in that person's standing before the assembly to proclaim Good News. The preacher, above all, must preach what s/he first has heard and believed as a member of the People of God.

Building on the insights of the first two points regarding the reader as co-creator and the identity of interpretive communities, it is possible to situate the office and person of the preacher as an integral part of the assembly who engages in the primary activity of "kerygmatic reinterpretation." Furthermore, as an instrumental voice by reason of office, the preacher also presents a focal voice within an "interpretive community." This prophetic voice brings unity to the self-understanding of that community and expands the horizons of that identity in light of the new context within which the word is uttered. To expand on this sacramental perspective, Fish's notion of the "informed reader" and Iser's similar but nuanced "implied reader"

---

[84] Bishops' Committee on Priestly Life and Ministry, *Fulfilled in Your Hearing*, 6. Kenan Osborne has commented on the need for clarification of such language as "fundamental sacrament" when he noted: "The Church is a basic sacrament, but not in the same way that Jesus is a basic or fundamental sacrament. The precise terminology for this distinction has not been found" (*Sacramental Theology: A General Introduction* [Mahwah, N.J.: Paulist Press, 1998] 98). Osborne prefers, in the meantime, to speak of Jesus as *Ursakrament* (75).

[85] See Rahner's second point in Chapter 2 above.

[86] Otto Semmelroth, *The Preaching Word: On the Theology of Proclamation* (New York: Herder and Herder, 1965) 232.

will provide a framework for understanding the responsibilities and competence that accompany the preaching vocation. Along with those duties, the attentive preacher embraces the humbling awareness that one is set in the midst of a holy assembly, the Church, in order to articulate a word *for them* which, as Hill asserted, is "really effective of redemption and salvation."

The "Informed Reader" and the Responsibility of the Preacher. Stanley Fish's concept of the "informed reader" emerged in the early stages of his theoretical project, when the text still made a claim on the activity taking place in the mind of the reader. The surface structure of the literary text (what Culler called "linguistic sequences" or the "'grammar' of literature"[87]) interacts in a "temporal flow" with the expectations of the reader and the overall intent of the author so that, *in the process of this event,* the deep structures of meaning are revealed. As Fish said:

"For we comprehend not in terms of the deep structure alone, but in terms of a *relationship* between the unfolding, in time, of the surface structure and a continual checking of it against our projection (always in terms of surface structure) of what *the* deep structure will reveal itself to be; and when the final discovery has been made and the deep structure is perceived, all the 'mistakes,' the positing, on the basis of incomplete evidence, of deep structures that failed to materialize, will not be canceled out. They have been experienced; they have existed in the mental life of the reader; they *mean.*"[88]

Part of the point Fish emphasized here is that "deep structures" are not the sole bearer of "the point" or "the meaning" of the text. Indeed, in Fish's later schema, the independence of the text as a vehicle of that meaning disappears into the "interpretive strategies" of the readers themselves. However, the complex process outlined above began to suggest to him that there must be an "idealized reader" of sorts who is aware of the dynamics at work, checks his/her expectations, and makes the "final discovery" that is the result of the "temporal flow" of this reading activity. This "idealized" reader, what he will officially call for precision an "informed reader," experiences the fullest possibilities of *meaning* the event can offer.

[87] Culler, *Structuralist Poetics,* 114.
[88] Fish, " Literature in the Reader," 48.

Fish laid out the criteria of this reader clearly and succinctly in "Literature in the Reader":

"The informed reader is someone who (1) is a competent speaker of the language out of which the text is built up; (2) is in full possession of 'the semantic knowledge that a mature . . . listener brings to his task of comprehension,' including the knowledge (that is, the experience, both as a producer and a comprehender) of lexical texts, collocation probabilities, idioms and other dialects, and so on; and (3) has *literary* competence. That is, he is sufficiently experienced as a reader to have internalized the properties of literary discourses."[89]

This "informed reader," he continued, is "a hybrid—a real reader (me) who does everything within his power to make himself informed."[90] This privileged reader's intentionality, to use Hill's vital characteristic of the preacher, demands a conscious attempt on the part of this reader to become the repository of the possible responses and to suppress what might be a narrow or idiosyncratic reading of those responses.[91]

As Fish noted, his thinking regarding the informed reader shifted with the recognition of interpretive communities and the effect that such communities have on the informed reader in their midst. Fish then noted the consequences of his shift in thought: "What I finally came to see was that the identification of what was real and normative occurred within interpretive communities and what was normative for the members of one community would be seen as strange (if it could be seen at all) by the members of another."[92]

Fish's informed reader, therefore, moves away from the context of the distanced critic to the more engaged and interacting "reader" who meets the text *"in the context of the critical community."*[93] The preacher, as a specific example of such an "informed reader" within the ecclesial community, illustrates the responsible position the informed reader occupies in Fish's thinking. Even though preachers are, rightly, not critics who distance themselves from the assembly

---

[89] Ibid.
[90] Ibid., 49.
[91] Ibid.
[92] Fish, *Is There a Text in This Class?* 15–16.
[93] See Steiner, "'Critic'/'Reader,'" 438–9; Fowler, "Who Is 'The Reader' in Reader Response Criticism?" 14.

and the text out of which they must speak, their role of reader is still not synonymous with the assembly as a whole. Preachers shoulder a responsibility in their position of "informed readers" that demands competence, study, awareness of the lives of the assembly of readers who listen, and an intentionality to speak a word which is expressive of what Fish calls "the community's perspectives." Those perspectives must be consistent with the self-identity of the community and the tradition of the *kerygma* passed on in the apostolic tradition. A dual role, therefore, exists within the preaching office. First, one must be a believer who seeks out what Steiner called the "real presence" within the texts, "*as if* the text was the housing of forces and meanings, of meanings of meaning, whose lodging within the executive verbal form was one of 'incarnation.'"[94] Second, those who preach must uncover, through responsible work, what Fish called "the repository of the (potential) responses a given text might call out."[95] In short, the preacher is both hearer and bearer of the word.

The preacher's dual role, therefore, truly makes sense according to Fish's notion of the informed reader as a hybrid of sorts. She does not speak for herself alone, or even for the sum total of consensual understandings within the community regarding a text, but she embodies an ecclesial voice enfleshed in the temporality of this liturgical enactment and the office the Church has given her. By reason of the intentionality of her position as bearer of the *kerygma* in all its fullness, and at the same time recognizing her deepest identity as a member of this body of Christ, the preacher finds herself, "in however deficient and instrumental way," in an awesome and humbling position within that ecclesial community. She must risk to be the voice that summons people to break down the barriers of distance from the Gospel proclamation and to allow themselves to be the community which itself, as Steiner said, is "being read" by the sacred text and formed by the dynamism of grace that word offers.

The Preacher as the "Frame of Reference" that Draws the Listeners "Into the World of the Text." Wolfgang's Iser's concept of the "implied reader" offers a nuance of Fish's "informed reader" that yields interesting results when explored from the perspective of the preacher's role within the liturgy. For Iser, the "implied reader as a concept has his roots firmly planted in the structure of the text; he is a construct

[94] Steiner, "'Critic'/'Reader,'" 440.
[95] Fish, "Literature in the Reader," 49.

and in no way to be identified with any real reader."[96] This would seem to pose a major obstacle to the reality of the person of a preacher who, according to the argument so far, truly is a "real reader" in his own right. Yet, if Iser's argument is followed to its conclusion, the application becomes clear. The authentic preacher's voice remains a communal one and not the expression of his or her own issues or projections. The assembly embodies the "real reader" in the context of liturgical enactment. How this dynamic emerges deserves closer inspection.

The role of Iser's "implied reader" is to be a frame of reference. This figurative role structures the text in such a way that the different perspectives, intentions, characters, and situations can be drawn together by the reader and, in the act of "anticipating the presence of the recipient," allows the meaning to "emerge during the reading process."[97] The implied reader, therefore, actualizes the dynamism that occurs within a reader that represents a creative intentionality. By means of this dynamic intention, the reader gathers within himself the world the text offers. This creative act allows the reader to be open to the transformation such a new perspective can bring to the limitations of his own experience and worldview. This intentionality engenders a wider vision and a richer experience of reading. As Iser explained:

"The text must therefore *bring about* a standpoint from which the reader will be able to view things that would never have come into focus as long as his own habitual dispositions were determining his orientation, and what is more, this standpoint must be able to accommodate all kinds of readers."[98]

Because, for Iser, the "*artistic* pole" of the text is always in concert with the "co-creating" role of the reader who actively draws together the "meaning from the perspectives the text provides,"[99] there is an act of creative articulation (the *aesthetic* pole) which the reader brings to the text. This presence to the text exhibits an act of openness which acknowledges that "the potential text is infinitely richer than any of its individual realizations."[100] That act of receptivity is a role that the

[96] Iser, *The Act of Reading*, 34.
[97] Ibid., 34–5.
[98] Ibid., 35.
[99] Donald Keesey, *Contexts for Criticism*, 2d ed. (Mountain View, Calif.: Mayfield Publishing Co., 1994) 125.
[100] Iser, "The Reading Process," 55.

157

real reader accepts from the text itself. As Iser said, "Thus the vantage point of the reader and the meeting place of perspectives become interrelated during the ideational activity and so draw the reader inescapably into the world of the text."[101]

Since Iser's implied reader is a "transcendental model" and not identified singly with any real reader, how does that evocative, invitatory role correspond with the preacher within a liturgical assembly, which is a structured body of "readers" in its own right? Clearly, every member of the assembly cannot and does not want to engage the text in the way Iser describes at such a creative level. The preacher accepts that role by reason of vocation and "office." When one is exercising the office of preacher, therefore, he maximizes that particular faculty of "intentionality" in order "to draw [the assembly] inescapably into the world of the text." As a result, the preacher opens up the world of the biblical tradition in order that the assembly might see in a new way—God's way—rather than being blinded by their own habitual dispositions and thereby missing the "meeting place," which Iser insisted *is* "the meaning of the text."[102] Sacramental life expresses this great encounter with God's saving acts in Jesus.

The preacher still speaks as a historically individuated person. *Caro salutis est cardo* ("The flesh is the hinge of salvation"), Tertullian reminds us. As a result, this ecclesial role "can be fulfilled in different ways, according to historical and individual circumstances," Iser said, so that "the process of fulfillment is always a selective one" which thereby "provides a frame of reference within which individual responses to a text can be communicated to others."[103] This selectivity and multiplicity of responses suggests that no single eloquent preacher and no isolated message totally encompasses the creative act of preaching. The charism of the office of preaching acknowledges the uniqueness of one's own personhood, while at the same time grounding itself on the humbling reality that one is an instrument of grace alive in the Church. The faithful exercise of such a charismatic sacramental office enables the whole community to continue to encounter God in the mystery of the sacramental event.

The preacher as a sacramental expression of the concept of implied reader, therefore, accepts a role that produces a "particular kind of

[101] Iser, *The Act of Reading,* 36.
[102] Ibid., 35.
[103] Ibid., 37.

tension" that enables the worlds of the text and of the assembly to meet in a fulfilling interchange. The prophetic nature of that tension impels the preacher to invite the assembly into a wider world—a world where the Gospel can transform hearts and invite the community of worshipers into a new way of living. Iser's fluid and expectant implied reader, even more than Fish's individualized and competent informed reader, rightly captures the mysterious role of one who uses human words and personal limitations as a vehicle of sacramental expression. Both critics, at the same time, provide models of responsible and committed readers who, in the event of proclamation, draw *out* the richness of the biblical text and draw the worshipers *into* the new possibilities the Scriptures offer. Text, context, and reader converge at this ritual moment. "We call this meeting place the meaning of the text," Iser said.[104] The preacher represents a creative partner in this sacramental encounter.

[104] Ibid., 35.

5

The Holy Preaching: A Sacramentality of the Word as "Fulfilled in Our Hearing"

In 1963, the year the Vatican Council promulgated the Constitution on the Sacred Liturgy, Jesuit Josef Jungmann argued for "the renewal of the *kerygma*" that embraces the Church's life and mission. Jungmann argued that the biblical understanding of *kerygma* as "that which is preached" draws its present-day authority and grace from "what Christ himself proclaimed and what his apostles proclaimed abroad as his heralds: that the kingdom of God had entered the world, thus disclosing salvation to [humankind]."[1] This foundation upon Christ and the apostles remains "the core and basis of all subsequent guidance and instruction of believing Christians." As a result, Jungmann concluded that preaching and sacramental worship—indeed, "every expression of the Church's life"—must be "led back to its unified original power, so that above all else it is the kerygma itself that is heard."[2]

Jungmann's clarion call was a challenge for a Roman Catholic Church in which the events of the Liturgy of the Word had been severed from the sacramental concerns of both theologians and worshipers. Two aspects of this re-appropriation emerged in Jungmann's thinking regarding the renewal of the *kerygma.* First of all, liturgical preaching must remember its foundation in "God's call and invitation," uniquely revealed in the life, death, and resurrection of Christ (1 John 1:1; Acts 4:20; Luke 24:47). This announcement concerns, first and foremost, an *event* of the word in which believers are invited to share and so "is more than just a doctrine." Second, liturgical

---

[1] Josef Jungmann, *Announcing the Word of God,* trans. Ronald Walls (New York: Herder and Herder, 1967) 59.

[2] Ibid.

proclamation, especially, must guard "against all excessive splitting up of the substance of faith within preaching, and against rank growth around the fringe," that is, what is preached is intimately related to the paschal mystery celebrated sacramentally at the table and the font.[3] To the Church, particularly the Roman communion, poised on the verge of a new era of self-understanding with the advent of Vatican II, Jungmann's concerns about "the shape of public worship"[4] in ecclesial life and the integral relationship between preaching and sacramental activity are clear and unambiguous. As he concluded, "The 'kerygmatic climaxes' must once more come into their own."[5]

This book has attempted to recapture and expand, in the light of contemporary sacramental and liturgical theology, the spirit of Jungmann's concerns about the "original, unified power" of God's self-disclosure through Christ in Word and Sacrament. It placed this theological perspective in constructive conversation with current literary theory about the relationship of text, context, and reader in order to appreciate the sacramental integrity of the proclamation of the word within the liturgical enactment itself. We can now review the arguments put forward and discuss some of the implications that arise in the arena of pastoral and liturgical practice.

In Chapter 1, the *mystery of God's action* in the lives and events of people struggling to appropriate their ecclesial identity as the body of Christ situated the complex path that resulted in the reform Jungmann envisioned. This *pastoral foundation* to the modern liturgical movement emphasized the focal role the *experience of worshiping people* played in the subsequent theology that informed the revisions of the liturgy at the time of Vatican II.[6] In Chapter 2, we anchored proclamation and preaching in *an ecclesial understanding of sacramentality.* From this unified perspective, Word and Sacrament are understood as indispensable expressions of the nature of the Church, itself the source and expression of the abiding presence in the world of Christ, the *Ursakrament.* In

[3] Ibid., 60–1.

[4] Ibid., 59.

[5] Ibid., 62. Jungmann adopted the term "kerygmatic climaxes" from Fr. Hofmann, *Theologie und Glaube,* XLVIII, 1956, 306.

[6] The Constitution on the Sacred Liturgy stated that "the rites be revised carefully in the light of sound tradition and that they be given new vigor to meet the circumstances and needs of modern times" (4). The council, in this first document, acknowledged the important relationship between scholarly research and the pastoral needs that fuel such study.

order to illustrate this, the work of Otto Semmelroth, Karl Rahner, and Edward Schillebeeckx in re-imagining traditional sacramental categories highlighted the following four points germane to sacramental life and the role of liturgical proclamation:

(1) *Word and Sacrament is a corporate activity of the Church, which expresses her identity as the basic sacrament of God's saving acts in Jesus.* The Church does not exist as a mere dispensary of grace; rather, it is the arena of encounter where God and human persons meet in a great redemptive dialogue where Christ is both *Wort und Antwort* (Word and Answer).

(2) *Word and Sacrament, because of this ecclesial foundation, share in God's decisive utterance on our behalf in Jesus, "bodied forth" in the Church.* The proclamation of the word and the sacramental actions which surround it embody a single work which bestows the grace of Christ's incarnation and redemption, the fullness of the paschal mystery. They represent focal moments in the great event of God's revelatory encounter uttered in history, in which Christ is personally present as savior and *Kyrios.* This unity discloses the mystery of this *kerygma* and engenders the faith to embrace it. Simply stated, what is heard in the word takes flesh in the sacramental activity.

(3) *The ritual event of proclamation shares in the sacramental bestowal of grace.* Because of God's self-revelation in Jesus, this grace-filled bestowal continues in the Church through the power of the Spirit that animates her *kerygma.* The incarnational activity of proclamation and preaching takes place in both preacher and assembly, each being what Semmelroth called "a collaborator in the symbolic act which the event of preaching represents."[7] Because of the irrevocable promise of God signified and rendered present in this event, the proclamatory act is the bearer of grace, revealed "in our hearing" and fulfilled at the table or font. We cannot divorce the temporal, bodily, and historical nature of this encounter from the content of the Good News. Consequently, event-full sacramentality demands a participatory quality to this encounter.[8] What is more, the event-fullness of proclamation

---

[7] Otto Semmelroth, *Church and Sacrament* (Notre Dame, Ind.: Fides Press, 1965) 58.

[8] In the end, we must admit that the mystery of God's grace supplies any lack in both content and expressive activity. However, the intentionality of both preacher and hearers of the word provides the concrete situation in which that utterance is received and communicated and which expresses the richness of the grace being offered.

emphasizes that the homily is not *about* God, but reveals God. The incarnate Word is speaking *to us* and *for us* in a sacramental encounter of grace. In Edward Schillebeeckx's terms, the revelation in word illumines the revelation in reality.[9]

(4) *Finally, Word and Sacrament, a redemptive dialogue incarnate in the world, participates in the paschal mystery itself.* Worship "in spirit and truth" (John 4:24) involves a summons in faith and an invitation to join in Jesus' own self-offering to the Father in obedient love. Christ, revealed as *Wort und Antwort,* remains present to the world through the Church's participation in the Spirit's life-giving grace, inviting the world into this saving relationship with God. The liturgical proclamation of the word, therefore, is trinitarian in nature and eminently involved with the saving reality it announces. Proclaiming and preaching the word express actions of both worship and sanctification (loving encounter and obedient response) and thus participate in the saving events of Christ himself, through the power of the Holy Spirit at work in the Church and the world. In this light, liturgical worship clarifies and makes explicit the multivalent, sacramental presence of Christ in the word.

Keeping the specific issue of the sacramentality of liturgical proclamation as an ultimate concern, Part II of this work attempted a more complex enterprise. Chapters 3 and 4 investigated the insights of literary theory in order to understand the *particular dynamics at work when the Scriptures are read* within the gathering of believers celebrating the saving mysteries of Christ. Literary theory, in the decades following the initial liturgical reform, has yielded a rich variety of critiques concerning what *happens* when a text with shared meaning encounters the specificity of readers in different contexts. As a result, New Historicism and reader-response criticism provided the following four perspectives on the sacramentality of liturgical proclamation:

(1) *Communal texts with a valued meaning for the sociocultural body are not static and univocal icons that are passed on from one generation to the next, or even from one "reading" to the next.* Mysterious transactions take place between the *author* or received tradition, the *readers and hearers* who experience the work in a setting apart from its initial creation, and the *cultural milieu* that shapes the attitudes, expectations, and beliefs of those who encounter them. In this vein,

---

[9] Edward Schillebeeckx, *Revelation and Theology,* vol. 1 (London: Sheed and Ward, 1966) 36–8.

we need to appreciate that sacred texts are social events that are negotiated, contested, and redefined in light of the contingent nature of human experience and the nature of social practices in which they are embedded. What endures in these works is their capacity as literary artifacts to convey a "life" that was originally encoded in them and which continues to be refashioned in every encounter.

From this critical perspective, the Church acts as a social institution engaged in a cultural practice of liturgical enactment in which proclamation is an integral part. Furthermore, the biblical texts themselves yield a rich variety of meanings in this liturgical setting. These dynamic meanings share the creative energy that circulates when ritual beliefs and practices of a community interact with these texts. Such an understanding frees scriptural proclamation from the deadening effects of abstract exegetical analysis and totalizing claims.

The sacramental characteristics of liturgical proclamation prioritize a personal encounter of a believing member of the community with the risen Christ, present in the word and inviting a human response. The sacramental nature of this encounter welcomes a schema that erodes the fixed boundaries "between literary text or performance and other social practices."[10] Contemporary sacramentality finds an easy conversation partner with a literary approach whose claims give privileged place to the interplay of text, context, and reader in an eventful and creative transaction. This dynamic energy at the heart of the community's grace-filled event of worship reveals the creativity of the God who continues to utter that word in love. God's creative grace endures through time and history; it is the "life" which grounds the sacredness of biblical proclamation.

(2) *Dynamic texts go hand in hand with the creative participation of those who encounter them.* Readers and hearers of a sacred text[11] are

[10] Brook Thomas, "The New Historicism in a Postmodern Age," *The New Historicism and Other Old-Fashioned Topics* (Princeton, N.J.: Princeton University Press, 1991) 39. Thomas is ferreting out the key issues of Stephen Greenblatt's challenge to "the text/context opposition."

[11] The complex notion of "sacred text" describes oral and written artifacts that claim to be revelatory of ultimate meaning and which, in turn, affect the self-identity of those who reverence them. See Robert Detweiler, "What Is a Sacred Text?" *Semeia* 31 (1985) 213–30. See also the Vatican document *Dei Verbum* VI:21, noted in Sandra M. Schneiders' *The Revelatory Text* (San Francisco: HarperCollins Publishers, 1991) in a section entitled "The Bible as Word of God: Sacrament," 40–3.

doing something when they retell the stories and dramas that make up the cultural poetics expressed in corporate, public worship. This remembering and re-presentation of the great paschal events convey the mystery and life-giving power that animates the community's ultimate concerns and desires. Liturgical enactment opens up both readers and hearers to be refashioned and transformed in the literary encounter. A "holy meeting" occurs in the convergence between the sacred text and those who encounter them.

Furthermore, literary theory illustrated how the biblical readings, as written or oral texts, never tell the whole story. The Scriptures contain gaps or blanks that are engaged by the assembly, who, in turn, co-create the text as a "new hearing." A word that is heard, believed, and appropriated "renders Christ present" and articulates the word as a grace-filled proclamation uttered by God precisely *for us* and *to us.* This relational presence to and with Christ seals the ecclesial assembly's sacramental identity as the spirit-filled body of Christ. Even though God first utters the word and remains the author of its life, the mystery of the incarnation locates that divine presence irrevocably within the historical contingencies that make up the community of believers, which is both sign and reality of this saving grace of Christ. The community's co-creation of the biblical texts in this sense simply means that God uses real lives and concrete situations as moments of grace-filled proclamation. Such co-creativity respects both the divine inspiration of the sacred Scriptures and the sacramental identity of the Church, whose worship and life embodies the *kerygma* that she proclaims.

The active agency of the reader, therefore, gives greater clarity to the sacramental character of liturgical proclamation, in which the *participation of the assembly* is crucial to its fruitful enactment. The worshipers' role as communal reader and hearer differs from that of a group of passive listeners. Even more, the sacred text embodies more than a message uttered thousands of years ago, passed on relatively intact, and about which comments are put forth or connections are made. Reader, text, and context, as an ensemble, incarnate the energetic word being offered. To be true to its sacramental self-identity, the liturgical assembly must draw near in an act of self-offering and trust, in order for the meeting of biblical text and assembly to take place in all the rich dimensions the grace of God makes possible. Clearly, an appreciation for the dynamism of the reader in these literary theories helps situate the assembly's role in God's creative activity among us.

166

(3) *The reading and hearing of sacred texts is never an individual enter-prise, but is embedded in an interpretive framework that is communal and which facilitates communication within it.* Endless, individualized re-interpretations of Scripture or the loss of the centrality of the Bible's canonical authority remain legitimate fears when one acknowledges the fluidity of text and interpretation. The hermeneutic of community addresses and even lessens such reservations, especially when em-ployed as the inevitable context for any reading activity. Individuals cannot escape their historicity or their embeddedness in a culture; for that matter, neither can the focal texts. This same historical and faith contextual dynamic, Schillebeeckx reminded us, manifests the founda-tional assumption of an embodied sacramentality.

The resonance of these embedded texts radiates from the midst of a community which, as an interpretive body, continues to negotiate the meaning and claims contained in them. The interaction sparked by this resonance shapes the community's ongoing relationship to the history, values, and beliefs that are crucial to its self-identity. From the perspectives of both New Historicism and reader-response, disagree-ments inevitably emerge as part of this transaction, different lenses can be respected and employed, and shifts of emphasis are expected to occur at different times and among different sociocultural bodies.

The dialectical and sacramental paradigms that shape ecumenical dialogue provide a classic instance that persons of different faith tra-ditions need not gloss over essential differences in order to remain talking to one another and deepening the evolving encounter with the word of God. Differing interpretations exist in the same body of Christ, yet the paradigms still posit the centrality of the Bible as the revealed and definitive word of God.[12] Individuals or groups who

[12] As Charles Rice explained in *The Embodied Word* (Minneapolis: Fortress Press, 1991), "For Barth, as for the Reformers, when we say 'Word of God' we mean Jesus Christ present to his people, and without that neither Scripture nor preaching opens toward God's eventful Word." Despite their dialectical emphasis, in contrast to a Roman Catholic sacramental perspective, Luther, Calvin, Barth, Bultmann, and Tillich represent a whole tradition that has yet to be fruitfully tapped in the community's "interpretive negotiations" about what it means for liturgical theology to speak of Christ's presence in the word. The citation from Barth is *Church Dogmatics* 1/1:208. Mary Catherine Hilkert asserts that each paradigm makes important contributions toward a fuller understanding of the liturgical dynamics involved in proclaiming the revealed Word of God. See Hilkert's "Revelation and Proclamation: Shifting Paradigms," *Journal of Ecumenical Studies* 29:1 (Winter 1992) 1–23 and chs. 1

cannot claim a particular biblical paradigm eventually shift to other interpretive frameworks, which are themselves communal in nature. The changing makeup of certain liturgical communities over a period of time attests to this mobility at different levels.[13] The focus of unity amid such diversity, however, rests on a common grace-filled encounter with the revelatory word of God.

Any community of interpretation employs patterned, communal structures to communicate the centrality of their common texts. Through its ritual enactment, the community names and reveres the narratives that embody its shared past, express its present life and meaning, and articulate its common future hope. Within this critical community, individuals meet the text. The ritual structures celebrate the individual's self-identity within that body while, at the same time, they heighten and clarify that one's scriptural heritage is first and foremost a proclamation to a people and not a private devotion. The community names the grace in the sacred texts, to use Hilkert's image, and the interpretive act of naming announces a shared revelation whose life was originally encoded in them.

(4) *Informed readers mediate the encounter between text and readers in a critical community and draw the members of that community into the wider world the text offers.* The preacher, as a believer who is also called to exercise a charism, shares these critical qualities and bears a responsibility to the community by reason of this office. Informed readers bring a unity to the self-understanding of the community and expand the possibilities of the richer vision the contemporary context brings to light. According to Stanley Fish and Jonathan Culler, these readers possess a measure of literary competence, employing creative tools of knowledge and experience that may not be readily available

---

and 2 in *Naming Grace: Preaching and the Sacramental Imagination* (New York: Continuum Publishing Co., 1998).

[13] The large number of "candidates for full communion" in RCIA programs in the Roman Catholic Church is evidence of one side of this mobility. Within Catholicism itself, the migration from one parish to another in large urban areas provides another example. In an age where the cultural boundaries are shifting so rapidly and community identity increasingly rests on a common vision and expression of belief, individuals change parish affiliation or worship communities as if the styles of celebration and the shared ethos were literally another denomination of religious faith. Once again, it is apparent that cultural practices and shifting boundaries play a major role in a person's sense of religious identity and therefore affect their interpretation of the focal texts that lie at their creedal center.

to those who encounter the texts occasionally or for the first time. Their responsibility especially informs works that are from different cultural, historical, or linguistic contexts. Literary competence does not negate the inescapable fact that the informed reader remains first and foremost a reader herself; she plays a mediating role as a hybrid reader, with communal duties toward the greater interpretive body as a whole.

A preacher's charism demands competence and intentionality to fulfill the responsibilities entrusted to him. Biblical and theological study, immersion in the lives of the community's concerns and beliefs, rhetorical skills critiqued and honed in accordance with personal gifts, and a critical knowledge of the sociocultural context in which the Church lives are part of the obligations of the informed preacher. Situated within the believing community, the preacher never speaks his own message or even the prevailing interpretations that contemporary consensus brings forth. Rather, the charism of preaching invites the difficult task of challenging the community to go beyond itself, while at the same time it affirms that the locus of God's revealed presence occurs at the heart of human experience.

Wolfgang Iser's "implied reader" demonstrated how the preacher can negotiate that subtle balance between challenge and affirmation. The preacher embodies a dynamic frame of reference from which the immersion into the traditional *kerygma* allows her then to call others into that same interaction. The dynamic meeting between revealed word and contemporary lives, between comfortable interpretations and alternate ways of experiencing the text, engenders within the community a wider vision and a richer experience of encounter. Reverencing the potential and inexhaustible riches of the biblical texts, the preacher speaks a fresh word to the assembly so that God's creative interaction can transform the event of hearing and allow the community to see in a new way, that is, God's way. This responsibility requires an intentionality on the preacher's part to remain open, to continue to expand the horizons of expectation concerning what the text reveals and how the community hears the proclamation in multiple life-situations. Even more, the concept of preacher as "informed reader" insists that such focal interpretations not be localized in one person or one event of critical engagement with the text. Preaching a fresh and vital word, therefore, *happens over time* and is enriched when that duty and responsibility are shared among a variety of persons competent in carrying out the responsibilities such a role entails. This perspective suggests that the Church must discern the parameters of the important office of preaching in new ways today, in order that the kerygmatic reinterpretation of the Gospel message is faithful to the sacramental dynamism from which it springs.

In light of the arguments outlined in this study so far, we can draw further conclusions and pastoral directions from the assertion that Word and Sacrament are complementary and supplementary moments which express the Church's sacramental nature. Their implementation would further enhance the worship and life of the Church so that, in Josef Jungmann's prophetic words, "above all else it is the kerygma itself which is heard."

(1) *Care given to the celebration of the liturgy creates an environment in which the proclamation finds its proper focus and enriches the sacramental encounter.* Congregations begin to expect to hear Good News with increasing vigor and expectancy when every aspect of liturgical worship radiates care and a unified focus. Shared ministerial roles, a mutual regard between a congregation and those who lead the prayer, and the attention given to ritual actions and language all signal the four-fold presence of Christ in its sacramental fullness. In addition, the reverence with which lectors and preachers embrace their charge to proclaim the word or to prepare and deliver homilies cooperates with this over-all respect for the mystery the community encounters in Christ. Everything coalesces to reflect the sacredness of the gifts of Word and Sacrament, the gathered assembly, and the liturgical time in which they gather. Care for liturgical enactment, therefore, is not the whim of experts or the concern of dilletantes. The entire celebration proclaims one word and work of God.

Given this intentionality, the community itself gradually hears with greater clarity the invitation to become what they receive. It brings to the meeting place of the sacramental encounter an intuitive understanding of *ex opere operato* and *ex opere operantis*, "doing what the Church intends" and "putting no obstacles in its way." As Peter Fink, S.J., described it, the community's "openness to the power of ritual is openness to the power of God who accomplishes his saving work in Christ according to the dynamics of the ritual itself."[14]

Simple details of liturgical performance also aid in this conscious intentionality. Amplification, lighting, and environment enhance the

---

[14] Peter E. Fink, *Worship: Praying the Sacraments* (Washington, D.C.: Pastoral Press, 1991) 32–3.

quality of celebration, and they augment the assembly's willingness to participate in these saving mysteries. As the critical theories discussed in this book attest, all the strategies and negotiations that make up the context of reading or hearing are part of the communicative event.

Additionally, lest a concern for conscious intentionality in pastoral practice and for aesthetic details appear to be beyond the concerns of serious liturgical and sacramental theology, history reminds us of the danger of decomposing sacramental life into static categories. Josef Jungmann's essay on the retrieval of the "original, unified power" of the Church's kerygmatic mission argued strongly against such bifurcating distinctions. Speaking at a time when liturgical reform was in its infancy, he noted a certain tension between the pastoral and dogmatic concerns in theology at the time:

"At all events it is striking that . . . lively discussion has arisen about this very tension, . . . that is, whether the demands, associated with the kerygma, for greater closeness to life, for emphasis upon the message of salvation, for Christocentricity, necessitate the construction of an autonomous theology alongside traditional scholastic theology. The necessity has been denied, with good reason. . . . We must resist the temptation to turn theology into a supernatural metaphysic and to treat the actualities of salvation history only in passing."

Jungmann ended his plea with the insistence upon the true task of both dogmatic and pastoral theology:

"Christ's resurrection is no mere past event, but continues in the activity of the Church and in the life of grace of the faithful throughout the ages. . . . Hence, theology, too, if it places Christ at its center and never loses sight of him, need lose none of its breadth of horizon."[15]

---

[15] Jungmann, *Announcing the Word of God*, 60–1. See also Geoffrey Wainwright, *Doxology: The Praise of God in Worship, Doctrine, and Life* (New York: Oxford University Press, 1980). As Wainright quoted Heinrich Ott in *Theology and Preaching* (London: Leavenworth, 1965):

"It may be necessary to affirm that dogmatics is the conscience of preaching and that preaching, again, is the heart and soul of dogmatics. In order to preach at all well, the preacher must engage in dogmatic reflection; while the dogmatic theologian, in order to teach dogma well and truly, must realize that he works with the intention of preaching, even though he himself does not have to mount the pulpit Sunday after Sunday" (22).

(2) *Given this conscious concern for liturgical preparation and enactment, the Liturgy of the Word must be ritually cohesive with the rest of the sacramental celebration which surrounds and expressively fulfills it.* At least a decade before the Vatican Council, Jungmann took great care to emphasize in *The Mass of the Roman Rite (Missarum Sollemnia)* that the proper and traditional setting in which the proclamation takes place is a liturgical one. He understood the ritual setting of the lections in the patristic sense of "breaking the bread of God's word to the people." The acclamations expressed upon hearing the word, he said, reflect "the prevailing tone *(Deo gratias)* that dominates the Roman liturgy" and that this eucharistic response indicates that one "has heard the summons." Such grateful consciousness permeates everything the Church says and does in worship, even the "simple act of choosing readings appropriate to the liturgical days and feasts."[16] Acknowledging that traditional connection between Word and Sacrament, the *General Instruction on the Roman Missal* notes that the "readings lay the table of God's word for the faithful and open up the riches of the Bible to them."[17] The liturgical dynamic of proclamation, therefore, provides multivalent means to nourish the common hunger in the world for an encounter with God. Protestant communions, with a traditional focus of the word, struggle with the same invitation to broaden their understanding of the nature of the feast that worship offers. As Richard Lischer cautioned his faith community in *A Theology of Preaching:*

"What else is liturgy but the recital of God's story—from the song of the angels in the *Gloria in excelsis* to the awesome chant of the cherubim and seraphim in the *Sanctus*—interspersed with kerygmatic interpretation? All this is to say, too briefly, that preaching lives, moves, and has its being in this environment. When it disregards its liturgical matrix, preaching becomes the individualistic, virtuoso performance with which many Protestants are familiar, and thereby diminishes both itself and the church."[18]

For Wainwright's full treatment of this subject in *Doxology,* see "Preaching as application of the message," 177–8.

[16] Josef Jungmann, *Missarum Sollemnia,* vol. 1, trans. Francis A. Brunner (Westminster, Md.: Christian Classics, 1988) 403–19, 421.

[17] *General Instruction on the Roman Missal* 34; see also no. 8 for the influence of patristic studies on the revision of the missal.

[18] Richard Lischer, *A Theology of Preaching: The Dynamics of the Gospel* (Nashville: Abingdon Press, 1981) 42–3. On the Liturgy of the Word as the

The arguments in this book have echoed that insistence, employing Roman Catholic sacramentality and contemporary literary theory as an integrating hermeneutic. The situational framework of the ecclesial celebration suggests that the movement of the liturgy is interrelated and progressive. One word and work of God proclaims the paschal mystery of Christ, and the Liturgy of the Word shares that overall internal dynamic. The rhythm ebbs and flows from the gathering of the assembly and collecting those present in prayer to the ritual juxtaposition of readings with responsive chant, with intermittent silence, spoken word and expressive gesture, from Gospel proclamation immediately to the preaching, and from the recital of the creed to the intercessory prayers.[19] Jungmann himself perceived the eucharistic foundation of this progression in the Liturgy of the Word: "The proclamation has been heard, the reading has been received, and the reply that resounds from the people is one which the Christian should use in every challenging situation in life: *Deo Gratias,* Thanks be to God."[20] Enacted within this significant matrix, the movements of the Introductory Rites and the Liturgy of the Word clearly provide a context for and an invitation to the table of the Eucharist.[21]

---

pattern or "ordo" for Christian life, see Gordon Lathrop, *Holy Things: A Liturgical Theology* (Minneapolis: Fortress Press, 1993) esp. 31–2.

[19] For the essential ritual strategy of "juxtaposition" and the particularities of preaching, see Lathrop's *Holy Things,* 10–11.

[20] Jungmann, *The Mass of the Roman Rite,* 421. Even within the context of the Tridentine rite as he knew it, Jungmann took great pains to note and document "the intrinsic relationship between the creed and the eucharistic prayer" (473, see also his n. 74). It is also important to note Jungmann's remarks about the focal role that the intercessions had in the earliest liturgies. The catechumens were dismissed before the intercessions were prayed and "are the first in which the neophyte takes part." As a result, Jungmann says that this prayer, "apart from the *eucharistia*—was from ancient times regarded as the most excellent prayer, the prayer, simply, of the Church" (479–80). This relationship to the Eucharistic Prayer chronicles a reaction against the unfortunate transference of the assembly's common intercessions into the private prayer of the canon in later centuries.

[21] The opening rites play an important role in this eucharistic progression in the Liturgy of the Word because they acknowledge the locus of the revelation taking place and the ecclesial foundation of sacramental life. As Mark Searle stated: "Ritual is rather like speech in that it consists of a sequence of sign-units and communicates effectively when the sign-units are not only carefully chosen but carefully ordered in sequence. Good ritual, like good speech, requires careful attention not only to vocabulary, but also to syntax." See also

Some further pastoral suggestions regarding the unity of ritual enactment and the Liturgy of the Word emerge from these conclusions. Lectors and preachers must cultivate a responsibility toward their ministry, both in preparation and in enactment. Such ministers communicate much more by deeds faithfully enacted week after week, rather than by voluminous commentaries that attempt to explain the liturgical connections between Word and Sacrament. Their reverent exercise of ministry suggests to the entire assembly that what is being done is holy and both "sign and reality" of the mysteries they proclaim.

Furthermore, continued and artful restatement throughout the entire celebration of specific images and metaphors from the day's Scriptures and from the homily need not be an exercise in liturgical deconstruction or an exercise of a presider's ego. Understood from the perspective of Robert Fowler's "mysterious merger of text, context and reader,"[22] such simple "poetics" expresses the interrelatedness of the proclamatory event with the totality of the paschal mystery being celebrated within a particular ritual time and space. The homily, as well, provides an expressive symbolic vehicle for integrating the many facets of this grace-filled encounter, which takes place through the instrumentality of word, elements, presider, and congregation. It can regularly and creatively name the reality of what is taking place in the gathering, acknowledging the moment as the sacramental *embodiment* of the saving events which the Scriptures and feasts proclaim. The poetic interweaving of text, context, and reader continues to forge an integral bond between what the assembly *hears* and what it *does* when the Church gathers to give thanks and praise.[23]

(3) *A historical lack of ecumenical dialogue around issues in sacramental theology left a large lacuna in Roman Catholic understanding of Christ's presence in the word,* affirmed so unequivocally in the Constitution on the Sacred Liturgy 7 and Paul VI's *Mysterium Fidei* 36. Semmelroth,

---

Searle's essay, "Semper Reformanda: The Opening and Closing Rites of the Mass," *Shaping English Liturgy: Studies in Honor of Archbishop Denis Hurley* (Washington, D.C.: Pastoral Press, 1990) 54.

[22] Robert M. Fowler, "Who Is 'The Reader' in Reader Response Criticism?" *Semeia* 31 (1985) 15.

[23] Jungmann himself, in *The Mass of the Roman Rite*, restated rather strongly the insistence of J. Hartog (*The Sacrifice of the Church*, vol. 1 [Baarn: Hollandia, 1939]) that "the sermon in the liturgy is not an *instruction* but an *initiation*, an introduction into the *mysterium*" (459, n. 23).

Rahner, and Schillebeeckx carried out their theological investigations at a time when a re-imagination of sacraments and preaching led them into new and tender territory. They do not engage Luther or Calvin, or even Bultmann and Barth, in attempting to posit proclamation and preaching within the unified sacramental expression of the Church's life. One simple reason for this was that they were in the process of overhauling a sacramental system *from within,* one that had not considered the sacramentality of the word as proper matter and form for discussion. The focus of their concerns, as David Power has noted, centered upon the imaginative shift from an understanding of sacramental representation as a "presence *of*" to a "presence *to,* or being present to another, *through* intermediary expression (of language and ritual)."[24]

On the Protestant side, the neo-orthodoxy of the first half of this century, largely the legacy of Karl Barth and his critique of "anthropocentric liberal theology,"[25] did not make dialogue with an incarnational sacramental imagination the most amenable enterprise. For Barth, the authority of any human structures to claim a vicarious relationship with Christ meant that "proclamation . . . is dehumanized; that is, it is drawn into a sphere . . . in which only in appearance can it signify a humanly assailable, responsible, surpassable and therefore subservient action."[26] A sacramental approach to

---

[24] David Power, *The Eucharistic Mystery: Revitalizing the Tradition* (New York: Crossroad, 1992) 321–2.

[25] The description belongs to Hilkert in *Naming Grace: Preaching and the Sacramental Imagination,* 20. Chapter 2, "The Dialectical Imagination: The Power of the Word" provides a concise synthesis of the word-centered approaches to theology.

[26] Karl Barth, *The Doctrine on the Word of God,* Church Dogmatics 1, trans. G. T. Thomson (Edinburgh: T. & T. Clark, 1936) 100. Otto Weber, in *Karl Barth's Church Dogmatics* (trans. Arthur C. Cochrane [Philadelphia: Westminster Press, 1953]), sets the parameters not only for the broad rift between the dialectical and sacramental imaginations, but also admits a possibility for a rapprochement from an ecclesial perspective. Weber said, commenting on Barth's passage rejecting any claim by human structures to cooperate as an embodiment of the word in the world:

"In this way Christ's Lordship over his Church has lost its real scope for action. It is no longer recognizable how Christ actually still is the ruler as a Person. However, those erroneous opinions cannot present the concept of the *'vicarius Christi'* (Christ's representative), applied to proclamation and to that extent to the Church, being also capable of a proper interpretation, when this

the word, therefore, sounded to him more like humankind endlessly responding one to another in a redundant circle hemmed in by its own finitude. Nor did Barth's critique of liberal Protestantism cut any less deeply. His fundamental critique of the tradition in which he had been schooled has been described "as though they were doing little more than speaking about man in a loud voice."[27]

What Barth did affirm in his notion of the word as "preached, written, and revealed" is the primacy of God's revelation. God defines all terms of that revelation, before it is filtered through the media of Scripture (which "points to it"), through the tradition (which canonizes it, but cannot hold it bound), and through the preaching of it (which is the "event" of its hearing).[28] For Barth, preaching, worship, and the practice of theology must maintain the unequivocal realization that "God—not human beings—is at the center of reality."[29] Later in his career, Barth's specific critique of Roman Catholicism's emphatic primacy of sacramental life over the power of the preached word eased a great deal. As a trusted editor of Barth's works clarified this later shift, "Barth himself did not wish in any way to minimize the sacrament; yet, preaching, he thinks, has priority and the sacrament serves as a confirmatory act."[30] Dominican Louis Marie Chauvet's work exemplifies a sacramental theology that takes great pains to include the Reformed tradition in his contemporary analyses. However, Chauvet still

---

representation is understood simply as subservient, a representation which acknowledges the free Lordship of Jesus Christ and permits it to rule."

[27] Daniel Jenkins, "Karl Barth," *A Handbook of Christian Theologians*, ed. Martin E. Marty and Dean G. Peerman (Nashville: Abingdon Press, 1984) 398.
 [28] Barth, *Church Dogmatics* I, 1 #4. As Barth said elsewhere in *Homiletics:*

"Preaching must conform to revelation. First, this means negatively that in preaching we are not to repeat or transmit the revelation of God by what we do. Precisely because the point of the event of preaching is God's own speaking *(Deus loquitur)*, there can be no question of our doing the revealing in any way. . . . All the action that takes place in preaching, which lies between the first advent and the second, is the action of the divine Subject. Revelation is a closed circuit in which God is both Subject and Object and the link between the two."

See *Homiletics*, trans. Geoffrey W. Bromiley and Donald E. Daniels (Louisville: Westminster/John Knox Press, 1991) 47.
 [29] Hilkert, "Revelation and Proclamation," 4.
 [30] Geoffrey W. Bromiley, *An Introduction to the Theology of Karl Barth* (Grand Rapids, Mich.: Eerdmans, 1979) 6.

wondered speculatively why the "christocentrism" so central to Barth's theology did not alleviate to a greater degree his lingering suspicion about the danger of confusing human actions with the actions of God.[31]

All of these concerns deserve more careful and scholarly investigation. Indeed, as Edward Kilmartin had pointed out, "the unfolding of a theology of the event of preaching in all its manifold possibilities," and especially the sacramentality of the word whose "theme of the *personal, active presence* of God in the event of preaching the word of God" is central remains a challenge of Vatican II's call for renewal. Ecumenical dialogue heightens the necessity for a sharing of the fruits of our respective traditions.[32] Despite efforts to fill that lacuna, Kilmartin stated, "the Council has certainly not said the last word on the subject."[33] Perhaps Paul Tillich's investigation into the Gospel as the response to the questions of ultimate human concern, in which "a reality of reconciliation and reunion, of creativity and meaning and hope" can be spoken, could be the bridge between these two perspectives, as Hilkert suggested.[34] Theological convergence around the multivalence of Christ's presence in the power of the Spirit acknowledges different modes of that encounter. We can recognize the communication of God's word as complementary in Word and Sacrament, rather than competing with each other for a greater share in the event of grace which the word in all its fullness announces. Though Rahner foresaw this, he did not engage his Protestant colleagues to deepen that initial instinct. In considering a sacramentality

---

[31] Louis Marie Chauvet, *Symbol and Sacrament: A Sacramental Reinterpretation of Christian Existence,* trans. Patrick Madigan and Madeleine Beaumont (Collegeville: The Liturgical Press, 1995) 538–9. See also Edward Kilmartin's overview in ch. 16 of *Christian Liturgy: Theology and Practice,* vol. 1 (Kansas City: Sheed and Ward, 1988) 284–301.

[32] William Hill notes in his essay "Preaching as a 'Moment' in Theology," *Search for the Absent God* (New York: Crossroad, 1992): "Faith today can be effectively communicated only in an ecumenical setting. An exclusively denominational ambience means not allowing a full Christian meaning to the mysteries preached" (184).

[33] Kilmartin, *Christian Liturgy,* 300.

[34] Hilkert, *Naming Grace,* 27. The quote from Tillich is from *Systematic Theology,* vol. 1 (Chicago: The University of Chicago Press, 1951) 49. Hilkert's concise treatment of both Protestant and Roman Catholic positions in her book lays the foundation for grounding a Christian sacramental proclamation in a theology of revelation.

of the word—particularly the manifold presence of Christ in the event of proclamation—the time for a re-appropriation of the rich offerings of the Lutheran and Calvinist traditions has come.

THE POSSIBILITY OF A NEXT STEP: TAKING LUTHER AND CALVIN AS A PRIMARY SOURCE FOR A RICHER UNDERSTANDING OF THE SACRAMENTALITY OF PROCLAMATION IN THE ROMAN CATHOLIC LITURGICAL TRADITION

We have acknowledged the lacuna in ecumenical dialogue in the first half of the twentieth century. How might we begin to bridge that gap? How might theology now employ specific insights of Martin Luther and John Calvin on their own merit, rather than merely pointing out and appreciating their different emphases in the theological traditions that followed upon them? Certainly, Martin Luther's foundational understanding of the *unity of the word of God*, that "it is a uniquely life-imparting power, a message communicated by [human persons] in whom the Scriptures had become alive," provides a point of contact. The harmonious singularity of God's message in Luther adds much-needed force and clarity to the kerygmatic nature of revelation that Schillebeeckx proposed, as well as the wholeness of the uttered word of God revealed in Christ that is so dynamic in Rahner and Semmelroth. As Luther said clearly in his *Smalcald Articles* (1537), "God will not deal with us except through his external Word and sacrament."[35] Sacraments, as such, "are not substitutes for the Word, instead they substantiate the Word and the intention of God."[36] In her nature as a fundamental sacrament, the Church expresses this relationship between the visible and the preached word so that, as Luther affirmed, *"Ubi est verbum, ibi est eccelsia."*[37] Luther's insistence on the primacy of the saving word, therefore, tends to level many arguments about the wisdom of excessive didacticism or moralism in liturgical homilies, and it situates the important issues surround-

---

[35] Martin Luther, *The Book of Concord*, ed. Theodore G. Tappert (Philadelphia: Muhlenberg Press, 1959) 313.

[36] E. Theodore Bachmann, introduction to *Word and Sacrament*, vol. 35, bk. 1 of *Luther's Works*, ed. Helmut T. Lehmann (Philadelphia: Muhlenberg Press, 1960–) xiii.

[37] Martin Luther, "Disputation at the Promotion of Johannes Macchabaeus Scotus," February 3, 1542, *D. Martin Luthers Werke*, vol. 39, II, Kritische Gesamtausgabe (Weimar, 1883), 176; quoted in Brachman, ibid., xvi.

ing authority and the office of preaching in the liturgical assembly today.[38]

In addition, the practical nature of Luther's injunctions about preaching are a welcome reminder to a Roman Catholic communion that is just finding its way to the pulpit in these years following the Vatican Council.[39] He insists that the grace of the liturgical gathering in Word and Sacrament is anchored in the enduring promise of God, in which the Church is its herald and embodiment and the preacher the servant. On the bestowal of faith in the hearts of believers, Luther said:

"That is God's work alone, who causes faith to live in the heart. Therefore we should give free course to the Word and not add our works to it. We have the *jus verbi*, but not the *executio*; we should preach the Word, but the consequences must be left to God's good pleasure."[40]

This reliance on God reveals the heart of the Church's action of praise and thanks in the liturgy and the ground of any spirituality of preaching. Luther's focal awareness of this brings the believing community to the centrality of Christ as *Wort und Antwort* of God's great promise. Christ's self-offering signals the great communion in which worshipers are invited to share in the liturgy in a personal and life-giving way. Hence, as Luther enjoined, rather than talking *about*

[38] Unresolved discussions about the sacramental role of women in the preaching event and a possible confusion of ministries, for example, take a different path when they are addressed in this ecclesial, word-centered light. The primary pastoral and canonical issue must remain focused on the necessity that the word in all its fullness is proclaimed. Furthermore, the preaching ministry flows from the ecclesial foundation and not an individualized one. Here, Luther and contemporary sacramental theology confirm each other's insights.

[39] For some examples of these references see "Conversations with Luther," *A Compendium of Luther's Theology*, ed. Hugh Thomson Kerr Jr. (Philadelphia: Westminster Press, 1943) 147–50. In his "Commentary on the Sermon on the Mount," noted here as well (150), Luther remarked quite pointedly in a way refreshing to Roman Catholics who have had to endure the malaise of preaching for so long: "These are the three things, it is commonly said, that mark a good preacher; first, that he take his place; secondly, that he open his mouth and say something; thirdly, that he know when to stop." Beneath the blunt and humorous admonition lies a deep and penetrating reminder to the preacher and the assembly that the Church is servant to the word and that God is doing something powerfully in our midst *through us* and that this word is personally *for us*. Rahner's affirmation of this same point could have profited from this practical nuance.

[40] Martin Luther, "The Eight Sermons at Wittenberg, 1522," *Sermons*, vol. 51, I of *Luther's Works*, 76.

Christ, as if facts and analyses of texts are the way to encounter, or as if Christ himself can be employed as a tool in an argument, the focus must be clearly on the holy meeting which the moment of proclamation occasions: "Rather ought Christ to be preached to the end that faith in Him may be established, that he may not only be Christ, but be Christ for thee and for me, and that is what is said of Him and what His Name denotes may be effectual in us."[41]

John Calvin's understanding of preaching as the primary mode by God's presence in the world highlights for liturgical theology the *actual event of communication* that literary studies agree is crucial to the meaningfulness of the text. The Platonic and Augustinian influence on Calvin regarding the relationship between the spiritual and the material has often been evaluated by Catholic theologians in terms of an excessive dualism no longer current. However, a re-investigation of the Calvinist insistence on the reality of *spiritual communion with Christ* might open new avenues for a retrieval of pneumatology in the liturgy. The Holy Spirit plays a crucial role in the encounter with Christ in worship and represents the agent of communion.[42] As Calvin said in the *Institutes:*

"For first, the Lord teaches and instructs us by his Word. Secondly, he confirms it by the sacraments. Finally, he illumines our minds by the light of his Holy Spirit and opens our hearts for the Word and sacraments to enter in, which would otherwise only strike our ears and appear before our eyes, but not at all effect us within."[43]

[41] Martin Luther, "A Treatise on Christian Liberty," *Career of the Reformer,* vol. 32, I of *Luther's Works,* 357.

[42] In *The Eucharistic Mystery* David Power remarked on the centrality of the Holy Spirit for Calvin:

"In appeal to the operation of the Spirit of Christ, he was able to stress the personal and relational aspect of the sacramental presence. Not only is the Spirit the agent of the presence, but it is the bond that exists between Christ and the believer who receives in faith" (253).

Both Power and Killian McDonnell (*John Calvin, the Church, and the Eucharist* [Princeton, N.J.: Princeton University Press, 1967]) stress in their treatment of Calvin that the spiritual presence is nonetheless real. As McDonnell explained:

"In Calvin's vocabulary spiritual presence means presence through the power of the Holy Spirit who guarantees the objectivity of the Eucharistic reality by giving the worthiness (that is, faith and love) to the believer, and by effecting the presence of Christ's body. Beyond the objectivity of the Spirit in act there is, in the sacramental economy, no objectivity" (364).

[43] John Calvin, *The Institutes of the Christian Religion* 4.14.10, trans. Ford Lewis Battles (Grand Rapids, Mich.: Eerdmans, 1989) 89.

Calvin's pneumatology and christology obviously have a transcendent pole that made him reject the role of the Church or the sacraments in the saving action of Christ and to stress the predestination of God for all believers.[44] Yet a preponderant immanence of God as a trinitarian communion radiates as well, a dynamic particularly related to the conclusions of this book. The preaching event, for Calvin, expresses an epiphanic moment. As such, Calvinist scholar John Leith insisted, the "human work of the sermon is critically important" for him.[45] This labor includes the responsibilities of the preacher as informed reader formulated in the previous chapter: exegesis, rhetorical skills, performance, choice of metaphors, and a sense of one's vocational role.[46] Noting the precarious balance between the

[44] McDonnell, *John Calvin, the Church, and the Eucharist*, 363–4. A recovery of pneumatology in western sacramental and liturgical theology has been fostered through the work of Edward Kilmartin, especially in the 1988 work *Christian Liturgy: Theology and Practice*, vol. 1, mentioned above, and in the posthumous work published a decade later, *The Eucharist in the West: History and Theology*, ed. Robert J. Daly (Collegeville: The Liturgical Press, 1998). Kilmartin's trinitarian approach to worship draws together the multivalent levels of participation of the Church in the paschal mystery of Christ: "The Holy Spirit, as Spirit of Christ, is the mediation of the personal immediacy of the assembly of the faithful to Christ and of Christ to the faithful because Christ and the believers are personally united in the one Spirit" (*The Eucharist in the West*, 374). The Spirit, therefore, is the agent of this union and communion in the Triune life of God.

[45] John H. Leith, "Calvin's Doctrine of the Proclamation of the Word and Its Significance for Today," *John Calvin and the Church: A Prism of Reform*, ed. T. George (Louisville: Westminster Press, 1990) 206–29, esp. 211–3.

[46] In *A Theology of Preaching*, Richard Lischer noted the importance of the "Oral-Aural Word." He cited the importance of works such as Walter Ong's *The Presence of the Word: Some Prolegomena for Cultural and Religious History* (New York: Simon and Schuster, 1970) and Ong's later *Interfaces of the Word: Studies in the Evolution of Consciousness and Culture* (Ithaca, N.Y.: Cornell University Press, 1977) as examples of "voices [that] are needed to remind us that the visual words we see are the representations of a more fundamental and primal reality, namely, the word as sound" (67). An insight of Ong's that attempts to situate proclamation in the event-fullness of sacramental encounter captures the mystery of the liturgical *Sitz-im-Leben* as it takes shape in the Liturgy of the Word: "In an oral culture, verbalized learning takes place quite normally in an atmosphere of celebration and play. . . . Sound situates [men and women] in the middle of actuality and in simultaneity, whereas vision situates [them] in front of things and sequentiality" (30, 128). The literary theories employed in this study suggest this rhythmic expression of grace. A fruitful direction would be to employ Ong's seminal works in a closer study

absolute dependence on God and the meager skills of human persons to communicate such a mystery, Leith commented:

"Calvin unites the work of God and the work of [humankind] in the sacrament and in preaching without separation, without change, and without confusion. In practice he may have claimed too much for the minister and the words of the sermon. Yet in doctrine he knew that the words of the sermon are at best frail, human words, but words that can by the power of the Holy Spirit become the occasion of the presence of God."[47]

Cooperating with God's initiative becomes the source and expression of what for Calvin is the fruit of the "exercises" of the sacraments: they "make us more certain of the trustworthiness of God's Word."[48] That trustworthiness instilled in his personal spirituality a "compelling sense of the presence of God" and a zeal for communicating that grace to those who came to hear him preach. As a result, Calvin "could paraphrase scripture with precision and clarity, translating it into the language of the common discourse of his own time." The impetus for that skill, Leith added, "must be in Calvin's own spiritual and theological resonance with the text."[49] We can never leave out pastoral zeal, accompanied by a liturgical spirituality that lives and breathes the mysteries the Church celebrates, as part of the "context" of the powerful, graced communication at work in the liturgy.

Calvin's own sermons furnish an eloquent testimony to this reality in his life and, as a number of Reformed studies have put forward, "a significant supplement to the theology of the *Institutes* and a corrective to the traditional as well as the Barthian interpretations of Calvin."[50] The Calvin who encountered God both in his heart and in the people in the pews realized the importance of the preaching medium for the communication of a sacred reality. Calvin affirms our

---

of the orality of preaching and the liturgical connotations for sacramental presence in that act.

[47] Leith, "Calvin's Doctrine of the Proclamation of the Word," 212. Leith mentioned as examples Calvin's Commentary on John 14:26, the Commentary on Ezek 2:2, and the Commentary on Isa 29:11.

[48] Calvin, *The Institutes of the Christian Religion* 4.14.6.

[49] Leith, "Calvin's Doctrine on the Proclamation of the Word," 212.

[50] Ibid., 207. Leith noted especially Richard Stauffer, *Dieu, la création et la providence dans la prédication de Calvin* (Bern: Peter Lang, 1978), and Rodolphe Peter, "Jean Calvin prédicateur," *Revue d'histoire et philosophie religieuses* (1972).

own pastoral conclusions that such care for one's responsibility, rooted in spiritual passion rather than in personal eloquence, must go hand in hand with the intentionality given to the entire celebration. The circulation of grace energizes every activity with spiritual possibility and minimizes none. Accepting that sacramental reality, worshipers can appreciate the real presence of Christ in the liturgy in its multivalent fullness. Roman Catholic sacramentality can then assent in Calvin's own words: "Therefore, let it be regarded as a settled principle that the sacraments have the same office as the Word of God: to offer and set forth Christ to us, and in him the treasures of heavenly grace."[51]

"THE HOLY PREACHING": THE SACRAMENTALITY OF THE WORD AND THE MISSION OF THE CHURCH

St. Dominic, the founder of the Order of Preachers, spoke of his early community as "The Holy Preaching" and "The Preaching of Jesus Christ."[52] The community as a collective *ecclesia* embodies the proclamation of God's Good News in Jesus, poured out upon the world in the power of the Holy Spirit. The imaginative framework out of which Dominic lived and worked integrated the identity of the community with the invitatory word that called each member into being. Every talent and gift, each act of service and prayer, participated in "The Preaching of Jesus Christ." This wisdom cuts to the heart of every aspect of this book. The Dominican charism, like every gift of the Spirit, mirrors an important feature of the rich face of Christ embodied in the Church and her mission. The liturgical gathering provides the ritual expression of that identity. Sacramental theology, as well, attempts to systematize the Church's engagement with the mystery at work in our midst. What we do and who we are is embedded in this complex interchange of grace that God initiates with the world. Even for systematic theology, therefore, the theoretical criteria of engagement need not be shunned. As we admitted at the outset, we must begin with a simple acknowledgement of the mystery. But the circulation of grace asks more of us: believing communities must embrace the gracious offer for communion in and with God embodied in every talent and gift, in each act of service and prayer. The community as "The Holy Preaching" expresses our

[51] Calvin, *The Institutes of the Christian Religion* 4.14.17.
[52] The Book of the Constitutions and Ordinations of the Order of Friars Preachers *(Liber constitutionem et Ordinationum Ordinis Fratrum Praedicatorum)* 100, I.

own faithful response to this covenant relationship. The Word became flesh and we become the Holy Preaching, molded by grace into Christ's own life. St. Dominic would rejoice in broadening his favorite name for his community to the whole Church. Engaged in the sacred act of embodying the word in our world, we participate in Christ's own answer of self-offering love to the One who utters it.[53]

Theory and practice remain uncomfortable partners in the experience of such mystery. Yet, Stephen Greenblatt's bold admission that contemporary theory "must situate itself" at the heart of the mystery, "in the hidden places of negotiation and exchange,"[54] confirmed for us that good liturgical instincts are always forged in the middle of such faithful practice. Such moments of grace we experience in the act of worship often yield important theological truths about our self-identity as a believing community.

To this end, we have focused on the liturgical dynamics of the event of proclamation and preaching because worship locates the primary arena of encounter for experiencing the grace and truth that the biblical texts offer the Church. The liturgical interchange of word, elements, assembly, and presider names the place where the vibrant transactions ensue. And so, in consort with Stephen Greenblatt's pursuit of "the marvelous at the heart of the resonant," we conclude that liturgical celebrations "make it easier imaginatively to recreate the work in its moment of openness."[55] For this reason, the conclusions that emerged in the course of this study of sacramental theology and literary theory simply open the door for more concentrated reflection upon the liturgical and pastoral issues that face the Church in the

---

[53] Edward Kilmartin, in his final work before his death, echoed the insights of Otto Semmelroth on the dialogic nature of the Christ event and the liturgical sacrifice:

"The special mission of the Word has two dimensions. There is the Incarnation of the Word, the expression of the Father's fidelity to his covenant: the sending of his only Son. And there is the response of the Son of Man in his humanity to the Father's work in him: the embodiment of the fidelity of humanity to the covenant relationship with the Father. In the special mission of the Word, the Holy Spirit is the divine source of the sanctification."

The dynamism of "The Holy Preaching" reflects this nature of an ongoing dialogue. See Kilmartin, *The Eucharist in the West*, 356.

[54] Stephen Greenblatt, "Toward a Poetics of Culture," *Learning to Curse: Essays in Early Modern Culture* (New York: Routledge, 1990) 159.

[55] Greenblatt, "Resonance and Wonder," *Learning to Curse*, 181, 171.

new millennium. The imagined possibilities for that reflection upon praxis suggest the following final points for consideration.

Contemporary communities of faith can enhance their understanding of "real presence," for example, by reverencing the "gaps" and "blanks" in ritual and narrative that draw them as a participating assembly into the dynamics of its reverent mystery. We need not explain away the mystery with endless commentary, and we cannot cover up our struggle with dissonant passages and exclusive liturgical practice on the grounds that liturgical enactment is immune from such negotiations. At the same time, believers can trust that God is faithful and at work, and our doing the work of worship continues the dialogue. The assembly's reverent silence at key juxtapositions expresses a powerful communal proclamation that honors these gaps and spaces so that the Spirit can breathe.

Furthermore, our imaginative recovery of the sacrificial aspects of Christ's self-offering in the Eucharist makes an interesting claim on the sacrificial character of grace-filled preaching. "The pulpit," Thomas Long reminded us, "is a hungry place,"[56] and a true offering of praise and thanks takes place there. The Table of the Word is also the place of meeting, where the community recognizes the need, breaks open its own hunger, and then miraculously feeds the neighborhood and the larger society around it. Accompanied by our movement to the Table of the Eucharist, these two focal points of encounter in Christ invite us all to the same apostolic commitment. In that vein, a fresh look at "transubstantiation" and "transignification" in ecumenical dialogue might yield a richer understanding of the sacramentality of the word as well. The Spirit's activity in this transformation of the gifts cooperates with the "circulation of social energy" that spirals around the dramatic event of sacred texts proclaimed in the midst of a believing assembly. Such issues stem from liturgical instincts that arise when the unity of Word and Sacrament are taken seriously.

The complex problems of ministry coalesce as well. Sacramental and liturgical theology needs to address how preaching during a eucharistic celebration in the absence of an ordained minister shares in the sacramental dynamism of a grace-filled event. The unresolved issues surrounding the relationship of preaching and presiding remain important issues in areas of liturgical formation as well. Our focus on the four-fold presence of Christ in the Liturgy of the Word removes

[56] Thomas Long, *The Witness of Preaching* (Westminster/John Knox Press, 1989) 177.

the discussion from the isolation of individual charism alone and orients that discussion toward the fullness of our communal identity as "The Holy Preaching."

Finally, from an engaged perspective of pastoral and liturgical ministry in our own communities, we admit the possibilities that powerful preaching has on the overall life of a worshiping assembly. "Preached communities," as I have come to call them, are those congregations whose experience of intentional and careful proclamation of the word has gradually engendered in them an expectation of Good News when they gather in liturgical assembly. They have all experienced a mysterious communal moment when the community itself and the proclamation merge in a great in-gathering of grace. These "preached moments" convince us that engagement and participation do occur through the medium of a single voice within a holy meeting. Such powerful communication reveals itself most faithfully when the intentionality given to the ministry of preaching is constant, shared by more than one person, and reverently integrated into the larger liturgical preparation that worship assemblies require.

All of these possibilities can seem daunting and presumptuous to us, if left completely to our own designs. Yet the tradition that nourished us and the faithful people who have embodied the hunger converge upon our own merger of text, context, and communal reading and sustain us with a grace-filled presence.[57] As both Catholic and Protestant traditions remind us with truthful abandon, God is at the heart of everything. This fact of God expresses itself most especially in the awesome ministry of proclaiming the Good News in the midst

[57] In *Corpus Christi: The Eucharist in Late Medieval Culture* (Cambridge: Cambridge University Press, 1992), Miri Rubin made the following comment about eucharistic practice that situates it right at the heart of things. It echoes the glorious risk that meaningful liturgical worship as a whole encompasses:

"The drama of the eucharist is the drama of human creativity and human frailty: its force deriving from the tension inherent in human action, between the capacity to construct meaning-laden symbols, and the consequent imperatives of living by them, adhering to them and maintaining their meanings when they become susceptible to the vagaries and vicissitudes of human interpretation" (1).

Rubin's concerns in her book are much like those of this study: "that religion can be best understood if it is not set apart from the social, not seen as an entity *sui generis* but rather as a culture, a system of meaning which represents and constructs experience and imagination" (7). The risk demands engagement with this creative exchange.

of the holy People of God. Dominican theologian William Hill, writing after years of faithful study and struggle with these great truths, provides an appropriate affirmation as a closing exhortation:

"The Word, which is the bearer of God's life and meaning for us, incarnates itself in human history, midway between the one who utters it and those who listen. But we must take seriously the fragility of the human situation here. God's act in history is a *kenosis*; [God's] intentions remain those of setting up the kingdom in and through the weak things of the world. And so, paradoxically, God cannot do without the stammering ways in which we strive to give utterance to that Word. It is part of faith to accept that."[58]

The presence of Christ stirs that faith in us and leads us deeper into the mystery we worship.
"Amen," we affirm, "So be it."

---

[58] Hill, "Preaching as a 'Moment' in Theology," *Search for the Absent God*, 186.

Bibliography

GENERAL SACRAMENTAL AND LITURGICAL THEOLOGY

Aune, Michael B. "Worship in the Age of Subjectivism Revisited." *Worship* 65 (1991) 224–38.

Baldovin, John F. "Biblical Preaching in the Liturgy." *Studia Liturgica* 22:1 (1992) 100–18.

_____. *Worship: City, Church and Renewal.* Washington, D.C.: Pastoral Press, 1991.

Barth, Karl. *The Doctrine of the Word of God.* Trans. G. T. Thomson, ed. G. W. Bromiley and T. F. Torrance. Church Dogmatics 1. Edinburgh: T. & T. Clark, 1975.

_____. *Homiletics.* Trans. G. W. Bromiley and Donald E. Daniels. Louisville: Westminster/John Knox Press, 1991.

Bishops' Committee on Priestly Life and Ministry. *Fulfilled in Your Hearing: The Homily in the Sunday Assembly.* Washington, D.C.: U.S. Catholic Conference, 1982.

Botte, Bernard. *From Silence to Participation: An Insider's View of Liturgical Renewal.* Trans. John Sullivan. Washington, D.C.: Pastoral Press, 1988.

Bradshaw, Paul F. "The Use of the Bible in Liturgy: Some Historical Perspectives." *Studia Liturgica* 35:1 (1992) 35–52.

Bugnini, Annibale. *The Reform of the Liturgy: 1948–1975.* Trans. Matthew J. O'Connell. Collegeville: The Liturgical Press, 1990.

Cahill, Michael. "Reader-Response Criticism and the Allegorizing Reader." *Theological Studies* 57 (1996) 89–96.

Calvin, John. *Institutes of the Christian Religion.* Trans. and annotated by Ford Lewis Battles. Grand Rapids, Mich.: Eerdmans, 1989.

Carroll, Thomas K. *Preaching the Word.* Message of the Fathers of the Church 11. Wilmington, Del.: Michael Glazier, 1984.

Casel, Odo. *The Mystery of Christian Worship.* Trans. Burkhard Neunheuser. Westminster, Md.: Newman Press, 1962.

Chauvet, Louis Marie. *Symbol and Sacrament: A Sacramental Reinterpretation of Christian Existence.* Trans. Patrick Madigan and Madeleine Beaumont. Collegeville: The Liturgical Press, 1995.

Chenu, M. D. "A Council for All Peoples." *Vatican II Revisited.* Ed. Alberic Stacpoole, 19–23. Minneapolis: Winston Press, 1986.

Collins, Mary. "Eucharist and Christology Revisited: The Body of Christ." *Theological Digest* 39:4 (Winter 1992) 321–32.

_____. *Worship: Renewal to Practice.* Washington, D.C.: Pastoral Press, 1987.

Congar, Yves M.-J. *Fifty Years of Catholic Theology: Conversations with Yves Congar.* Ed. Bernard Lauret. Philadelphia: Fortress Press, 1988.

_____. *Report from Rome on the First Session of the Vatican Council.* The Christian Living Series. London: Geoffrey Chapman, 1963.

_____. "Sacramental Worship and Preaching." *Concilium* 33. Ed. Karl Rahner, 51–63. New York: Paulist Press, 1968.

Cooke, Bernard J. *The Distancing of God: The Ambiguity of Symbol in History and Theology.* Minneapolis: Fortress Press, 1990.

Corbon, Jean. *The Wellspring of Worship.* Trans. Matthew J. O'Connell. New York: Paulist Press, 1988.

Craddock, Fred P. *Overhearing the Gospel.* Nashville: Abingdon Press, 1978.

Crichton, J. D. *Christian Celebration: Understanding the Mass.* 3d. ed. London: Geoffrey Chapman/Cassell Publishers Ltd., 1993.

_____. *Christian Celebration: Understanding the Sacraments.* 3d. ed. London: Geoffrey Chapman/Cassel Publishers Ltd., 1993.

Dalmais, I. H. *Introduction to the Liturgy.* Trans. Roger Capel. Baltimore: Helicon Press, 1961.

Duffy, Regis A. *Real Presence: Worship, Sacraments and Commitment.* New York: Harper and Row, 1982.

Eigo, Francis A., ed. *The Sacraments: God's Love and Mercy Actualized.* Villanova, Pa.: Villanova University Press, 1979.

190

Eslinger, Richard L. *A New Hearing: Living Options in Homiletic Method.* Nashville: Abingdon Press, 1987.

Faith and Order Commission. *Baptism, Eucharist and Ministry.* Geneva: World Council of Churches, 1982.

Ferrara, Dennis Michael. "In Persona Christi: Towards a Second Naiveté." *Theological Studies* 57 (1996) 65–88.

Fink, Peter E, ed. *The New Dictionary of Sacramental Worship.* Collegeville: The Liturgical Press, 1990.

_____. *Worship: Praying the Sacraments.* Washington, D.C.: Pastoral Press, 1991.

Hilkert, Mary Catherine. "Bearing Wisdom: The Vocation of the Preacher." *Spirituality Today* 44:2 (1992) 143–60.

_____. *Naming Grace: Preaching and the Sacramental Imagination.* New York: Continuum, 1997.

———. "Naming Grace: A Theology of Proclamation." *Worship* 60:5 (September 1986) 434–49.

_____. "Preaching and Theology: Rethinking the Relationship." *Worship* 65 (September 1991) 398–409.

_____. "Revelation and Proclamation: Shifting Paradigms." *Journal of Ecumenical Studies* 29:1 (1992) 1–23.

Hill, William J. "Preaching the Word: The Theological Background." *The Proceedings of the Catholic Theological Society, 28th Convention.* Ed. Walter J. Burghardt, 167–80. Washington, D.C.: Catholic Theological Society of America, 1973.

_____. *Search for the Absent God: Tradition and Modernity in Religious Understanding.* Ed. Mary Catherine Hilkert. New York: Crossroad, 1992.

Hoge, Dean R., Jackson W. Carroll, and Francis K. Sheets. *Patterns of Parish Leadership: Cost and Effectiveness in Four Denominations.* Kansas City, Mo.: Sheed and Ward, 1988.

International Commission on English in the Liturgy. *Documents of the Liturgy 1963–1979: Conciliar, Papal and Curial Texts.* Collegeville: The Liturgical Press, 1982.

Irwin, Kevin W. *Context and Text: Method in Liturgical Theology.* Collegeville: The Liturgical Press, 1993.

_____. "Method in Liturgical Theology: Context Is Text." *Eglise et Théologie* 20 (1989).

Jones, Cheslyn, ed. *The Study of the Liturgy.* New York: Oxford University Press, 1992.

Jungmann, Josef. *Announcing the Word of God.* Trans. Ronald Walls. New York: Herder, 1967.

_____. *Liturgical Renewal in Retrospect and Prospect.* Trans. Clifford Howell. London: Burns and Oates, 1965.

_____. *The Liturgy of the Word.* Trans. H. E. Winstone. London: Burns and Oates, 1966.

_____. *Missarum Sollemnia: The Mass of the Roman Rite.* Vols. I and II. Trans. Francis A. Brunner. 1950. Reprint, Westminster, Md.: Christian Classics, 1988.

Kavanagh, Aidan. *On Liturgical Theology.* New York: Pueblo, 1984.

_____. "Textuality and Deritualization: The Case of Western Liturgical Usage." *Studia Liturgica* 23 (1993) 70–7.

Keifer, Ralph A. *To Hear and Proclaim: Introduction, Lectionary for Mass.* Washington, D.C.: National Association of Pastoral Musicians, 1983.

Kilmartin, Edward J. "The Catholic Tradition of Eucharistic Theology: Towards the Third Millennium." *Theological Studies* 55 (1994) 405–57.

_____. *Christian Liturgy: Theology and Practice.* Vol. I, *Systematic Theology of Liturgy.* Kansas City: Sheed and Ward, 1988.

_____. *The Eucharist in the West: History and Theology.* Ed. Robert J. Daly. Collegeville: The Liturgical Press, 1998.

LaCugna, Catherine Mowray. *Freeing Theology: The Essentials of Theology in Feminist Perspective.* San Francisco: HarperSan Francisco, 1993.

_____. *God for Us: The Trinity and Christian Life.* San Francisco: HarperSan Francisco, 1991.

Lash, Nicholas. *His Presence in the World: A Study of Eucharistic Worship and Theology.* Dayton, Ohio: Pflaum Press, 1968.

Lathrop, Gordon. *Holy Things: A Liturgical Theology.* Minneapolis: Fortress Press, 1993.

_____. *What Are the Essentials of Christian Worship?* Minneapolis: Augsburg Fortress Press, 1994.

Leith, John H. "Calvin's Doctrine of the Proclamation of the Word and Its Significance for Today." *John Calvin and the Church: A Prism of Reform.* Ed. Timothy George, 206–29. Louisville: Westminster/John Knox Press, 1990.

Lischer, Richard. *A Theology of Preaching: The Dynamics of the Gospel.* Abingdon Preacher's Library Series. Ed. William D. Thompson. Nashville: Abingdon Press, 1981.

_____. *Theories of Preaching: Selected Readings in the Homiletical Tradition.* Durham, N.C: Labyrinth Press, 1987.

Long, Thomas. *The Witness of Preaching.* Louisville: Westminster/John Knox Press, 1989.

Luther, Martin. *A Compendium of Luther's Theology.* Ed. Hugh Thomson Kerr Jr. Philadelphia: Westminster Press, 1943.

_____. *Luther's Works.* Ed. Helmut T. Lehmann. Philadelphia: Muhlenberg Press, 1955–1986.

_____. *Selections from His Writings.* Ed. John Dillenberger. Garden City, N.Y.: Doubleday, 1961.

Marmion, Dom Columba. *Christ in His Mysteries.* London: Sands and Co., 1939.

_____. *Words of Life: On the Margin of the Missal.* St. Louis: Herder, 1939.

Martimort, A. G., ed. *The Church at Prayer.* Vol. II, *The Eucharist,* by Robert Cabie. Trans. Matthew J. O'Connell. Collegeville: The Liturgical Press, 1986.

Mazza, Enrico. *Mystagogy: A Theology of Liturgy in the Patristic Age.* Trans. Matthew J. O'Connell. New York: Pueblo, 1989.

McDonnell, Killian. *John Calvin, the Church, and the Eucharist.* Princeton, N.J.: Princeton University Press, 1967.

Megivern, James J., comp. *Official Catholic Teachings: Worship & Liturgy.* Wilmington, N.C.: McGrath Publishing Co., 1978.

Melloh, John A. "Preaching and Liturgy." *Worship* 65:5 (September 1991) 409–20.

Ong, Walter J. *The Presence of the Word: Some Prolegomena for Cultural and Religious History.* 1967. Reprint, Minneapolis: University of Minnesota Press, 1981.

Osborne, Kenan B. *Sacramental Theology: A General Introduction.* Mahwah, N.J.: Paulist Press, 1988.

Palmer, T.H.L. *Calvin's Preaching.* Louisville: Westminster/John Knox Press, 1992.

Paul VI. *Mysterium Fidei* (3 Sept. 1965) (The Doctrine and Worship of the Holy Eucharist). Trans. Austin Garvey. London: Catholic Truth Society, 1965.

Pecklers, Keith F. *The Unread Vision: The Liturgical Movement in the United States of America: 1926–1955.* Collegeville: The Liturgical Press, 1998.

Pelikan, Jaroslav. *The Vindication of Tradition.* New Haven, Conn.: Yale University Press, 1984.

Power, David N. *The Eucharistic Mystery: Revitalizing the Tradition.* New York: Crossroad, 1992.

Rahner, Karl. *The Church and the Sacraments.* Vol. 9, *Quaestiones Disputatae.* New York: Herder and Herder, 1964.

_____. "Considerations of the Active Role of the Person in the Sacramental Event." *Theological Investigations* 14. New York: Seabury Press, 1976. 161–84.

_____. *Encyclopedia of Theology: The Concise Sacramentum Mundi.* New York: Seabury Press, 1975.

_____. *Hearers of the Word.* Trans. Michael Richards. New York: Herder and Herder, 1969.

_____. "The Word and the Eucharist." *Theological Investigations* 4. New York: Crossroad, 1960. 253–86.

_____, ed. *The Renewal of Preaching: Theory and Practice.* Concilium 33. New York: Paulist Press, 1968.

Ramshaw, Gail. "Typology and Christian Preaching." *Liturgy: Preaching the Word: The Journal of the Liturgical Conference* (Fall 1989) 28–33.

Rice, Charles R. *The Embodied Word.* Minneapolis: Fortress Press, 1991.

Schillebeeckx, Edward. *Christ the Sacrament of the Encounter with God.* Kansas City, Mo.: Sheed, Andrews and McMeel, 1963.

_____. *Revelation and Theology.* Trans. N. D. Smith. New York: Sheed and Ward, 1987.

_____. "The Sacraments: An Encounter with God." *Christianity Divided: Protestant and Roman Catholic Theological Issues.* Ed. Daniel J. Callahan, Heiko A. Oberman, and Daniel J. O'Hanlon. New York: Sheed and Ward, 1961.

_____, and Boniface Willems, ed. *The Sacraments in General: A New Perspective.* Concilium 31. New York: Paulist Press, 1968.

Schneiders, Sandra M. *The Revelatory Text: Interpreting the New Testament as Sacred Scripture.* San Francisco: HarperCollins Publishers, 1991.

Semmelroth, Otto. *Church and Sacrament.* Trans. Emily Schossberger. Notre Dame, Ind.: Fides Publishers, 1965.

————. *The Preaching Word: On the Theology of Proclamation.* New York: Herder and Herder, 1965.

Simcoe, Mary Ann, ed. *The Liturgy Documents: A Parish Resource.* Rev. ed. Chicago: Liturgy Training Publications, 1985.

Skelley, Michael. *The Liturgy of the World: Karl Rahner's Theology of Worship.* Collegeville: The Liturgical Press, 1991.

Stacpoole, Alberic, ed. *Vatican II Revisited: By Those Who Were There.* Minneapolis: Winston Press, 1986.

Trulear, Harold Dean. "The Sacramentality of Preaching." *Liturgy* 7:1 (1988) 15–21.

Vorgrimler, Herbert., ed. *Commentary on the Documents of Vatican II.* Vol. I. Trans. Lalit Adolphus, Kevin Smyth, and Richard Strachan. New York: Herder and Herder, 1967.

————. *Karl Rahner: His Life, Thought, and Works.* Trans. Edward Quinn. London: Burns and Oates, 1965.

————. *Sacramental Theology.* Trans. Linda M. Maloney. Collegeville: The Liturgical Press, 1992.

Wainwright, Geoffrey. *Doxology: The Praise of God in Worship, Doctrine and Life.* New York: Oxford University Press, 1980.

Waznak, Robert P. "The Homily Fulfilled in Our Hearing." *Worship* 65:5 (September 1991) 29–37.

Wood, Susan K. "Priestly Identity: Sacrament of the Ecclesial Community." *Worship* 69:2 (March 1995) 109–22.

LITERARY AND CRITICAL THEORY

Anderson, David R. "Razing the Framework: Reader-Response Criticism after Fish." *After Poststructuralism: Interdisciplinarity and Literary Theory.* Ed. Nancy Easterlin and Barbara Riebling, 155–76. Evanston, Ill.: Northwestern University Press, 1993.

Bell, Catherine. "The Ritual Body and the Dynamics of Ritual Power." *Journal of Ritual Studies* 4:2 (Summer 1990) 299–313.

————. "Ritual, Change, and Changing Rituals." *Worship* 63 (January 1989) 31–41.

————. *Ritual: Perspectives and Dimensions.* New York: Oxford University Press, 1997.

_____. *Ritual Theory, Ritual Practice.* New York: Oxford University Press, 1992.

Culler, Jonathan. *Structuralist Poetics: Structuralism, Linguistics and the Study of Literature.* Ithaca, N.Y.: Cornell University Press, 1975.

Dean, William. "The Challenge of the New Historicism." *Journal of Religion* 66:3 (July 1986) 261–81.

Detweiler, Robert. "What Is a Sacred Text?" *Semeia* 31 (1985) 213–30.

Eagleton, Terry. *Literary Theory: An Introduction.* Minneapolis: University of Minnesota Press, 1983.

Easterlin, Nancy, and Barbara Riesling, eds. *After Poststructuralism: Interdisciplinarity and Literary Theory.* Evanston, Ill.: Northwestern University Press, 1993.

Fish, Stanley F. "Consequences." *Critical Inquiry* 11 (March 1985).

_____. "Interpreting the *Variorum.*" *Critical Inquiry* 2 (Spring 1976) 465–85.

_____. *Is There a Text in This Class? The Authority of Interpretive Communities.* Cambridge, Mass.: Harvard University Press, 1980.

_____. "Literature in the Reader: Affective Stylistics." *New Literary History* 2:1 (Autumn 1970) 123–62.

_____. *Self-Consuming Artifacts: The Experience of Seventeenth-Century Literature.* Berkeley: University of California Press, 1972.

Felperin, Howard. "Canonical Texts and Non-Canonical Interpretations: The Neohistoricist Rereading of Donne." *Southern Review* 188:2 (November 1985) 235–50.

_____. "Making it 'Neo': The New Historicism and Renaissance Literature." *Textual Practice* 3 (Winter 1987) 262–77.

Fowler, Robert M. "Who Is 'The Reader' in Reader Response Criticism?" *Semeia* 31 (1985) 5–21.

Goody, Jack. *The Interface Between the Written and the Oral.* Cambridge: Cambridge University Press, 1987.

Graff, Gerald, and Bruce Robbins. "Cultural Criticism." *Redrawing the Boundaries: The Transformation of English and American Literary Studies.* 419–36. New York: MLA, 1992.

Geertz, Clifford. *Local Knowledge: Further Essays in Interpretive Anthropology.* New York: Basic Books, 1983.

196

Gill, R. B. "The Moral Implications of Interpretive Communities." *Christianity and Literature* 33:1 (Fall 1983) 49–63.

Greenblatt, Stephen J. Introduction to "The Forms of Power and the Power of Forms in the Renaissance." *Genre* 15 (1982) 3–6.

_____. *Learning to Curse: Essays in Early Modern Culture*. New York: Routledge, 1990.

_____. *Renaissance Self-Fashioning: From More to Shakespeare*. Chicago: University of Chicago Press, 1980.

_____. *Shakespearean Negotiations*. Berkeley: University of California Press, 1988.

Greene, Thomas M. *The Vulnerable Text: Essays on Renaissance Literature*. New York: Columbia University Press, 1986.

Groden, Michael, and Martin Kreiswith, eds. *Johns Hopkins Guide to Literary Theory and Criticism*. Baltimore: Johns Hopkins University Press, 1994.

Halpern, Richard. *The Poetics of Primitive Accumulation: English Renaissance Culture and the Genealogy of Capital*. Ithaca, N.Y.: Cornell University Press, 1991.

_____. "Shakespeare in the Tropics: From High Modernism to New Historicism." *Representations* 45 (Winter 1994) 1–25.

Holub, Robert C. *Crossing Borders: Reception Theory, Poststructuralism, Deconstruction*. Madison: University of Wisconsin Press, 1992.

Howard, Jean E. "The New Historicism in Renaissance Studies." *English Literary Renaissance* 16:1 (Winter 1986) 13–43.

Iser, Wolfgang. *The Act of Reading: A Theory of Aesthetic Response*. Baltimore: Johns Hopkins University Press, 1978.

_____. *The Implied Reader: Patterns of Communication in Prose Fiction from Bunyon to Beckett*. Baltimore: Johns Hopkins University Press, 1974.

Jay, Gregory. "Ideology and the New Historicism." *Arizona Quarterly* 49:1 (Spring 1993) 141–56.

Johnson, David E. "Voice, the New Historicism, and the Americas." *Arizona Quarterly* 48:2 (Summer 1992) 81–116.

Keesey, Donald, ed. *Contexts for Criticism*. 2d ed. Mountain View, Calif.: Mayfield Publishing Co., 1994.

Lentricchia, Frank. *After the New Criticism*. Chicago: University of Chicago Press, 1980.

Leitch, Vincent B. *American Literary Criticism from the Thirties to the Eighties*. New York: Columbia University Press, 1988.

_____. *Cultural Criticism, Literary Theory, Poststructuralism*. New York: Columbia University Press, 1992.

Liu, Alan. "Local Transcendence: Cultural Criticism, Postmodernism, and the Romanticism of Detail." *Representations* 32 (Fall 1990) 75–113.

Montrose, Louis. "New Historicisms." *Redrawing the Boundaries: The Transformation of English and American Literary Studies*. 392–418. New York: MLA, 1992.

_____. "Renaissance Literature and the Subject of History." *English Literary Review* 16:1 (Winter 1986) 1–12.

Porter, Stanley E. "Reader-Response Criticism and New Testament Study: A Response to A. C. Thistelton's New Horizons in Hermeneutics." *Journal of Literature and Theology* 8:1 (March 1994) 94–102.

_____. "Why Hasn't Reader-Response Criticism Caught On in New Testament Studies?" *Journal of Literature and Theology* 4:3 (November 1990) 278–92.

Ricoeur, Paul. "The Model of the Text: Meaningful Action Considered as a Text." *Social Research* 38 (Autumn 1971) 529–62.

_____. *Time and Narrative*. Vol. 3. Trans. Kathleen McLaughlin and David Pellauer. Chicago: University of Chicago Press, 1984.

Steiner, George. "'Critic'/'Reader.'" *New Literary History* 10 (Spring 1979) 423–52.

Stout, Jeffrey. *The Flight from Authority: Religion, Morality and the Quest for Autonomy*. Notre Dame, Ind.: University of Notre Dame Press, 1981.

Suleiman, Susan, and Inge Crosman, eds. *The Reader in the Text: Essays on Audience and Interpretation*. Princeton, N.J.: Princeton University Press, 1980.

Thomas, Brook. *The New Historicism and Other Old-Fashioned Topics*. Princeton, N.J.: Princeton University Press, 1991.

Tompkins, Jane P., ed. *Reader-Response Criticism: From Formalism to Post-Structuralism*. Baltimore: Johns Hopkins University Press, 1980.

Veeser, H. Aram, ed. *The New Historicism*. New York: Routledge, 1989.

Index

dialogue, redemptive
   liturgical enactment as, 3, 16, 163,
   164
Dominic, St. *See* The Holy Preaching

ecumenical dialogue, 174–83
ex opere operantis, 11, 26, 35, 170
ex opere operato, 11, 26, 153, 170

Felperin, Howard, 75, 93, 94
felt community, 117, 120
Fink, S.J., Peter, 11, 12, 13, 15–6, 170
Fish, Stanley, 129, 135–7, 139–41, 168
   on communities of interpretation,
   88, 144–8, 159; *see also* reading,
   the activity of
Foucault, Michael, 75, 133
Fowler, Robert, 132–3, 142, 144, 147,
   174
Fulfilled in Your Hearing, UCCB
   document, 136, 152–3

Gallagher, Catherine, 75, 93
Geertz, Clifford, 111–2, 133
Gill, R. B., 151
Greenblatt, Stephen. *See* New
   Historicism
Guéranger, Abbot Prosper, 6

Halpern, Richard, 99, 112
hermeneutics, biblical, 101
Hilkert, O.P., Mary Catherine, 100–1,
   102, 168, 175, 176, 177
Hill, O.P., William, 135, 152, 154, 155,
   177, 187; on kerygmatic
   reinterpretation, 141, 143, 170; *see
   also sensus plenior*
Holland, Norman N., 150
Holy Preaching, The
   community as, and the early
   Dominicans, xv, 183–7
Howard, Jean, 108, 109, 111

implied reader (Iser), 135; preacher
   as, 156–9

informed reader (Fish), 135, 153;
   preacher as, 154–6, 159
interpretive communities. *See*
   communities of interpretation
Irwin, Kevin, 115
Iser, Wolfgang, 135, 137–41, 156–9

Jauss, Hans Robert, 134
Jay, Gregory, 75, 120
Johnson, David E., 75, 86
Jungmann, S.J., Josef, 6, 10, 161–2,
   170, 171, 172, 173, 174

kerygma, 40, 47, 59, 130, 131, 141,
   142, 161, 163, 171
Kilmartin, S.J., Edward, 15, 177, 181,
   184

Lathrop, Gordon, 115, 173
Leavitt, David, 124
Leith, John, 181, 182
Lentricchia, Frank, 74
lex orandi et lex credendi, 5, 115
Lischer, Richard, 172, 181
literary competence, 149, 168–9
literary texts
   and theater, 73–4, 80, 104–19
   and their relationship to the
   reader, 137–41, 145–51
   as social events, 71, 102, 107, 111,
   116, 118, 139
   as vulnerable, 124–5
   negotiation and manipulation in,
   91, 101, 112, 148, 151, 185
   semiotic approach to, 149–50
literary theory
   in dialogue with liturgical praxis,
   17, 70, 75, 100–4, 173; *see also*
   New Historicism, reader-
   response criticism
liturgical movement, the modern, 6–11
   leading to Vatican II reform, 3–5, 162
liturgy, the
   as meeting place, 158–9, 170, 166,
   180, 185

on proclamation as part of the one
whole word of God, 37–44
on the Church as a starting point
for sacramentality, 33–7
on the Church as fundamental
sacrament, 31–3
reader-response criticism, 70, 129–59
and the interpretation of sacred
texts, 136–7
and the liturgical assembly as
corporate reader, 131
See also implied reader, informed
reader, Stanley Fish, Wolfgang
Iser
reading, the activity of, 73, 85,
129–59
reception theory, 134
resonance and wonder, 77
as a way of encountering texts,
119–27, 167
Rice, Charles, 167
ritual dissonance, 100
Rubin, Miri, 186

sacramental theology, 11–3, 85
mid-twentieth century revival of,
13–6, 162, 172, 174–5. *See chapter 2*
sacramentality
and collective contingency, 84, 97
and human personal encounter,
43–8, 50–1, 61, 84, 172
as revelatory event, 60–3, 92, 129,
152, 164, 168
of the word, 20, 43, 61–3, 131, 165,
183–7
patristic notion of, 13–6
sacraments
as events, 41, 91–5, 181
as expressions of the true nature of
the Church, 23–5, 33, 92
eccelsial foundation of, 92–4. *See*
Part I
sacramentum et res sacramenti, 30, 35,
39, 92, 94

sacred texts, scriptures as
contemplative gaze of, 125–7
contingency of, 64, 100–4, 141, 166,
174
dynamism of, 69–70, 86–7, 90,
93–4, 96–100, 123–4, 149, 156,
165
Schaeffer, John D., 117–8, 119
Schillebeeckx, O.P., Edward, 44–64,
81, 93, 98, 99, 131, 141, 164, 167
on proclamation as a focal point of a
revelatory sacramentality, 54–64
on sacramentality as revelation, 46–8
on the humanity of Jesus as basis for
a sacramental encounter, 48–51
on the Trinitarian structure of
ecclesial and sacramental life,
51–4
Schneiders, I.H.M., Sandra, 101, 165
Searle, Mark, 173–4
Semmelroth, S.J., Otto, 20–7, 63, 92, 163
and the notion of Christ as *Wort
und Antwort*, 27, 103, 163, 179
on the nature of the Church, 22–5
on the relationship of Word and
Sacrament, 25–7
sensus communis, 117–8, 119. *See* Vico,
Giambattista
sensus plenior, 141, 150
sermon, 26, 62, 181. *See* preaching
and the proclamation of the word
Shakespeare, William, 79, 84–5, 95,
99, 112
Steiner, George, 142, 155, 156
Suleiman, Susan, 134, 150

Tertullian, 48, 158
Thomas, Brook, 67, 71, 74, 86, 107,
165
Tillich, Paul, 167, 177
Tompkins, Jane, 86, 133, 134, 149
Tracy, David, 81, 124
tradition, 89–90, 109–10, 121
Turner, Victor, 111